JOAN
The Reluctant Kennedy

By LESTER DAVID

Ethel: The Story of Mrs. Robert F. Kennedy

Ted Kennedy: Triumphs and Tragedies

JOAN
The Reluctant Kennedy

A Biographical Profile

by LESTER DAVID

FUNK & WAGNALLS
New York

Designed by Dennis J. Grastorf

Manufactured in the United States of America

Library of Congress Cataloging in Publication Data

David, Lester.
  Joan—the reluctant Kennedy; a biographical profile.
  1. Kennedy, Joan Bennett. I. Title.
CT275.K4575D38   973.92'092'4 [B]   74-7243
ISBN 0-308-10122-7
          3   4   5   6   7   8   9   10

To Irene with love

Contents

1. "How Glamorous Can Life Be?" 1

2. The Golden Girl of 14 Eastway 16

3. "Have I Got a Girl for You!" 32

4. The Marriage 45

5. The Selling of the Candidate's Wife 60

6. Senator's Lady 92

7. Square Peg 106

8. Showstopper 125

9. The Tragedies 147

10. On Her High Horse 177

11. To Find Herself 192

12. Sex and the Married Senator 211

13. Joansie 234

Index 258

Resolve to be thyself: and know, that he
Who finds himself, loses his misery.

MATTHEW ARNOLD

1

"How Glamorous Can Life Be?"

1. Summons Home

THE PLANE RIDE from Germany had been agonizing.

Once before she had flown home from Europe, summoned by a family tragedy. That was when Robert Kennedy was murdered in California while she was touring in France. This time her eldest son, Teddy, Jr., the twelve-year-old who has her blue eyes and soft blonde hair, was gravely sick.

Joan Kennedy had been traveling abroad most of that summer and fall. Her husband, Edward Kennedy, had vacationed in Colorado and Hyannis Port—"baby sitting" there, she had told a newsman, while she journeyed around the capitals.

The second week in November, 1973, he had called her from their home in McLean, Virginia, telling her the bad news about their son. She had rushed home as soon as she could arrange for transportation.

It hadn't hurt a great deal at first, Teddy told her when she arrived, just a nagging pain, worse when he was running or riding a bike. Then it had got real bad, and he told his governess about it. There was a lump on the lower part of his right leg, which looked and felt like a bruise.

The governess had called Dr. Philip Caper, a family friend and a physician on the staff of the Senate health subcommittee, of which Senator Kennedy is chairman. Dr.

Caper hadn't liked the looks of the swelling and suggested an examination by specialists.

On Friday, November 9, the boy had been taken to Georgetown University Hospital, a complex of red brick buildings in southwest Washington. There the doctors found enough medical evidence to cause deep worry, evidence that Teddy could have a cancerous growth on the lower part of the leg, adjacent to the shinbone. If it was confirmed, the only treatment to avoid spread of the malignancy was amputation.

He had been sent home from the hospital the following morning, and on the next day Joan arrived. The family remained secluded, Joan and Ted in despair yet masquerading with cheerful looks and lighthearted manner when they faced their children. Kara, a beautiful girl of thirteen with long dark blonde hair, and Patrick, six and still wraith-thin, could sense something was wrong, but they weren't told.

The weekend crept slowly. The doctors called and told the Kennedys they wanted Teddy back in the hospital on Tuesday for further testing. On Sunday, the 11th of November, Ted called Luella Hennessey Donovan, the tiny coppery-haired nurse he had known since his own childhood. Luella had assisted at the birth of his three children and twenty-four other grandchildren of Rose and Joe Kennedy. Whenever there is a birth or serious sickness in the family, a call is put through to Luella.

She answered the phone in her spacious garden apartment in Norwood, Massachusetts, a pleasant suburb a few miles outside Boston. The senator started to explain, but he broke down. Then Rosalie Helm, Joan's dark-haired, unflappable social secretary took the phone and told Luella the news. Would she come at once?

Luella flew down with her husband, George Donovan, and prepared to take over the nursing care as briskly and as competently as she has for forty years.

On Tuesday, Joan and Ted took Teddy back to the hospital. Leading bone specialists from the Mayo Clinic and other major medical centers were there, conferring with Dr. George W. Hyatt, director of the division of orthopedic surgery. They confirmed the earlier diagnosis.

The lump was a chondrosarcoma, an extremely uncommon type of cartilage tissue tumor. It grows less rapidly and spreads more slowly than a more common form of bone cancer, osteogenic sarcoma, which arises in bone cells. But it is nonetheless considered highly malignant. Daughter cells can loosen from the original cancerous cluster, enter the bloodstream and invade other parts of the body, most likely the lungs, where they can lodge and grow and eventually kill.

There was no longer any doubt. To save Teddy's life, Joan and the senator were told, the leg had to be removed.

The boy still did not know. His father, in a replay of a previous incident, had ordered the radio and television removed from the room, telling the surprised and disappointed boy that he needed to rest and that the sets would be returned in a day or so. Ten years earlier, in Hyannis Port, Kennedy had ripped the wires from the TV and pretended it was broken to prevent his father from hearing the newscasts of President Kennedy's death until he could tell him more gently.

Friday evening, Senator Kennedy walked alone into his son's hospital room and told him what must be done the following morning. Joan remained in a nearby room.

"It was probably the hardest thing I ever had to do," Kennedy said afterward. The boy began to cry. The fears surfaced: Would he be able to go camping again? Could he sail his boat? Could he ski with the family again? The senator held his son and wept with him.

Next morning Teddy was wheeled to the operating room on the fourth floor where Dr. Hyatt removed the leg in an hour-long operation. Joan and Ted were told that the surgery went well. They saw their son at 10 A.M. after he had awakened from the anesthesia and was returned to his room at the rear of the hospital, overlooking the campus of Georgetown University. There were three nurses for round-the-clock care, and Luella.

Despite the anguish she felt, Joan's face was still cheerful and smiling, her voice still light whenever she entered the room where the boy lay.

Luella Hennessey Donovan: "She and the senator and Rose Kennedy were just as gay as they could be, putting up a good front for the boy. It was 'how are you?' and 'look at the flowers' and 'say, who sent you that football?' —all said very lightheartedly. But I know that Joan's heart must have been breaking, because it's very difficult as a mother who has had Teddy as a little boy to see this tragedy of having a leg amputated at such an early age. She and the senator were so brave in controlling their feelings. Neither one broke down in front of any of the doctors and nurses, but I'm sure they did when they got home.

"It had happened so fast. Everyone was more or less in a state of shock, including myself, because it was so final. It wasn't as if it were an operation and would get better. There was this terrible finality of amputation. Everybody tried to support each other."

While Kennedy was at the hospital almost constantly, Joan went back and forth to McLean, twenty minutes away, to care for the other children. The senator kept only one engagement, the wedding of his twenty-two-year-old niece, Kathleen, to David Lee Townsend, who was twenty-five and a Harvard graduate student.

Twenty minutes after he saw his son, Kennedy left the hospital. Shortly afterward, he drew up in a limousine with the bride at Holy Trinity Church a few blocks away, helped her alight and escorted her up the steps. He was smiling. But as he knelt in prayer after taking communion, he pressed his fingers into his closed eyes.

Standing beside Ethel Kennedy, his brother Robert's widow and the mother of the bride, he watched Kathleen and the bearded groom exchange marriage vows and heavy gold rings, Gaelic-inscribed, made by Townsend himself. Caroline Kennedy, daughter of the slain President, was a bridesmaid and her brother, John, an altar boy. Immediately after the ceremony, Kennedy slipped quietly away and returned to the hospital.

The first day after the surgery, Teddy, Jr. was off the bed and standing. That same day, attendants fitted him with a temporary artificial leg consisting of a foot resembling a shoe tree and an aluminum pylon. Ted looked at it ruefully and commented: "They told me they'd give me a new leg and look what they gave me." He was assured that he would receive a far more efficient prosthesis before too long.

Meanwhile, Teddy's doctors were calling the division of cancer treatment at the National Cancer Institute in Bethesda, Maryland. Were any treatments recommended as a precaution to make certain all cancer cells were destroyed? What was the status of chemotherapy? Dr. Stephen K. Carter, associate director of the division, reported that the malignancy that struck Ted was X-ray resistant.

The best drug available so far was adriamycin, an anti-tumor antibiotic. It was not considered wise to expose the patient to its possible harmful side effects.* It is available, however, in the event of a recurrence. Doctors don't know the cause of chondrosarcoma. Some 70 percent of those afflicted survive for ten years, after which the malignancy is unlikely to recur. Dr. Carter reports that a few have had recurrences as late as twelve years.

During his hospitalization, young Ted went to the physical therapy division daily, sometimes twice in one day, to learn how to walk with his temporary limb. The first day he used parallel bars, then crutches. Just a few days after the operation, he was able to go down to the sundeck by himself.

Less than a week after the operation, Joan got her first really good news.

Dr. Donald A. Covalt, associate director of the Institute for Rehabilitation Medicine of New York University Medical Center, had been called down for consultation. He had examined the boy and watched him at physical therapy. Then he answered the questions put to him by Joan and Ted:

How would the amputation affect their son's movements? How well would he walk and run? Would he be able to engage in the sports he loved?

Here is what the doctor told them:

---

* Several months later, young Teddy entered Children's Hospital in Boston for a series of experimental treatments with methotrexate, a potent anti-cancer drug, to decrease chances of a recurrence. He also received citrovorum to counteract the drug's side effects. "There's a finite chance that the cancer could recur," Dr. Caper pointed out. "We don't know what it is, but we think it is very small. So we are doing something to reduce it even further."

"The boy will be able to walk, run and play. After a period of training he will be a young boy again.

"I believe he will be able to ski. I have many young patients who are amputees and who are skiing. I expect he will have no handicap as far as his limb is concerned.

"Afterward, when your son meets somebody who doesn't know he has had an amputation, that individual would never know he has had one. He will walk perfectly, normally, and without a limp."

"He'll do extremely well," agrees Dr. Howard A. Rusk, director of the Institute. "About the only thing he may not be able to do is play football and other heavy contact sports."

The doctors' predictions were correct; a few months later he was riding a bike and skiing.

And the famous Kennedy touch football games? Will young Ted be able to join the other active young Kennedys?

"Of course," say both doctors.

2. Kennedy Woman to Watch

SHE ARRIVED IN Washington only a decade before, radiantly happy, stunningly beautiful, eager to please. Life was beautiful.

She told me: "When you're twenty-six and there's been no tragedy in your life and you're the sister-in-law of the President of the United States and your brother-in-law is the attorney general and your husband has just become the senator from Massachusetts—I mean, how glamorous can life be?"

But almost at once the tragedies came into her life like big waves pounding against a seawall.

Seven months after she set up housekeeping in the Capital, the President's infant son, Patrick, died in a Boston hospital of a respiratory disease thirty-nine hours after his birth.

Three months later the President himself was dead, struck down by an assassin's bullet on a Dallas street.

Seven months afterward, in June of 1964, the wound hardly healed, her husband broke his back and almost lost his life when his light plane crashed in an apple orchard on his way to a political nominating convention in Springfield, Massachusetts.

In June of 1968, Robert Kennedy was murdered in a Los Angeles hotel pantry, plunging her husband into black despair, the worst he had ever experienced. He had worshipped John, who was twelve years older, but he had been closer to Bobby, six years his senior and his adviser, protector and guide since childhood.

In July of 1969 her husband had driven off a wooden bridge on Chappaquiddick Island in the dead of night following a cookout. A young woman riding with him was drowned and a scandal erupted that tarnished his name and hurt her grievously.

In between there had been three miscarriages and several painful illnesses. On another level, different assaults came her way—rumors, stronger every year, that her husband was unfaithful; stories that she drank too much to ease her growing tensions. Gossip had been simmering hotly ever since the accident on Chappaquiddick Island that her marriage had become hollow and soon would end. In fact, in the summer months before Teddy lost his leg, rumors were circulating that she and her husband were about to separate after fifteen years of marriage.

The excitement, the glamour, the people who created the special wonder and style of those early days, all are gone from the scene if not from life itself. Everything has changed for the lovely girl Ted Kennedy brought to Washington in 1963, changed as much as she has herself.

Once she was all round face and innocent look, the Virgin Mary in her high school Christmas pageant, a sweetheart of Sigma Chi blonde beauty straight out of a Warner Brothers musical of the uncomplicated 1950s. At thirty-seven, in harsher times for her, the fat pads of her cheeks have receded, giving her face length and depth and the truer beauty that maturity and crises can imprint upon it. There are fine lines below the cheekbones and around the chin, and the mouth seems too wide now that the moonface of first youth is gone. Her hair, thick and yellow, drops like a cataract, swirling and eddying around her neck and shoulders.

Her long brown legs are set into full, 37-inch hips; her slender waist arcs into a 34-inch bust. Her forehead is high and sloped, her green eyes deep set, her brows kept full. Her back is a gracefully curved orthopedist's dream. (One literary friend, paraphrasing a long-forgotten writer of light verse, rhapsodizes irreverently though accurately: "With that absolutely perfect nose and her equally faultless backside, some divinity must have shaped her ends.")

We talked for a long time one afternoon in January, before Teddy's illness.

Joan had arrived at her McLean home a half hour late for the appointment, breathing regrets. A few weeks before she had astonished me by telephoning me in Long Island in response to my request for an interview. "I think we'll get along," she had said. "Most people like me."

Then one of these horrible mistakes happened, a shuddery thing one hates even to recall; and yet, in the light of

what was to become unraveled, a thing of no little significance. She had spoken so softly I had misunderstood her
words. "Why?" I had asked, puzzled. I had *thought* she
said: "Most people *don't* like me."

There was a gasp. And a silence. "Why?" she repeated,
in a voice like the widening of eyes, shocked, and a little
frightened. And again, "*Why* do they like me? What do
you *mean?*" In that brief moment, Joan Kennedy told me
something important about herself: about her pathetic
small-girl wish to be liked and to have friends, and her
terror that she would not.

Quickly I realized my mistake and apologized for mishearing her, and the moment passed.

The call from her was unusual. Generally, members of
the Kennedy family agree to interviews through their
press or social secretaries, and between campaigns when
they have no need of the publicity, they do not agree
often. Joan has the services of Dick Drayne, her husband's briskly competent press aide, and Rosalie Helm,
the social secretary. Both are adroit at fending off journalists, but Rosalie, who has lived all over the world as the
wife of a Foreign Service officer and for whom diplomacy
is a way of life, is more skillful by far. Drayne can be
abrasive at times, but Rosalie protects Joan with such
genuine "I'm so-o-o sorrys" that many journalists end up
by apologizing for asking. One told me: "It was twenty
minutes after I hung up that I realized I'd been refused."
Rosalie not only knows where Joan will be weeks ahead
but can forecast her mood and state of weariness. ("We'll
make it for after January 20. Congress will be in session
and they'll all be back from Palm Beach where they'll be
spending Christmas, the children will be in school and
that will be off her mind and she'll really be able to concentrate on it.")

Although I had written two books about the Kennedys, I had never met this youngest wife who had become one of the most talked-about women in Washington. It is only fifteen minutes from the heart of the Capital to Chain Bridge Road, a two-lane, tree-bordered artery that cuts through the estate section of McLean, north of the town center. Only a number nailed to a tree trunk marks Ted and Joan Kennedy's $500,000 antique-filled home, 131 feet wide and 92 feet deep, built on five heavily wooded acres on a high bluff overlooking the Potomac.

No need to linger long upon its magnificence, for it has been described many times. Enough to say that, from the road, the house looks like "throwaway architecture," the words of Keith Irvine, who did the interior design. "All the drama is saved for those who come into the house," he says. "The view is private." And so it is. From the road, beyond the unpaved crescent driveway, behind the plain wooden fence, the gray-shingled, wood and glass house looks to be comfortable, doctor-owned, upper-middle-class, nice but not spectacular or even impressive. No fancy cars parked there either, only a blue Toyota used mostly by the governess to shop and to chauffeur the children. (Joan has a late-model white GTO.) Even the plantings, the dogwood, birch and wildflowers, are simple, artfully designed to look natural.

It was moving on toward four o'clock. Patrick, with the orange-red hair and delicate features, then four years old, came to greet his mother. Usually bouncy and talkative, he seemed listless. He put his head in her lap and remained there; she ran her fingers through his hair and smiled down at him: "Poor Patrick. He's got a dreadful cold." Soon Patrick wandered away.

As Joan talked, Teddy, Jr., neat in the blue blazer worn by students at St. Albans School for Boys, where he was in the fifth grade, came home from school. He was red-cheeked, smiling, his blonde hair cropped at ear-lobe length. I called out a hello, and then blundered badly. "I see you got yourself a haircut. At the Cape last summer it was way down to there"—pointing to his shoulders. Teddy, then ten years old, looked at his mother and smiled. Or was it a grimace? I had touched a sore point. After Ted had gone, Joan explained that St. Albans did not permit boys to wear their hair long, and Teddy had had to sacrifice his locks. (Had there been a scene in the Kennedy home, too, as in so many others when a young male is ordered shorn? Let us not pry further.)

Her face, still burned by the sun and wind of Sun Valley, was in shadow as she sat on a yellow-white chintz couch backed against tall glass walls. She was dwarfed in the vast living room, lost among the five couches, the dozen upholstered chairs, the baby grand and the side tables, small beneath the twenty-foot high ceiling supported by arched beams hewn by hand, chosen to match the grain of the solid oak flooring, and not a nail in any of them. Symbolism? Maybe, but the thought hits hard that she seemed small and fragile and, yes, lost there in the bigness. Behind her, there was a wide sundeck, barren of furniture, and below it, down the bluff, the Potomac River, full and surging.

That afternoon she talked in a tape-recorded interview until it grew dark in the house. The only glow in the yellow-walled room came from the log fire, lit hours ago in the white marble-faced fireplace and now long past its prime. She did not notice the dark nor move to switch on a light but spoke, sometimes urgently, leaning forward and clasping and unclasping her hands.

She talked about the emotional struggle she underwent

to become a Kennedy, the quiet and simple times of her life, the tragic times, the fascinating though hardly placid present and the questions that must be faced and resolved in the years ahead.

She is the Kennedy woman to watch.

No other is in her special position now: the rest are only sentimental favorites of a sadly decimated family, extinct volcanoes, as Lady Astor once called herself. Rose is the "venerable old wine" (her phrase) brought out by the family on ceremonial occasions; Ethel is the brave widow trying desperately hard to raise eleven fatherless children and not doing well with some of them; and Jackie has stepped out of the magical Kennedy circle. No grandsons or granddaughters are even close to a political career and Sargent Shriver, Eunice's husband, has retreated once again into the background after his vice presidential bid with George McGovern and will stay there until Teddy Kennedy decides what he will do in 1976. Of them all, only Joan is left to reign as queen of a restored Camelot, should the moving finger write the story.

A sheltered girl from an upper-middle-class home in the suburbs, Joan Kennedy was never reared for the vortex into which she plunged when she married Edward Moore Kennedy. From a life that was all college weekends, slumber parties, music recitals and cotillions, she was thrust all at once into a world of glittering personages who moved on a global stage, a stage of enormous wealth and of vast power, of intense ambition, intrigue, venomous hatreds and tragedy.

With a father whose chief delight after work was to act in amateur theatricals on high school and church stages, and a mother who enjoyed sewing her own clothes, Joan was bewildered by a family who talked about a son becoming President of the United States. And actually made it! Quiet, unathletic, shy, she had little in common with the relentlessly competitive, energetic, headstrong Kennedys.

She was unready, too, to cope with the emotional blows that came soon after her marriage. Unlike the Kennedys, death and human suffering had not touched her or even come close in her early years. She had developed no stoicism, no fatalism toward events; all she could do was react in horror and have fits of terrorized weeping from the thought that her husband, too, might be murdered as had his brothers, John F. Kennedy and Robert F. Kennedy.

In the other, quiet world there was privacy and freedom of movement. Nobody stared or gossiped, or if some did, it wasn't anything she couldn't handle. In this world, she has become the choicest rumor target in Washington, and most of the stories eventually reach her ears. She hears all the latest tales about Ted's "romances," the ugly outpourings sent to them through the mails, frightening threats against their lives.

Instead of taking pride in herself as a woman of true accomplishment, Joan opted for competing with the Kennedys. And she failed. She didn't have the strength, inner or outer, nor the cynicism ingrained in a family by a father who had lifted himself to fabulous wealth by his bootstraps, nor the fatalism, nor the chutzpah. The more she tried, the worse she failed and the stronger her feelings of inadequacy. Her ego should have grown strong and healthy enough to admire the Kennedys' genuine talents and applaud their achievements while at the same time being clearly aware of her own worth as a human being.

Instead, her ego withered as she continued to measure herself by their yardstick.

All the Kennedys have been grievously hurt by their tragedies, of course, but this sensitive young woman has been wounded in a special way. How it all happened, why it happened and the steps she has taken toward healing is the substance of this book.

2

The Golden Girl of 14 Eastway

1. Harry and Ginny

ON A SPRING DAY in 1939, Harry Wiggin Bennett, Jr., arrived at Building No. 8 of Midland Gardens with his wife, Ginny, two small daughters and a vanload of furniture, barely enough to fill his new four-room apartment.

Midland Gardens, a red-brick apartment complex in a corner of Bronxville, New York, is the kind of place an upwardly mobile, young executive will install his growing family while he saves enough money to buy a home. For Harry Bennett, Midland Gardens was a step up from Riverdale, a few miles southward beyond the busy, cluttered city of Yonkers, but more importantly it was a step toward roots he could put down. Harry strongly believed that his daughters—Virginia Joan was three and Candace one—should have the security of a permanent home in a good suburb where they could meet nice children like themselves and live a good life.

Harry's own father, then seventy-three, was never a rooted man. The elder Mr. Bennett would come around now and then to visit his grandchildren and see how things were with Harry and Ginny, but he didn't come often nor stay too long. He was too busy traveling and getting into, and out of, business ventures. For Harry, Sr., a restless adventurer in the tradition of the nineteenth-century fortune-seekers, wandered all over the face of the world in his eighty-six years and now and then changed some of it.

And he came from pioneer stock. Ted Kennedy's first American forebears caught the boat from Ireland when his great-grandfather, Thomas Fitzgerald, was driven from County Wexford by the devastating 1845 potato famine, but his wife Joan can trace her ancestry to the wave of emigrants that followed the *Mayflower* by only a few decades. Moreover, she has a former high official of a New England colony, one Thomas Wiggin, on her family tree.

The first of the Bennetts arrived in the Colony of Massachusetts Bay about a generation after the Pilgrims planted the first settlement in Plymouth in 1620. But by the time the Bennett progenitor reached these shores, nearby Boston was already being actively settled, and Charlestown, Medford, Watertown, Roxbury and Lynn were beginning to bustle. Eager to start in virginal land, he trekked northward through the wilderness toward Dover, the first of the settlements in New Hampshire, where a handful of colonists were busy building homes, farming land and fighting Indians.

There they remained, spawning active Bennetts down the generations who farmed, engaged in commerce and ultimately produced a music teacher. This Bennett married one Belle Wiggin, a descendant of the colonial official, who bore him three sons—Tom, Dick and Harry.

Harry, Joan's grandfather, was the incredible one. He began his business and professional life at the age of four after a foreshortened childhood on Alton Bay at the edge of Lake Winnipesaukee in New Hampshire. Born in 1866, his father hovered over his cradle, waiting for him to learn to talk. The moment he began, he was giving him voice lessons, which produced quick results. Young Harry had a sweet piping treble that earned him engagements at local festivals and ultimately led to a busy, though minor, career as a child performer in theaters throughout New England and even in New York City.

Inevitably, the vocal cords thickened, the soprano descended into a rasping bass-baritone and Harry's life as a professional entertainer ended almost overnight. It was just prologue to a life of adventure that, from the age of fourteen, careened along like the events in a picaresque novel.

After an apprenticeship in a grocery store in Dover, he wandered west to Toledo, Ohio, where he went to work for a spice company. Soon he was heading farther west to open a branch office in Kansas City, where he remained a few years before taking off once again, this time searching for his fortune deep inside Mexico. From there, he went to New York City as an investment broker, then left for Cuba to begin a sugar business—all this before he was fifty years old.

In Cuba, he built a railroad eastward to the harbor at Guantánamo, returned for a while to the sugar business, then tired of it and headed for the States where he bought a gold mine in New Hampshire, quickly following it with another gold mine in Alaska and a silk mill in New Jersey. He conceived the idea of baking bone-shaped biscuits for dogs, started up a business and sold it to the National Biscuit Co. After a long trip around the world, having fun and searching for more new ideas, he went into the business of producing tung, a fruit from which tung oil, used in waterproofing paints and varnishes, can be processed. With the profits, he went into real estate development, opening Tung Acres in Gainesville, Florida, where his widow, Andasia, his second wife, was still living in 1973.

"He was an adventurer who never saw a red light in his entire life," Andasia says. "He never saw a thing to stop him." Harry, Sr., died in 1952, still dreaming of places to go and worlds to conquer. He had made—and lost—several million dollars in his active lifetime, and by the time he died there was little left. "I inherited nothing but fond memories," Harry says.

Harry Bennett possessed his father's flair for business but was a gentler man whose life-style was keyed considerably lower. If he was no Harry, Sr., neither was he ever a Joe Kennedy, whether bossing a staff of employees or heading a family. The difference between Harry and Joe is striking and, in the light of later events in the life of his eldest daughter, significant. If Joseph P. Kennedy, the father of John, Robert and Ted, was aggressive, competitive and hard-driving, who pushed his children to the ultimate of achievement under the motto of "second best doesn't count," Harry Bennett pushed nobody around and let his children move at their own pace. If Joe was feared and often hated by those with whom he did business, Harry was almost unanimously regarded as a "nice guy."

So "nice" that when a beer company, one of Harry's accounts, was dissatisfied with the way sales were going, it waited until he left on vacation before firing the agency. Bryan Houston, the agency head, says the company's president visited him the day after Harry had gone and told him with a sad shake of his head: "He's such a nice man. We didn't want to hurt his feelings." In the hard world of business, the incident is not often duplicated. Certainly nobody has come forward with a similar story about Joe Kennedy. One businessman who had dealings with the clan's founder put it this way: "Everybody I know tried to screw the old bastard but the trouble was he screwed everybody first."

Harry Bennett's business career was unspectacular, though successful enough. He was born in 1907, the son of Harry, Sr., and the former Agnes Pattie Smith, and was graduated from Cornell University in 1932. Luckier than most young men thrust into the world during those depression years, he was able to land a job almost at once with the National Biscuit Co. as a trainee.

He remained two years, then moved to the Beech-Nut Packing Company as a salesman. Fired up by the advertising business, he joined the big Compton Agency and advanced to account executive, working zealously for eleven years, which were interrupted by two years' service as a medic with the Coast Guard. Ultimately, he rose to a $50,000 a year job—as executive vice president with the firm of Bryan Houston, Inc., where he bossed a staff of twenty people and personally handled the big Colgate-Palmolive-Peet account, an $18,000,000 annual billing. In addition, Harry also had overall supervision of the operations of the entire agency, which placed $32,000,000 worth of advertising every year.

An important executive in a high-pressure business, Harry kept his profile low and his disposition even. Recalled Houston,* elderly but still putting in three or four days of work in what he called semi-retirement: "He was very quiet, not shy but certainly not outgoing. He wasn't the hearty type, as so many admen are, or phony, he was just nice. There's that word again, but it's hard to find another that fits him so well."

Harry was a handsome man, six feet three inches tall

---

* Houston died early in 1974.

and weighing 210 pounds, with light brown hair, a healthy glow in his cheeks and a deep, resonant voice, an "actor's voice," his neighbors in Bronxville said. He made use of it, too, on the stage. For Harry was an active member, eventually becoming chairman, of the Westchester Spot Players, an amateur community theatrical society.

Joan was born early in the morning on September 5, 1936, in Mother Cabrini Hospital, not far from Harry and Ginny's Riverdale apartment. She was named for her mother, the former Virginia Joan Stead, daughter of William Albert Stead, who had married Harry on June 8, 1935.

Ginny was a beauty, five feet four inches tall, a slender woman with delicate features in a smiling, round face. She was an excellent seamstress and, despite an ample family income, made most of the dresses Joan and Candy wore to school in the growing-up years. Ginny taught Joan to sew and did a good job of it, for Joan would sometimes come to school in her own home-made pinafores, jumpers and aprons, while other girls were wearing the latest fashions from the Pondfield Road stores, Saks and Best & Co. Joan's taste in clothes, by her own admission, was "terrible." "It was so bad," she once said, "that my mother took me into the cheapest stores and told me to pick out anything I liked from the $3 and $5 racks."

After a few years at Midland Gardens, Harry Bennett had saved enough to buy a Mediterranean-style house of gray stone and pink stucco on a quarter-acre plot at 14 Eastway. Eastway lay between Southway and Northway, and all the Ways were lined with beautiful, expensive homes, widely separated on their capacious, gardener-maintained lawns.

Bronxville, which registers Republican by four to one and votes the party just as solidly, is unique among affluent suburban communities. Wedged between Yonkers and Mt. Vernon, a few miles above the working-class neighborhoods of the Bronx, it has always been, as author Stephen Birmingham has described it, "an insulated, isolated pocket of wealth." Bronxville was *planned* to be isolated; its streets curve, dip and dart, discouraging excess traffic; there are no sidewalks for strollers in the residential sections.

If Massachusetts has its doggerel about the Lodges speaking only to the Cabots and the latter speaking only to God, so too has Westchester:

> *Here's to Westchester County,*
>   *Society's uppermost shelf,*
> *Where Scarsdale speaks only to Bronxville,*
> *And Bronxville just talks to itself.*

Joan Kennedy spent the formative years of her life in this rich little enclave, sheltered by its invisible walls from the realities of the world outside.

Two old sycamores shaded the orange-tiled roof of Harry Bennett's new house, and a driveway led to the arched entrance. Inside, off the center hall, were a dining room, a vast living room with a stone fireplace and a kitchen and serving pantry. A circular staircase with a wrought-iron banister led to four upstairs bedrooms.

It was not a splendid home like the eleven-acre estate in Greenwich, Connecticut, where Ethel Skakel lived before she married Bobby Kennedy. Nor did it approach in elegance the Bronxville mansion where—coincidence of coincidences—Ted Kennedy spent the first few years of his life only a mile and a half away! (Joe Kennedy, too, had moved from Riverdale to Bronxville, but by the time the Bennetts came to town, Joe had built his sprawling house at Hyannis Port and taken his brood there. When the

Bennetts arrived, the five-acre former Kennedy estate had been cut up into smaller lots.)

There were no cooks, governesses and chauffeurs at 14 Eastway, as in the Kennedy houses, but it was a good, comfortable, upper-middle dwelling where Joan lived a good, comfortable, upper-middle life until she met and married Ted Kennedy.

2. Growing Up Easy

LIFE WAS PLEASANT, undemanding. Tears were never caused by anything more serious than a tumble from a swing or the sight of despised braces staring back from the bathroom mirror. Her routine was suburban-conformist, a life-style that, in the 1950s, was producing a homogenous breed of child, all alike as though stamped out on a cookie cutter: She was taken to New York often to the theater and concerts and dinner in a restaurant; she was invited to elaborate birthday parties where the hostess would provide, along with the ice cream and cake, a magician or puppeteer to entertain the small guests; later, there were Sweet Sixteen parties at swank places like the Siwanoy Country Club; she spent her summers at a private beach club on Long Island Sound, where the Bennetts were members, and at a vacation home that Harry acquired at Alsted, New Hampshire, near a sparkling mountain lake.

When she was nine, she received an invitation to attend Miss Covington's Dancing School. One had to be *asked* to Miss Covington's and only the children from the best families in Westchester received bids. Classes were held in the Womens Club building on Midland Avenue, once a week in the afternoon for younger children, in the evening for older ones. The girls wore long dresses, the boys jackets and ties.

Joan looked forward to these sessions, not because of the boys, in whom she had no great interest for the time being, but for the sheer fun of dancing, which she loved. But it was music she loved even more. Ginny, herself an accomplished pianist, began teaching Joan before she was four, handing out little gold stars for pieces well practiced and played. Joan, gifted with perfect pitch, progressed so rapidly that Ginny sent her for further lessons to Maude Perry, a renowned piano teacher. Miss Perry, who died in the mid-1940s, was an inspiration to Joan, more important to her small pupil than either could possibly realize at the time. For Maude Perry, with her unique ability to communicate her own love of music and her skill at teaching it, laid the groundwork for Joan's lifelong devotion to the piano, which was to be a solace in times of stress and, even more, a significant factor in helping her win self-confidence at a critical time in her life.

Joan was to continue piano studies all through her high school and college years. Later she would say: "I credit my mother for this. By the time they reach fourteen, most girls get tired of the chore of practicing. Dates and other interests get in the way. But my mother was smart—she encouraged my piano teacher to let me play pop—that's what they called it in those days—and this kept my interest alive. I'd play all those wonderful tunes, the ones from *South Pacific* especially, and then I'd have even more friends because everyone would gather around the piano and sing the old songs, 'Down by the Old Mill Stream,' that kind of thing, while I played."

Harry Bennett's role as family head was entirely different from Joe's. He led no political discussions around the dinner table, as Kennedy did, assigned his children no newspapers to read and report upon and conducted no detailed postmortems of athletic contests in which they had engaged to determine why some did not win. Harry, now in the construction business in Florida, recalls: "We chatted about everyday things, what happened in school, the movies, the radio shows, just ordinary family talk."

There was no pressure. For the most part, Harry, a staunch Republican, restricted his political arguments to lunch tables in midtown Manhattan restaurants with other admen and left his children to pick up whatever political knowledge they could, which wasn't much. Joan grew to young womanhood with scant understanding of, or interest in, public affairs. Candidly she would admit: "My lowest grades in college were in current events courses." And Harry never wanted to know why his daughters didn't win at sports because neither daughter engaged in them to any significant extent. Candy was better than Joan, which is faint praise because Joan wasn't much good at anything athletic. She couldn't ski, played tennis only fairly well, didn't sail and was allergic to horses, though she was, and still is, a good swimmer. Later, helped by Ted, she was to become fair to good at some of these. (For their part, the Kennedy children were expert at sports: They were given swimming lessons at the age of four, tennis lessons at six and at eight were put in the hands of a golf pro.)

As with the Kennedys, disciplining the children was mostly a maternal duty. Harry Bennett wasn't away from home as often or as long as Joe Kennedy, but he too spared the rod. Not so Ginny. Rose often said that "physical punishment is rather a good thing" and Ginny was of similar mind. Where Rose Kennedy had her coat hanger or ruler to mete out smacks to the deserving, Ginny had her hairbrush, and it was used. She hung it on a wall with a bright pink ribbon as a constant reminder to would-be transgressors. "I had Joan and Candy bring the hair brush to me and tell me whether they needed one or two whacks to remember not to do it again," Ginny recalls.

Ginny and Rose Kennedy handled the problem of schoolwork differently, however. Ginny would go to the teachers and exhort *them* to put pressure on her children. Rose would do it herself. Homework had to be done at the Kennedy house at a regularly scheduled hour, and it had to be shown to a parent.

The Kennedy children needed the prodding because their grades in the early years were often woefully low. Even the brilliant John was a late bloomer who didn't rise to peak achievement until the last half of his college career. But Ginny needn't have had any concern for Joan, who was bright, had her homework properly done and her hand constantly raised with the answers.

In conferences with her daughters' teachers, Ginny Bennett worried that the children were not made to work hard enough. John F. Parker, who taught Joan in the seventh grade, would receive messages from her almost monthly for talks about Joan's progress.

"She was very uptight about the child," recalls Parker, now retired, who is still living in his home across the road from the Bronxville school. "You could tell there was an undercurrent of worry all the time. Ginny would also stop me when we met on the street and the first thing she would say was, how are things with Joan and shouldn't she be doing more work? She always felt that I wasn't making her buckle down enough."

All through school Joan remained the quiet one. She rarely quarreled with anyone and minded her own business. After classes, she would go to the school library and burrow into books, kicking off her black and white saddle shoes and crossing her bobby sox at the ankles; or she would walk home, go upstairs and, munching an apple or eating a Yankee Doodle with a glass of milk, do her homework and then go downstairs to practice her piano.

Candy was different. Plumper than Joan, dimple-cheeked, shorter, she was joyously outgoing. She bounced and bubbled and attracted scores of friends who followed her home. Joan would be upstairs doing French verbs while Candy and a half-dozen boys would be listening to Rosemary Clooney singing "Come On-A My House" and Johnny Ray sob out "The Little White Cloud That Cried" and in between yak about that newcomer to the movies, Marilyn Monroe, and about those scary flying saucers.

As a child, Joan felt deeply but could not be demonstrative. Harry Bennett remembers: "When I'd come home from work, Candy would be halfway down the block to greet me and would throw herself at me. But Joan would sit and wait in the living room. She would be just as happy to see me—I could tell—but the happiness was bottled up inside."

A strong bond developed over the years between Joan and her father. (The Bennetts were always "Harry" and "Ginny" to the girls, never mom and dad.) On a date to a restaurant or a nightclub, she would write him a message on the postcards placed on the tables: "Dear Harry, Having such a nice time. Miss you. Joan." The cards would arrive on Monday morning at his office.

Once, when Joan was sixteen, Harry Bennett had to make a week-long business trip to Florida. He decided to take her with him.

Harry Bennett: "I thought it might be fun to take my little girl away with me and have her all to myself. I was working like crazy at the time. I was busy ten, fourteen hours a day. I knew I wasn't giving my family enough time and attention, but I was so busy earning a living. I decided that from the moment we left the front door of

our house, she would no longer be my daughter but my
date. We saw everything there was to see in St. Peters-
burg, Tampa and Gainesville; we went fishing and we
went swimming and once she stayed up all night with me
at nightclubs for the first time in her life, and she drank
champagne for the first time, and we just had one great
ball. On the plane coming home, she looked at me and
said, 'I never thought adults could be so much fun.' "

Looking back, Joan is grateful now for those years of
solitude. She believes they added a dimension to her life
she might otherwise never have acquired: the ability to
be self-sufficiently alone for long periods without bore-
dom or a desperate need for company. By contrast, her
sister-in-law Ethel cannot tolerate being alone even for
short periods. She must be surrounded by people and if
she is not, she will have lengthy telephone conversations.
Joan is different, and thankfully so. She told me: "Early
one morning, in an airplane returning from a skiing trip
in Sun Valley, I suddenly found myself thinking of my
girlhood. It was two o'clock and I couldn't sleep. I was
reading Joseph Lash's book, *Eleanor and Franklin*, the
part where she talks about her homeliness, her plain appearance. The author commented that if she had been
beautiful and self-assured and just skimmed along on the
surface of life, as many beautiful young girls do—you
know, been very popular—she might never have
acquired true depth.

"That brought my own early life to mind, and I'm glad
it went the way it did. If you had asked me when I was
sixteen, I wouldn't have agreed it was good, but now that
I'm over thirty-five I'm grateful I wasn't pushed into
growing up too soon. I had those extra years many girls,
especially teen-age girls today, don't have. They're propelled into early dating and too-early sophistication. I

didn't do that and I think I learned a lot of things that stood me in very good stead in my life since I've been married."

By senior year, though, things changed dramatically. Dateless much of the time in her early and mid-teens, Joan's lanky form filled out, the braces came off and a young beauty emerged. The boys took note. She became one of the most sought-after dates to Ivy League fraternity weekends and accepted many at Yale. She even got dates with Yale men for Candy.

It was great mid-1950s fun . . .

About noon on Friday, Joan and Candy would catch a New Haven train and chug into the station where dozens of Yale men were lining the platform, waiting for their girls. (For Joan, Raoul would be waiting; he was a handsome, dark-eyed young man from a wealthy exiled Cuban family, an early beau, who would soon disappear from her life.) They would be taken to private homes, where the boys had arranged for rooms, and then to dinner.

Later, there might be a play or a concert at the university or in town or parties in the residential colleges, where the food was plentiful and the liquor and beer flowed freely, though not in Joan's direction. She and Candy stuck to soft drinks. If there was carousing, and often there was, it had to end at midnight because those were years when colleges still acted *in loco parentis*. Next morning there would be a late breakfast at George and Harry's and, huge chrysanthemums pinned to their coats and blue and white Yale banners in their fists, Joan and Candy would get aboard the old open trolleys for the jolting ride to the Yale Bowl.

After the game, another trolley ride to town, enlivened by the "hot penny" game that has diverted Yale men for decades. Small boys would line the trolley route and scramble for coins tossed by the students, some of whom would heat pennies with matches and took delight in watching the children pick them up and quickly let go with yelps. Dinner might be in suburban Branford, along the Sound or at the tables down at Mory's. Then more partying and a late sleep on Sunday morning. Lunch might be in the college dining hall, then still another party or some touch football on the lawns and, in midafternoon, down to the station for the trip home.

They were all like this, those early years. One searches vainly through them for high drama or even evidence of mischievousness or escapades.

Her reputation was sterling among the toughest judges of all, the high school boys. Dorothy Day, dramatics and recreation director, would be on duty in the recreation room after classes when the boys would drift in and, over bottles of soda, discuss the parties they had attended and the girls they dated. Miss Day admits she would pretend she wasn't listening, but her ears "were flapping in the breeze." One afternoon her flapping ears heard a boy ask the group if anyone had ever gone out with Joan Bennett. One had. "But," he said, "you could never make out with her." Not, he said, like you would with . . . and the names and reputations of a half-dozen young Bronxville belles were left shredded on the rec room floor.

Joan's rapidly expanding social life cut into her extra-curricular activities, though she was careful to give a full measure of attention to her piano and school studies. Once, when a production of Gilbert and Sullivan's *The Sorcerer* was announced, she auditioned for a part, got it but dropped out of the cast a few weeks later, though she still appeared in the chorus. "She was too busy to make the weekend rehearsals," says Miss Day. She did have time for work on the scenery committee for several shows with Barbara Bain, the chairman, who later was to become a Miss Rheingold. Nor would she give up her work as assistant news editor on the school newspaper, *The Bronxville Mirror*, which she enjoyed hugely.

Nonetheless, her accomplishments in school and town were modest and Joan, the teen-ager, left no deep imprint on Bronxville. Most residents hardly remember the shy blonde girl who grew up in their midst. But Joan, the wife of the controversial Ted Kennedy, is an entirely different matter. A visitor wandering through the community, talking to people he meets, hears expressions of sympathy for her, sharp criticism of him: She is decent, her husband is not. She is the suffering wife, he the unfeeling husband. She is so obviously in love, he so obviously not in love with her. At the Chamber of Commerce office on Pondfield Road a woman expresses a typical view: "I'm so sorry for her. Why do people talk about her so much? It seems to me that she's been thrown to the wolves down there in Washington and it's such a shame. She's a small-town little girl. People can be so cruel."

Dorothy Day: "She should have married a lawyer, like her sister Candy, and settled down to raise babies in a nice suburban home somewhere. [Candy, the wife of Robert M. McMurrey, lives in a nice house in Houston, Texas, and is raising three sons.]

"I have a great deal of pity for Joan now, knowing what she once was and what she has to face now. I just pray she will be strong enough to take this life she has to lead.

"She's changed—oh, how she's changed. I see her now on television and it shocks me. She was once so quiet and gentle and serious, but she seems so harsh now, brassy even. I can't believe it's the same Joan Bennett I watched grow up."

3

"Have I Got a Girl for You!"

1. Manhattanville

JOAN GRADUATED FROM Bronxville High with excellent grades in June, 1954, and headed for college, venturing only a dozen miles beyond the enclave. Harry was a Protestant and Ginny a Catholic; both children were being reared in her faith. Ginny wanted Joan to attend Manhattanville College of the Sacred Heart, which only two years earlier had moved from Morningside Heights in New York City to a beautiful new campus in Purchase.

Joan was happy at Manhattanville. She had many friends there, girls like herself, bright, well-bred daughters of wealthy Catholic families. (Man-huntingville, the boys from surrounding colleges called it, a put-down of wicked accuracy, for many of the girls were oriented, not to a career, but to a home and husband, both preferably of high quality.) Her courses were rigidly prescribed, for the unstructured academic era had not yet begun at colleges: English, history, mathematics, science, music, religion and religious philosophy, even a required course in Gregorian chant in her freshman year. Manhattanville was in the mainstream of Roman Catholicism, where Rose Kennedy and her daughters Eunice Shriver and Jean Smith were educated; where, in the words of one alumna, "Catholic mothers sent their daughters first to be protected and schooled in the ways of the church and second to get a liberal arts education." As in Rose Kennedy's day, many years before, nuns wearing long black habits and white wimples taught most of the classes and influenced the girls in the direction of strict, pre-Pope John Catholicism.*

Social rules were as rigid as the curriculum. Joan had to be in her room by ten every weekday night. And weekend leaves were not granted unless she could present a permission slip signed by her parents, guaranteeing that a proper chaperone would be present wherever she went.

Joan fitted uncomplainingly into the mold, finding the organized, sheltered life agreeable and comfortable. With the high stone wall enclosing its 250 acres, Manhattanville had the protective feeling of a convent about it.

She was to emerge from this chrysalis almost entirely unschooled in the practicalities of life. A music major, she kept on reading and studying and playing the piano and, in free time, enjoying the fifties' college scene: the fraternity parties with their beer busts, the Big Games, the trips to New York. Unlike the Kennedy children, who were taught early that one must compete hard in a world that gives little quarter, she trusted in the essential goodness of humankind. She had no cause to feel otherwise. Never having been hurt, she grew no protective calluses. Joe Kennedy admired physical courage above most other virtues and drilled it into his children from the beginning so that personal bravery was as important to them as winning. Rose Kennedy, too, knew that life could be hard

* Manhattanville has undergone a major transformation since Joan's day. It is nonsectarian and co-ed; the "of the Sacred Heart" has been lopped off and the curriculum totally revised. Most standard course requirements have been dropped and—to the dismay of some older alumnae—curfews have been eliminated and some dorms have gone co-ed. Its roots are still Roman Catholic, but the faculty consists largely of lay professors.

and tricky. One of six children of a rambunctious politician who made his way in a era of rough and tumble political in-fighting, she learned early that one must tread warily, something she communicated to her children along with their catechism. They learned from Rose that nothing comes easily, everything good required hard work and that nobody can find an easy way out of any place, anywhere. Nor was Joe the only parent, as many believe, to insist on winning. Rose, too, has candidly stated: "We would try to instill in them the idea that no matter what you did, you should try to be first."

It was different with Joan. Ginny fretted and fussed about her but was ineffectual in teaching her about life, and Harry didn't care whether she landed in first place or second or sixth. The night before she left for college, he told her: "Joan, your college days should be the happiest time of your life. Don't plug away at the books all the time. We're not going to expect you to come home with all A's and B's."

Overprotected by her environment, indulged by a fond father, living in a happy, moneyed world filled with sunshine and stardust and all the good things that come to a very pretty girl, she grew up vulnerable, a word she was to apply to herself many years later when the realities of life began to close in around her.

As Candy once said of her sister: "Joan learned the hard way."

2. Coming Out

THREE MONTHS AFTER her college career began, on a misty and cool Thanksgiving night, Joan Bennett was Introduced to Society. She was, in fact, introduced twice, first at the fifth annual Gotham Ball and, about three weeks later, at the nineteenth Debutante Cotillion and Christmas Ball, both gala affairs in New York's social whirl.

It was no great record: Some girls were still having as many as three or four debuts, although the coming-out party, once an indispensable rite of passage for marriageable young girls in American society, was already in steep descent and accelerating.

Getting to be accepted as a "debutante" was never an easy matter. In the 1920s, the publication *Town Topics* would grade the year's crop of debs like beef—prime, choice and utility. *Town Topics* used a letter grade to classify the girls: "A" ratings were given those whose families could be traced back at least three generations and who had an adequate amount of money (the amount not specified) and, in addition, were beautiful, vivacious and charming. Young ladies who met the family and financial test but lacked charm or personal attractiveness were graded "B," and the "C" girls were from the *nouveau-riche* families.

It wasn't that way by the time Joan came on the scene, but it wasn't easy either. Joan was not an automatic deb, like the daughters of the reigning social families; she had to pass a rigid screening by the committees in charge.*

The Gothams were strict. Months before, Joan had to submit an application, together with letters of recommendation from previous Gotham debs and others of high social standing. It was approved. Next, she was summoned for observation and evaluation in a personal interview, an ordeal which, at eighteen, was not unlike a session be-

---

* By Joan's day, individual coming-out parties were being increasingly supplanted by organization-sponsored mass debuts, although a number of girls from socially prominent families had both.

fore the Spanish Inquisition. One girl remarked after being
paraded before a screening committee that show dogs in-
spected by judges at the Westminster Show in Madison
Square Garden have a happier time of it than prospective debs before an evaluation committee.

But Joan passed and, in due course, received one of the
forty-two coveted invitations, along with a list of instructions and a bill for $1,000. The bill covered the din-
ner and ball for Joan, her parents and two escorts. The
instructions were explicit about the dress she should
wear. It was the era of the strapless evening gown, but the
Gotham people firmly said no: shoulders and upper arms
must be covered and under no circumstances could there be
even a suspicion of cleavage.

It was a night to remember.

Joan, Harry and Ginny arrived early in the day at the
Plaza, where they had taken rooms for the night. By
seven Joan was dressed in a white bouffant ball gown and
had drawn on her long white gloves, the traditional
costume for debutantes the country over, and, carrying a
bouquet of cardinal red blossoms, was in the foyer of the
ballroom for pre-dinner cocktails. Flocking around her
like court attendants were her two escorts and three stags,
the five males alloted to each girl to ensure proper attention
during the evening.

Dinner in the ornate, chandeliered Terrace Room was
magnificent: Boula Boula grapinée, a turtle and pea soup,
charcoal-broiled filet mignon with béarnaise sauce and a
huge bombe for dessert with, of course, appropriate wines.
After dinner, back to the ballroom for the presentation to
Francis Cardinal Spellman who, in his robes of office,
stood at stage center. Joan, on Harry's arm, walked to the
stage, curtsied, kissed the Cardinal's ring and walked off
the other side, where she was met by her two escorts.

She danced until 3 A.M., then, with her friends and escorts, went out on the town until dawn.

There wasn't much respite from the partying. By mid-December they began again for the second debut, an endless series of luncheons, teas and dinners; and then, on Monday, December 20, in the same white gown, Joan stood nervously in an anteroom of the Grand Ballroom of the Waldorf-Astoria for another presentation, this time with 103 other young girls. Jamming the room for the Debutante Cotillion, the largest mass introduction of debs in the country,* were some highly publicized young ladies, the daughters of oil-heir Laurence Rockefeller and the famous songwriter Irving Berlin. There was also an effervescent girl named Cary Latimer, whom New York society editors, in their quest for startlets, had named the season's Number One Glamour Deb.† Most of the girls, however, were, like Joan, little ripples in the social pool, "unknown," as *Time* magazine wrote, "beyond the limits of Scarsdale and Greenwich."

In March and April, students who could afford the fares and hotel rates flocked to Bermuda for spring recess, which would occur at different times depending on college schedules. It was pleasant fun and games, highlighted

---

* Though hardly the most fashionable. Stephen Birmingham, who knows about such things, says the Grosvenor Ball (for the benefit of Grosvenor Neighborhood House) is more exclusive by far; so are the Junior League Ball and the Junior Assemblies.

† Both Bouvier sisters, Jacqueline and Lee, were considered the leading debs of their coming-out years. Before she went off to Vassar at the age of nineteen, Jackie was named Queen Deb of the Year by the foremost society writer of the day, Cholly Knickerbocker of the Hearst newspapers. Jackie made her debut in Newport. In 1951, her sister, Caroline Lee, later Princess Radziwill, was generally accepted as the year's top deb.

by an all-day party at Elbow Beach in Paget Parish on the
south shore. There would be free hot dogs, soft drinks,
a band blaring and, as the highlight of the day, a contest
to select a College Queen.

Joan and a few friends went down in April. When the
contest was announced, she found herself propelled to the
stand where, with about a dozen other girls in bathing
suits, she was paraded before the hundreds of cheering
students. Her stunning figure, bright blonde hair and
fresh-faced beauty easily won her the most applause and
she was crowned forthwith.

There were more beauty honors to come. From the
college queens chosen in the spring, the Bermuda Chamber of Commerce would pick a queen for its annual floral
pageant the following year. Joan was an easy winner. On
March 2, 1956, the Mt. Vernon *Daily Argus* headlined the
story:

BRONXVILLE GIRL TO BE QUEEN
OF BERMUDA'S FLORAL PAGEANT

On April 5, in a ceremony at Hamilton, the Bermuda
capital, Joan was crowned queen of the pageant with a
tiara of pink and white carnations. Forty-eight floats,
blazing with tropical and semi-tropical flowers, were
drawn up before the coronation stand. After the ceremony, Queen Joan entered the lead float, a horse-drawn
coach decorated with 5,000 lily blooms; beside her were
her page boy, one Steve Masters, and a flower girl named
Cindy Young. The parade wound through Hamilton, Joan
smiling and waving to the throngs. In New York, the
Journal American published a two-column photo of Joan
in her royal coach under the caption: "NEW YORK GIRL
CAPTIVATES BERMUDA."

3. Model

ONE MORNING IN 1957, Candy Jones was conferring with Harry Bennett in his midtown Manhattan office on a new advertising campaign for a soap product. Candy had been one of the country's foremost models, thirteen times on magazine covers and in dozens of television commercials. Now she was the wife of Harry Conover, head of one of the two most important model agencies in the business (the other was John Robert Powers), and also director of a training school for models and career girls as well as beauty consultant for Colgate, Harry's most important account.

When the business part of their talk was finished, Harry leaned back in his chair, cocked his head and said to Candy:

"Have I got a girl for you!"

Candy, always interested in new modeling discoveries, asked: "Who is she?"

"My daughter, Joan."

Candy Jones: "How many times have I heard that from a proud father! They're all convinced that their little girls are God's gift to the modeling business but nearly always the beauty is in the eyes of the parent. Harry said he'd send this daughter of his over and I said fine, fine, I'd love to talk to her—the usual.

"But then one day around Thanksgiving time this golden girl walks in, this astonishing girl with a deep tan, and glorious eyelashes, sort of wheat color and so long. Her hair was a streaked blonde, the kind that women to-day spend hours in beauty parlors to match, only hers didn't come from chemicals. She had fine facial bone structure and a strong-looking, glowingly healthy body, a refreshing change from the gaunt, emaciated girl, a half step from anemia, we had all been accustomed to seeing at the agency.

"She was one of those rare beauties we get infrequently. I found myself comparing her to an Ingrid Bergman when she was Joan's age.

"I said to myself, 'This can't be for real. Okay, she's beautiful, but she'll probably turn out to be a lisper or would have a voice like a calliope or a terribly sibilant *s* or something horrible like that.' But she spoke as divinely as she looked, softly, with good, clear enunciation.

"I asked her to walk across the room for me and I saw right away that she didn't know how to walk at all. She loped like a cowgirl. Oh-oh, I thought, she'd be awful on a runway, so I immediately decided that, with her astounding beauty, her main value would be in photography and television. Let the others do the clothes modeling. Joan appeared to have the essential qualities advertisers insisted upon to sell their products, naturalness, sincerity that shone through clearly and an appealing personality.

"I asked her why she wanted to become a model and she answered quickly and frankly: 'To make some money to pay for a trip to Europe.' Fair enough. I wanted to know if she would have time, what with classes and all, and she assured me that with intersession, and the holidays, Easter and Christmas, she could manage some engagements, though certainly not on full time.

"I accepted her and we went to work."

First step was an evaluation of Joan's physical assets and liabilities. She was five feet seven and one-half inches tall, weighed 132 pounds and had a 36-inch bust, 25-inch waist and 37-inch hips, all duly noted in Candy Jones's records.

Miss Jones also wrote down her appraisal: "Needs brows groomed slightly" (underlining the slightly), "needs lipline reshaped—shade is too dark."

Candy felt that 132 pounds was a bit heavy for modeling, but on Joan they were well distributed. ("This girl wasn't a bit fat; her flesh was firm.") However, the 37-inch hipline was a little too much. Joan giggled as Candy instructed her on how to slim it down:

"Go down to Lamston's, the five-and-ten cent store," she told her, "and buy an old-fashioned rolling pin. Put some baby oil or any lubricant on your skin and roll, roll, roll up along the hip and backside."

Up at Manhattanville, Joan showed her friends the rolling pin and explained what Candy Jones had suggested. They were enthralled and ordered her to bring back rolling pins for them too. She did, buying up dozens, and soon most of the dorm was doing what Joan did nightly, anointing themselves with oil and rolling excess fat from their derrières and outer thighs. As an alternate, Candy had suggested a fanny roll on a hard floor. They did this too.

It worked. Within a few weeks, Joan had whittled her hips down two inches. The total hip reduction achieved at Manhattanville was not computed, but it must have been considerable, thanks to Joan.

Photographs were taken—Joan in a scoop-neck knit jersey with a single strand of pearls, Joan in shorts, Joan in a long tight black dress—and sent to advertising agencies. Her first job came within a couple of months after her initial interview.

Maxwell House sent out a call for an outdoor-type of girl, blonde, about twenty years old, for a top network television commercial. Joan was sent down and was dismayed to discover about one hundred other outdoor-type twenty-year-old blondes overflowing the reception room. When models are sought for a particular assignment, she was to learn, companies broadcast calls to dozens of agencies around town. Candy Jones had sent ten of her girls; the Powers agency fifteen.

One by one the candidates were called to audition. Hours later a short-sleeved assistant called out Joan Bennett's name.

For that one-minute commercial, her first, she was paid $2,500.

After that, the calls came frequently. Soon the entire Bennett household was acting as her booking agent, taking calls and relaying them to Joan at school. She did straight photographic modeling for beauty products, foods and shampoos, and a number of other television commercials. She was the Revlon Girl on the Perry Como show. She appeared on "Coke Time" with Eddie Fisher.

But she lost a few too. Once, after she had been accepted for an especially lucrative assignment, the director asked her to cut her hair above the shoulders. Joan refused point-blank. "My father would kill me," she told Candy Jones. "As much as Joan enjoyed making money," Candy says, "she kept her hair and the job went to somebody else."

Another time, the Perry Como variety show wanted a pretty young blonde for a cigarette commercial. Joan, who was wild about Como, desperately wanted the assignment, which called for her to inhale and exhale and look relaxed and lovely at the same time. But Joan was not a smoker. On the way to the agency, she bought a pack of cigarettes and, while waiting to audition, practiced puffing. Dozens of other girls were doing the same thing, making the reception room look like a smoking car in rush hour. When she was called before the director, all she could manage were some little billows of smoke and a pained, slightly dizzy look.

Candy Jones: "We taught her to get rid of that lope and to walk properly, to float a little more instead of putting all her 132 pounds on the floor at one time. She became quite light on her feet. Many of our other girls would drive us and the agencies crazy, forgetting accessories they were told to bring and being late for appointments. But Joan was very businesslike, very professional. She was on time, got her instructions right and followed them perfectly.

"At the beginning, I handled her bookings personally, but when it became apparent she was going to have a real career as a model, I took her by the hand and brought her over to the Harry Conover agency, which was better equipped to handle the larger volume of calls she was getting.

"Joan's modeling career lasted eighteen months and she made many thousands of dollars."

The Conover and Candy Jones offices were at 52 Vanderbilt Avenue, opposite Grand Central Terminal. On Friday afternoons the boys from Harvard, Yale and other schools in the area would get off the train and meet their dates at the famous rendezvous spot, under the clock at the Hotel Biltmore at 43rd Street and Madison Avenue. Some would show up at the model agency to pick up their dates.

One day Candy returned to her office and brushed by Joan Bennett who was in earnest conversation with a hatless young man. As she sat down at her desk, she turned to her secretary and asked: "Who's that fat kid with Joan?"

He was Ted Kennedy, six feet one and heavier than he was when he played football for Harvard, up from Charlottesville, Virginia, where he was in the third year of law school. Candy, who had never heard of him, was unimpressed.

"I thought Joan could do much better than that," she says.

4

The Marriage

1. "I Never Heard of the Kennedys"

Joan Kennedy: "There is this huge building on the Manhattanville campus, the Kennedy Physical Education Building, which is the center for sports and social events. Mr. Joseph Kennedy, who was a fitness enthusiast his whole life, contributed a large sum toward its construction and in 1957, in my senior year, it was finished and ready for students to use.

"So the college invited many notables to the dedication ceremonies. Afterward, there was a tea and reception in the Benziger Building, and all the seniors had to go because it was in honor of Cardinal Spellman and most of the Kennedys were there—my mother- and father-in-law, Bobby and Ethel, all my sisters-in-law. Everybody was there but me. I was upstairs in my dorm doing an English paper. Margot Murray, my roommate, rushed in and said they were missing me and maybe, if I came down real fast, the student government girl who gives out the demerits would see me and assume I'd been there through the whole ceremony.

"So I got out of my old bathrobe, jumped into something appropriate and ran over. Then the next thing I remember, I was standing with Margot, and Jean Smith, Ted's sister, came up to me and said, 'Oh, aren't you Joan

Bennett?' And I said yes. And she said, 'Remember we met last August?' The irony is that I had met her at Ethel Skakel Kennedy's brother's house. That's George Skakel in Greenwich, and I had been brought there to a big party by not one but two dates. They were never serious. They were just kind of two very best friends who liked taking a young girl to a party and not feeling it was a date. I won't mention their names now but they were both very, very good friends of Steve and Jean Smith's.

"Well, the Smiths came over to me to see who the new girl was that these two guys had at the party. Jean and I got to talking, and Jean said: 'Hey, you go to Manhattan-ville? I was there too. What class are you?' [Jean and Ethel were roommates at Manhattanville, both graduating in 1953.] I told her I was getting out in '58 and we got into a very girl-to-girl conversation, talking about the old nuns and what courses I was taking and how's old Manhattanville now. And then she said: 'You live in Bronxville, don't you?' and I said yes and she said, 'Oh we used to live in Bronxville too. Where do you live?' Well, I figured out that she used to live about three and a half blocks from where I lived! So you can see there was a lot of 'Gosh, small worlds!'

"Well, when she spotted me at this reception and came over to talk to me, I didn't know Jean Smith was one of the Kennedys. I had never even heard of the Kennedys. *I'd never heard of them!* I just took no interest in current events; my lowest grade in college was in current events, though I got very good grades in everything else. I didn't know what was going on in the real world.

"Anyway, Jean said to me she'd like me to meet her little brother or her younger brother, and I'd almost ex-pected to meet someone *that* high [holding a palm at knee length]. So she introduced Ted to my friend Margot and me. The great fun thing is that Margot, who roomed with me for four years, knew a lot of Ted's friends, and so the two of them started talking, 'Do you know who and this and that.' I mean, it really was kind of a small world. So they picked up the conversation and I too knew a lot of these people because Margot, who is now Margot Murray O'Mara, had a summer home in Southampton and I used to visit her there.

"Anyway, Ted was in a rush to get back to Charlottesville, Virginia, where he was in law school, and there was only one flight he could get out of La Guardia Airport, so Margot, who had a car on campus, said she'd drive him to the airport. So the three of us went and it was kind of fun, the excitement of rushing. Little did I realize that I'd be chasing to airports for the next fifteen years of my life.

"Ted got back to Charlottesville and that night, or the next night, he phoned me to chat. Didn't ask me out on a date at all. Just phoned to visit. As a matter of fact, there were several phone calls just to say, 'hi,' and 'how are you' and this and that. Then a couple of weeks before Thanksgiving vacation he said, 'I'm going to be in New York for a couple of days over the holidays. Could I see you then?' We had a luncheon date in New York and then he drove me back to Bronxville. That was our first date."

Less than a year later, in June of 1958, Ted walked with Joan from his father's big house at Hyannis Port to the shores of the sound and asked her to marry him. The engagement was announced on September 21.

Ginny fluttered all over Bronxville and New York with Joan, buying and fitting the long-sleeved, ivory-satin wedding dress, conferring with the caterer at the Siwanoy Country Club where the reception was to be held and arranging for the flowers. She wanted everything to be in perfect taste, she told Mrs. Morgan's Flower Shop on Parkway Avenue, simple fall blooms and hangings.

They were married November 29 that year at St. Joseph's Roman Catholic Church in Bronxville. It was an important wedding, not the most social of the season but one of the most newsworthy. No other bride and groom had their photograph published on the front page of the New York *Daily News*, America's most widely circulated newspaper.

Joe Kennedy, whose fortune by then was reputed to be greater than $300,000,000, had asked his friend Francis Cardinal Spellman to officiate. Forty-four years before, he himself had been married by a cardinal, William O'Connell, Archbishop of Boston. Cardinal Spellman had accepted and arrived at the rectory on Meadow Lane, around the corner from the church's main entrance, shortly before ten o'clock that frigid morning. The rectory staff, enormously excited, had spent the day and most of the night scrubbing and sweeping the large rooms and polishing the brass and silver, for the cardinal had never visited the church, much less conducted a wedding there.

The presence of His Eminence was a coup for the Kennedys, but Joan, though impressed, secretly wanted to be married by Father John Cavanaugh, the president of Notre Dame University. Ten years later she would blurt out this confession to a campaign audience in Indiana as she introduced Father Cavanaugh as "the best priest-friend Ted and I ever had." She said: "We wanted him to marry us but Cardinal Spellman said he should be the one to do it."

Joan apparently never insisted, yet the point was not without significance in terms of what it portended. The incident was telling her, if she was heeding, and in the excitement of the preparations she probably was not, that her life as a Kennedy woman would be governed not by her preferences but by the wishes of the Kennedy family, whose desires and welfare would determine any choice or any course of action.

Curiously, the presence of the Cardinal in their midst created much less stir among the residents of Bronxville than did the presence of the Kennedys and their important guests. Nobody was outside the rectory when he arrived but, despite the mid-teen weather and the biting wind that made it seem even colder, several hundred persons had collected on Kraft Avenue to await the exuberant Kennedys and the hundreds of judges, senators, diplomats and other celebrities they had invited.

A few minutes before eleven o'clock, the church was filled with nearly five hundred guests, among them Senator John F. Kennedy and his wife, Jacqueline, whom he had married five years before in Newport, Rhode Island, Robert and Ethel Kennedy and five of their six children; and a large group of hulking young men looking uncomfortable. They were Ted's football teammates from Harvard where he had played on the varsity, fellow jocks more at home in sweat pants than the morning coats and striped trousers that the Kennedys had rented for them for the day and which, for the most part, fitted badly. Only Richard Clasby, who had been captain of the team when Ted was an end and who was serving as an usher, had received a suit that hung well. He was preening before a mirror when John Kennedy walked by. Kennedy looked terrible in the outfit handed him. The trousers were too snug and he could barely button the coat.

Kennedy argued, sensibly enough, that since he was best man it was more important that he look better than Clasby, a mere usher. How about swapping? Clasby took one last, admiring look in the mirror and resignedly undressed, squeezing into Kennedy's too-small suit. He could barely sit down all day.

Harry Bennett, who wanted the entire wedding recorded on film, arranged for a friend to light up the interior of the church like an M-G-M sound stage, with floodlights at the sides and in front of the altar. The bride and groom had microphones hidden in their clothes. Bennett escorted his daughter, radiant in her gown of ivory satin, with a sweetheart neckline adorned with rose-point lace and a fitted bodice, with long sleeves and full skirt. Candy was maid of honor and her other attendants were Margot Murray, Danne Brokaw and Jean Kennedy, who was married to Stephen Smith. Bobby Kennedy was an usher, along with Webster E. Janssen, Jr., Joan's cousin; LeMoyne K. Billings, a Choate School classmate of John Kennedy's and a family friend; Joseph Gargan, a Kennedy cousin who was to remain in the shadows until the incident on Chappaquiddick Island eleven years later; Claude E. Hooten, Jr., Garret Schenck, Varrick John Tunney and Clasby. Hooten was to become a congressman and Varrick Tunney, Ted's roommate at the University of Virginia Law School, was to become John Varrick Tunney, a senator from California.

The camera ground and the lights shone, illuminating the stained-glass Crucifixion scene above the Italian marble altar. Joan and Ted became man and wife, in color and sound.

2. *Decision*

ONLY ELEVEN MONTHS after her marriage, Joan Kennedy was already struggling with one of the most crucial decisions of her life.

The choice was thrust upon her suddenly. In October she realized, for the first time, what lay ahead.

Like many young couples who have not yet found a home or apartment of their own, she and Ted had moved in with in-laws, his parents at the Cape Cod compound. For Joan, unused to sudden changes, the months since their marriage had been tumultuous. There had been three shiny, all-too-brief days of honeymooning on Lord Beaverbrook's estate in Nassau. "He was always telling Ted's father to send the children down to see him," Joan says, "so this time he did. He sent us." On the fourth day they had flown to Charlottesville and Joan had become a campus wife. Then graduation, and after a deferred wedding trip that took them through most of South America, they returned to the Cape.

The Kennedys loved her right away. Strikingly beautiful, she could have been secretly envied by the other Kennedy women, but she caused no resentment because she was genuinely unaffected. Jean, a tall and slender young woman, said: "We consider Joan fantastically pretty and tease her constantly about her perfect figure, especially the men. The amazing thing about her is that she is so unaware of her good looks and so unspoiled by them." The Kennedy girls looked upon her as the ideal wife; she was devoted to Ted, never complained, never blew up. Rose, whom she called "grandma," accepted her warmly. The girls included Joan in all their activities—the sports she was trying to learn, which included several sets of tennis daily, golf, water-skiing, sailing. Meanwhile, Ted was pondering his future.

He sat in on the long series of conferences with his brother John and their staff of advisers. In October they had all agreed that John, the senator from Massachusetts,

should seek the Presidential nomination the following
July. Ted made up his mind without waiting a day. Having
received his law degree and been admitted to the
Massachusetts bar, he would neither practice law nor business but devote himself, at least for the foreseeable future,
to active political work on behalf of his brother's candidacy.

Joan knew at once what it meant. Ted would be away
from home almost constantly. She could stay at home and
wait for his infrequent visits, or she could go with him.

Christmas at Hyannis Port was always the gayest and
most exciting of times. The tree in the large living room
was ceiling high and the house, smelling of fish chowder
and warm bread, was filled with her new in-laws and
dozens of bright-eyed, noisy nephews and nieces, some of
whom she still couldn't tell apart from their friends. In the
midst of all this, she wrestled with her problem, taking
long inward looks, weighing alternatives, and at last chart-
ing her life role.

"I decided," she would say later, "to be ready to go
anywhere and to accommodate myself to my husband's
schedule."

Throughout the years that were to follow, she was to
make heroic efforts to match Ted's long strides—to keep
learning about his world and his work so that she might
avoid the tragedy of a marriage in which husband and
wife move along parallel paths that never converge.

In the fall, when wet winds began blowing in from
Nantucket Sound and the wide lawns browned out, the
Kennedys closed down the compound for the season and
scattered to their inland homes. Joan went back to 14
Eastway for the birth of her first child.

By this time, most of her friends had married and moved
away, and there wasn't much to do but read, play the

piano and await the nightly telephone calls from her campaigning husband.

Ted was home on an infrequent visit late in February when signs appeared that the baby was on the way. He took Joan to the hospital, then telephoned Luella. No Kennedy has a baby without calling on Luella, who married George Donovan, a union organizer, in 1971.* Only a severe virus could stop her from being present at the arrival in March, 1955, of Christopher, the first child of Patricia and Peter Lawford, who have since been divorced. Luella came to work for the family in 1937 as governess for the growing brood, remained until the mid-1940s and has had steady assignments since. ("I don't suppose there will be many more grandchildren," she says, "but some of *them* are pretty grown up now and may marry soon. I'll be ready.")

In Walpole, Massachusetts, where she lived, Luella was awakened by the telephone at 2:30 in the morning, heard the clanking of coins in the box and then Ted's flat Bostonian tones, somewhat breathless: "Luella," he said, "the baby's on the way. Can you come down?" In her new Falcon, presented to her by Rose and Joe, Luella was driven by a friend to Hartford, Connecticut, where Ted was pacing in the cold outside a Howard Johnson restau-

---

* Luella Hennessey Donovan, R.N., does more than watch over Kennedy mothers. She is the director of the Kennedy Center for Programs in Early Development in Wrentham, Massachusetts, where, under a grant from the Joseph P. Kennedy, Jr., Foundation, she is developing techniques for the training of retarded children. Rosemary, eldest daughter of Rose and Joe, is a retardate and is now being cared for in a Wisconsin convent. The foundation was named after the eldest brother who was killed over the English Channel during World War II.

rant. He drove her to Bronxville Hospital, where Kara
Anne arrived at nine in the morning on February 27.

By spring, Joan was ready to move into her new
world. Beginning in late March and continuing into deep
fall, she went to the mining towns of West Virginia, where
the smoke from the steel furnaces throws a eerie pink
glow into the sky, flew up into the bleak Wisconsin farming communities, still snowswept in late April, on into
Arizona, New Mexico, Wyoming, Washington State and
California. She visited carnivals, ate at barbecues, rode in
motorcades, slept in motels where the water ran too luke-
warm for a proper hairwash and stood in the endless reception lines, pumping hands and greeting people, keeping
the smile where it was though her feet hurt calamitously.

After July, when John Kennedy became the nominee,
things became even more lonely-hectic—lonely when she
was back in Bronxville watching the baby grow and relaying her progress to Ted over the telephone at night,
impossibly hectic when she joined him and the other
Kennedy women on (a new phrase that had entered her
vocabulary and was to roost there forever) the campaign trail. It was all wearying, sometimes agonizingly so,
but an experience entirely new and different for Joan, who
had never even campaigned for president of the junior
class at Bronxville High.

In the winter of 1960, with John Kennedy now President of the United States, Joan and Ted moved into their
first home, a duplex apartment in Louisburg Square, the
most exclusive part of Beacon Hill. It was in a four-story
red-brick townhouse on a cobbled street, overlooking a
private park shaded by century-old elms. There had been
some pillow-talk about settling down out west someplace
to get out from under his brother's shadow, but the plan
never got anywhere, partly because they both realized

John's shadow now stretched nationwide but mostly because Ted's father would have nothing of the idea and summoned him back to the family lineup.

And so, soon after the November elections, the youngest Kennedy went to Europe for a six-week fact-finding tour with a Senate Foreign Relations Committee unit. When he returned, he took a job as a dollar-a-year assistant district attorney of Suffolk County in Massachusetts, which embraced most of Boston.

Meanwhile, Joan went house-hunting and finally found one she wanted—"a skinny, narrow Boston brownstone," she called it—in Charles River Square near fashionable Beacon Hill, just off heavily trafficked Storrow Memorial Drive, which runs parallel to the river. It wasn't brownstone but ivy-covered old red brick and, though skinny indeed, it was hardly modest, costing $70,000. Like the fifteen others in that horseshoe-shaped enclave, it was a three-story, renovated townhouse with high windows, an iron-railed balcony looking out on a narrow strip of greenery and an unmistakable air of quiet elegance.*

Walk up the five worn stone steps, go through the door painted "Kennedy blue," a sea color the family seems to have adopted, into a small hallway panelled with mirrors on each side. To the right, the stairs to the second floor; straight ahead, a small living room; to the left, the dining room and kitchen. Joan had the entire first floor carpeted in deep gold. Upstairs, another hallway, three bedrooms and a much larger sitting room with bookshelves lining the walls. Ted and Joan brought in books by the trunkful, filling the shelves from top to bottom.

They settled in as young marrieds. For a brief time, life

---

* The Kennedys sold the house in 1972 after using it intermittently for twelve years.

was placid again, upper-class Boston normal—he walking to the office in the morning, swinging his briefcase, she taking care of the house and baby, with two to help. He would be back at 7:30 and they would have a quick dinner.

They lived simply and entertained quietly. There were a few dinner parties in the chandeliered dining room on the main floor, mostly Ted's Harvard and law school buddies. Several nights a week, Ted would be off on speaking engagements; Joan would go to a concert with friends or stay at home in the large upstairs den.

Joan found herself busy constantly but enjoying every minute. Happily, she shopped for chair covers and knick-knacks to put on end tables, picked out pictures for framing and hanging on the walls that lined the staircase, and even cooked. Ethel had trouble making hamburgers and Jackie never entered a kitchen except to give orders to the cook, but Joan, besides being an excellent seamstress, became more than passably proficient, though like most brides she learned the hard way. In Charlottesville, where she and Ted had rented a three-bedroom house on Barracks Road, she was inept and totally disorganized at first, but, with the help of cookbooks and determination, she managed some palatable meals. Mrs. E. Gerald Tremblay, wife of a Charlottesville attorney who had been a classmate of Bobby Kennedy's at the University of Virginia Law School and later got to know Ted well, was a frequent guest at their home. "Joan wanted to show she had learned to keep house and wanted to do it herself," Mrs. Tremblay recalls. "Once there was a dinner party at their house, and they invited almost fifty people. Joan prepared all the food herself, with no help from anyone. It was a buffet, delicious and beautifully organized. She glowed with pride when we all told her how well it went."

The interest in cooking carried over to Boston. She would spend hours in the long, narrow kitchen with the window at one end that overlooked a small, tree-shaded terrace. She'd shell peas and make exotic preparations such as Hollandaise sauce for her fish and egg dishes. Then she made a discovery: that S. S. Pierce, a Boston food concern, "carried a Hollandaise sauce every bit as good as mine, and that Ted couldn't tell the difference between frozen peas and fresh ones, or between my gravies and the ones that come in cans." Her enthusiasm for gourmet cookery waned quickly.

She loved to take long walks with Ted in the evening on the banks of the Charles or stride with him along Beacon Street to the Public Garden and around Boston Common. Not yet a celebrity, she could wander at will into a famous jewelry store that advertised gifts slashed to half their original cost after Christmas and thriftily buy up presents for next year's Christmas.

She was comfortable and content. It was almost like Bronxville without the lawns and sidewalkless streets. Life was good, there were no problems she couldn't manage.

Spring came around once again and by May Joan already knew that the pleasant life was only a temporary lull.

In March of 1961 they had settled into another home, a four-bedroom summer house on a high bluff called Squaw Island (though not really an island at all) overlooking Nantucket Sound. Harry Bennett knew that area well; as a boy he had spent summers in a small cottage literally only a stone's throw away. The compound was a mile away: Go down a little winding road, drive across the half-mile causeway, turn left again. But though not linked physically, the new house was still very much a part of the Kennedy enclave; it was connected to it with a special telephone line and family members were constantly streaming back and forth.

Rose would call Joan several times each day, a habit that has persisted through the years. She would ask about the children, invite them to dinner, offer suggestions about meal planning and remind her of forthcoming religious observances. Ethel would be receiving similar calls and suggestions.

Joan had received many attractive wedding presents, among them expensive jewelry from Joe and Rose, an oil painting and, from Bobby, a five-foot model of an old sailing ship. But she was somewhat short of china, a deficiency Rose quickly corrected from her well-stocked cupboards. Occasionally, too, when Joan had more than fifteen house guests for dinner, she would run short of cutlery and a call would go out to the other Kennedys to bring some. Surprised guests would note that the silverware looked as though it were picked up in odd-lots from a flea market.

Her dinners were Kennedy-style outdoor things for the most part, lobsters steamed in huge kettles or a huge roast—one time it was a twenty-four-pound rolled roast beef. She had no help other than a college girl she hired as a combination part-time cook and all-around helper. She was learning early, too, about Kennedy solidarity. One Sunday she and Ted decided to have dinner by themselves instead of driving to the compound. For days the sisters teased her about being a "recluse."

That spring and summer, Joan was pregnant with Edward, Jr. She was on the Cape when she went into labor and was driven to St. Elizabeth's Hospital in Boston. In the labor room, Joan told the attending doctor: "Ted is a very heavy sleeper. It may be very difficult to reach him." Ted, at the Charles River Square house, had called the hospital and was told that the baby wouldn't be along for hours. "Get some sleep," the doctor advised. He went to bed, put the phone at his side and adjusted the bell to its loudest ring, or so he thought. He had shut it off instead. When he awoke it was nearly eight in the morning. He called the hospital and learned that his second child had been born three hours earlier.

During her pregnancy, Joan had learned from inside the Kennedy political structure and, of course, from talks with Ted, what the rest of Massachusetts was already beginning to suspect: The youngest Kennedy son was being groomed to run for the United States Senate in 1962, the seat once held by his brother, now the President.

With a sad smile, she would talk ruefully in later years about her skinny little townhouse where she had led, for such a brief time, the kind of life she loved: "I thought that's where we would settle down, but it didn't turn out that way at all. It's never really been home, but a way station."

But she was game. Her decision had been made and she wasn't turning back. Already something of a campaigner, she had rather enjoyed the new experiences despite the rigors and inconveniences. Most important of all, she was in love with her husband and wanted what he wanted.

And yet, that 1960 campaign was only a warm-up operation for Joan, an out-of-town tryout. A much bigger show, and a vastly enlarged role, lay ahead for her.

5

The Selling of the Candidate's Wife

1. The Diamond Mine

PRIVATE POLL SOUNDINGS in early summer of 1961 by the Kennedys showed that more women than men favored Ted's candidacy. The meaning was clear, his advisers pointed out: He and members of his family must concentrate on the women voters as his brother John had ten years before when he survived the Republican landslide that had swept Dwight D. Eisenhower into the Presidency.

Old Joe Kennedy had shaken his head when campaign strategists had suggested that the Kennedy women, Rose especially, plunge into the race. When John E. Powers, who headed up the Democratic drive in Boston, wanted Rose to speak at a series of rallies for John in the city, Joe had roared: "For heaven's sake, she's a grandmother!" But Powers retorted: "She's also a Gold Star mother, the mother of a congressman and a war hero, the beautiful wife of Ambassador Joseph P. Kennedy and the daughter of John F. Fitzgerald—which means that she's hot stuff in Boston. I need her and I've got to have her."

Rose had already shown what she could do. In John Kennedy's first political campaign in 1946, when he ran for the House of Representatives, she and Eunice co-hosted a reception at the Hotel Commander in Cambridge which drew an astonishing 1,500 persons, most of them adoring women. "That was the clincher," admitted Mike Neville, Kennedy's primary opponent who had been expected to take Cambridge in a landslide but barely won out. Kennedy defeated a field of ten in the primaries and went on to an overwhelming victory in November over Lester Bowen, his Republican opponent.

Joe capitulated and Rose went in. The daughter of John (Honey Fitz) Fitzgerald, a former mayor of Boston and one of its most colorful political personalities, she knew all about politicking. She would address a formal gathering in a silk gown and wearing fine jewelry—then race across town to a rally in a union hall, changing in the back seat of the car to a simple frock or skirt and blouse. "She wowed them everywhere," Powers remembered happily. "She greeted the Italians in the North End with a few words of Italian and told them how she grew up in their neighborhood. In Dorchester, she talked about her days in Dorchester High School. At a high-toned gathering of women, she'd talk for a few minutes after Jack and then she'd say, 'Now let me tell you about the new dresses I saw in Paris last month.' They loved her."

And they loved the other Kennedy women too. Patricia, Eunice, Jean, Ethel, all crisscrossed the state. They appeared at women's clubs, spoke at street corner rallies, rang doorbells and greeted women at dozens of tea and coffee parties, even on television in two programs called "Coffee with the Kennedys."

Kennedy beat his opponent, the incumbent Senator Henry Cabot Lodge, Jr., by 70,737 votes—drowning him, his opponents ruefully conceded, in almost precisely that many cups of tea and coffee. (Polly Fitzgerald and Helen Keyes, who had staged the receptions, later computed that 75,000 women had attended them.)

In 1960 they did it all over again and once more it worked. Everyone conceded that the Kennedy women were political gold mines for their men.

In 1962, when Ted got under way, the organization found itself another mine, this one diamond. Joan Kennedy.

Plans to use Joan in the campaign received the highest priority. Joan was eager to start—"I'll do anything to help Ted," she said over and over to every organization man she met, gladdening their hearts. She began inauspiciously when someone allowed her to commit a blooper that still ruffles a venerable fortress of respectability in Boston, the Harvard Musical Association.

The association (which has no connection with the university) was formed in 1837 and numbers many of Boston's elite among its members. On the second floor of the association's building, in the Jordan Marsh Room, are two pianos where serious players are permitted to practice for one and a half hour sessions. In the spring of 1962 Joan signed up for a session and arrived with a newspaper photographer who snapped picture after picture as she played. The next day a story appeared in a Boston newspaper: Joan Kennedy, wife of the candidate for Senate, comes regularly to the Harvard Musical Association to practice her piano . . .

Actually, it was the first time Joan had ever been there, and she was to come only once more. It was plain that the story had been intended purely as publicity for Ted's candidacy, to the annoyance of many members of the association. A spokesman, who still bridles at the incident, says: "We don't like to have the place used as a vehicle for publicity. It was an unnecessary use of a very tenuous connection. Ted Kennedy has never been a member, nor has any member of his family. They are not particularly musical. Such unauthorized staging simply doesn't go with the character of the association."

At least one major Kennedy aide worried about her. Gerard Doherty, a mild-mannered, quietly efficient young lawyer who was Ted's campaign manager, had become attached to the young couple and, over the years, was to become a friend and close associate. He knew far better than Joan the enormity of the task she faced and was unsure of how intensive politicking might affect her.

Doherty: "The other Kennedy women took to politics like ducks to water and little wonder, considering their natures and heritage. But we had to remember that Joan was a duck who had never been in water like this, and here she was being dropped into a very full lake. She had to prove to everybody that Teddy wasn't just a smart-ass kid."

No easy trick, considering her husband was just thirty years old, the Constitutional minimum for a senator, only three years out of law school with almost no experience and was seeking one of the most prestigious elective offices in the land. Beyond all this, his brother was President of the United States and he had a father worth $300,000,000 who, everyone knew, would spend and spend to elect him. Joan herself, an almost total stranger to the voters of Massachusetts, had to make herself known and liked before she could even begin to do any convincing.

Joan was put in the hands of seasoned professionals for merchandising. One of these was Donald J. Dowd, at thirty-two already one of the shrewdest in the Kennedy apparatus. A slender, sharp-featured man, Dowd was one of five "overall coordinators" of the Massachusetts campaign.

As convention time approached, the coordinator's main

function was to compile a dossier on every delegate and feed the information to the main campaign headquarters in Boston. These vital statistics included every fact that could be learned about the delegate—his age and education, his comings and goings, his worries and those of his family, his job and hobbies, whether he was favorably disposed to the Kennedys, wavering or opposed, his hopes, his financial standing. Nothing was omitted.

If a delegate went to a church social and was overheard saying something vaguely uncomplimentary about Ted, Boston headquarters knew about it the next day. Someone would be on the phone, instructing a worker to talk to the delegate; or, if it sounded bad, Ted himself would speak chummily to the man. Once when Gerry Doherty discovered that an uncommitted delegate was active in Little League, he sent a volunteer to infiltrate the league, become friendly with him over discussions of the team's merits and shortcomings and begin the job of persuasion. On another occasion, a coordinator reported that a delegate was unable to attend an important rally because her son was sick and she was taking him to a doctor. The next day headquarters sent word to Ted Kennedy who called the delegate at her home, asking about the health of the boy. Touched, she commented: "You don't find men like that in today's politics."

Few were more efficient at coordinating than nattily dressed Don Dowd, who, with the late Edward J. King, was in charge of the western part of the state from Worcester to North Adams. In addition to collating information about delegates, Dowd had another key function: to sell them on the candidacy of Edward Kennedy. In late March word came down from Boston headquarters to step up this phase of the campaign and go into "comprehensive exposure" of the candidate.

This meant, of course, comprehensive exposure of the candidates's wife as well. Don Dowd and Ed King did their jobs with enormous technical skill.

Dowd: "The way the Kennedys work, each community, each town, has a Kennedy secretary, a permanent resident who acts as our ears there. From headquarters in Boston we would pick a place for a day or two of campaigning and then we would get in touch with our man or woman there and we'd say: 'We're coming to Springfield on August 18 and 19.' Then we'd call neighboring towns, like Chicopee, West Springfield, Northampton and Holyoke, and say the same thing: 'What can you set up for Mrs. Kennedy when we get there?'

"In a few days our people would report in with suggestions, like they'll take her for a few hours to a hospital to go in and see the kids, or a visit to a housing project for the elderly where she could chat in the recreation room with the old-timers, and then a luncheon with a local civic group.

"On every trip we'd have those coffee hours we knew would pull in the votes. They were incredibly successful. We'd contact our man or woman, say, in Springfield and say: 'We're looking for a coffee hour in Ward Three. Who's your coordinator there?'. Our secretary got us the name right away. Santos Acia or Jimmy Gimaldi. Jimmy was also the state representative from the ward. So we'd call up Santos or Jimmy. 'We're looking for a home in your district, a lady who would be willing to sponsor a coffee hour for Mrs. Kennedy.'

"So in a day or maybe just a few hours he'd call right back and say he's got a Mrs. Garcia on Lebanon Street glad to do it, and she'll take care of inviting the people to drop in. Mrs. Garcia would get right on the phone and by evening she'd have thirty to forty people lined up. So everything would be ready for Joan when she showed up. She'd circulate among the people, just smiling and talking small talk, and then in an hour she'd be off.

"The Kennedys work at perfection. The whole tour has to be carefully scheduled. Ed King and I would draw up a timetable and send it to Gerry Doherty and Larry Laughlin in Boston for their okay, and even Ted Kennedy would look at it and see just exactly what Joan would be doing and where she would be going.

"And then, to make sure there'd be no messing up, we'd have an advance man, sometimes Ed or me, make a dry run of the whole trip from start to finish, to see everything would go just right."

By August, Ted Kennedy had hurdled the first big obstacle, endorsement of the Democratic Party over the opposition of Edward J. McCormack, favorite nephew of the powerful House Speaker, John W. McCormack. Older by ten years and considerably more experienced—he had served as the state's attorney general—McCormack was furious at the audacity of the youngest Kennedy and the campaign was growing increasingly bitter on both sides. Though denied the party's designation at the nominating convention in June, McCormack had decided to enter the state primaries on September 18. Every weapon was being sent into the battle. For the Kennedys, one of the biggest and newest was the suddenly discovered Joan, who was sent out almost daily to win votes.

This is how it was on two of those days.

2. Merchandising Joan

SOON AFTER SEVEN on August 17, an oppressively hot and humid evening, Joan Kennedy arrived in East Long-meadow, a town of some 10,000 inhabitants near the southern tip of Springfield. With her was Sally Fitzgerald, one of her closest friends, a cousin by marriage. Sally, auburn-haired, slender, with unmistakably Irish good looks, is a niece of former Governor Paul Dever of Massachusetts and the wife of Robert Fitzgerald, Rose Kennedy's nephew. The two young women were met by Don Dowd who packed them quickly into his dark blue Impala and drove them to Smith Road where 400 residents, mostly middle-aged housewives, were jamming St. Michael's parish hall and craning their necks toward the door.

Promptly at 7:30, Joan walked in, Don and Sally close behind. She sat on a folding wooden chair and watched a fashion show. Models, young matrons from the community and a few well-developed schoolgirls, glided out and pirouetted in new fall outfits provided by local shops to a commentary delivered in monotone by a mistress of ceremonies. Joan applauded politely after each number.

Soon the show ended and a reception followed. Joan wandered among the guests, chatting, smiling, shaking hands. Don, moving with her, glanced frequently at his watch and at ten minutes before nine he tapped her on the shoulder and whispered to her. Still smiling, she edged toward the door, said good-bye to the women closest to her and stepped out into the night.

Dowd piled them again into the Impala and drove nine miles into West Springfield to a card party in a hospital meeting room where 250 women had gathered. Joan walked from table to table greeting them. ("Hi, I'm Joan Kennedy. How are you. So nice to meet you.") When she moved away, they kept staring; then, as she passed beyond earshot, they leaned forward toward each other and whispered.

Just before eleven, Don motioned to Joan, who caught

his eye and gesture and edged toward the door. Don drove
Sally and Joan to the West Springfield Motel on Riverdale Road, near the Mass Pike, where they retired for
the night.

By 8:30, when Don came to pick them up, the day was
already shimmering hot. It wouldn't be long before Joan's
white dress would lose its crispness and the tiny beads
of perspiration would form in her hairline and on her
upper lip as she went uncomplainingly through the schedule
Don and the Kennedy staff had set up for her.

Dowd drove Joan to an ancient four-story red brick
building on Cypress Street, which housed the Springfield
newspapers, the *Daily News, Union* and *Republican*.
Visits to newspapers and radio and television studios,
where Joan would be interviewed, always had top priority on a tour.

Dowd: "You have to start at the newspapers early in
the morning to make the deadlines. This is very important in politics. You get going early and you make a
tour. She'll sit with the editors and just talk and have her
picture taken, and then she'll go around shaking hands with
members of the newspaper's staff, and then go into the
bookkeeping and accounting departments or any type of
office and shake hands with the people. Here in Springfield, she started out on the second floor where she toured
the press room and met the printers.

"In Springfield they've got a morning paper and an
afternoon paper, and you've got to hit them both. So in
the morning she visited the *Daily News,* which comes out
in the afternoon, and then we had to bring her back at
four o'clock to meet the editors of the *Union,* which was
published in the same building. It was the same procedure,
pictures and all. She did beautifully. They gave her a

great spread in the paper and later Ted kidded her about it, saying he didn't get that when he was there.

"In between these visits, we took her to a local television station in Agawam a few miles away where she spent a whole hour on a program called 'At Home with Kitty,' a talk show on Channel 22. She just sat and chatted informally about herself and her husband and how the campaign was going."

After the morning visit to the paper, Don's Impala, followed by aides in a backup car in case of a breakdown, took Joan to the day's first coffee hour. There would be three more. This one was set up for in a small house in Gimaldi's Ward Three, the Italian section in West Springfield. The sponsor donated the coffee and cake, the Kennedy organization provided the dozens of paper cups with "COFFEE WITH TED" printed in bright red. The homeowner had cleaned up the place for company, prepared the coffee, spread the cakes and, by nine, already had more than forty guests overflowing the small living room when Joan arrived.

She circulated for forty-five minutes, chatting about Ted, babies, campaigning, clothes and the heat, then left. After emptying their cups, most of the women put them in their purses to take home as souvenirs.

Dowd: "From there we went to the Shriners' Hospital in Springfield where these crippled children were and she went around the cribs and beds and talked to the kids. We left it to the officials about where they wanted her to go in the hospital because actually, one thing about the Kennedys, when they go into a school or hospital, they let the people in charge direct them as to where they want them to go. We don't go in like Gangbusters and say, 'Hey, we want to go there.' We say, 'We're at your disposal. You

tell us what you want us to do here, not we tell you.'
So the staff escorted Mrs. Kennedy to the wards, and she
spent more than the usual time there because she felt for
these youngsters.

"So we left there and went to an old-age community in
Carew Street in East Springfield where we had set up an
hour.

"Everywhere she went, she was always saying, 'Do you
think I did the right thing?' or 'Do you think he would
be happy with what I said?' She was very conscious of
that and she always tried to improve herself as she went
along the campaign trail."

Next they whizzed to the television studio for the hour
with Kitty and then it was time for lunch, never in a
fancy place but in an ordinary restaurant in a shopping
center or on main street where office workers, housewives
and blue collar people might go. This time, it was a
Friendly shop, one of a large chain of ice cream and sandwich restaurants, which originated in New England, where
Joan would be sure to be recognized. (Don Dowd: "We
try to go where she'll create a lot of excitement, because
once people say, 'Are you Mrs. Kennedy?' word gets
around.")

After lunch they drove to the Forest Park section of
Springfield where Mrs. Rita Scibelli and seventy-five
guests were waiting in the backyard of her home for a
reception in Joan's honor. Mrs. Scibelli had set up um-
brella-shaded tables and loaded them with cakes, cookies
and teacups. Joan made a little informal talk, chatted with
the ladies and, after ninety minutes, left with Don to go to
Holyoke, a few miles to the north, to visit retired nuns
living at the "Mother House," Mount Marie on Soring-
field Road. She remained for one hour.

Following the four o'clock tour of the newspaper, Don

drove her back to the motel to freshen up and dress for dinner and the evening's schedule.

In an hour, Joan, who had changed to a blue dress, and Sally drove down Riverdale Street, a busy thoroughfare lined with pizza parlors, gas stations and hamburger stands, to Vincent's Steak House, a gabled black and red structure, where a table had been reserved. There were some local celebrities, like Daniel M. Keyes, Sr., judge of the district court in Chicopee, and Representative Edward P. Boland from the Second District, both close to the Kennedys, on hand.

Joan ordered steak but could only peck at her food. There had been no time to think much about the biggest event of the entire trip, but now that it was only a couple of hours away she had become very nervous. At 8:30 she was to make a speech before 700 women at the American Legion post auditorium in Springfield, the first time in her life that she had ever appeared before a gathering of such size.

But it was friendly territory. The legion post, a huge two-story red brick structure, had been dedicated by John F. Kennedy himself in the late 1950s when he was a Massachusetts senator. And it stood on Liberty Street in the Irish-dominated Hungry Hill section, which is the Springfield equivalent of South Boston, one of the most impregnable of the Kennedy strongholds.

Joan had been told to expect a "good crowd" but gasped when she entered the hall. "It was wall-to-wall people, well over a thousand," says Phoebe Dowd, Don's wife who had joined the party. Ed Boland, sent back again and again by the voters of the district, delivered a ringing speech on behalf of Ted's candidacy and then introduced Joan.

Applause rolled at her as she approached the podium

and unfolded a few sheets of paper. Glancing now and then at some words she had written, she began speaking in a small voice that was carried by amplification into the auditorium. It was a simple talk about her husband, what he planned to do as senator, why he would be a good man in Washington for the people of Massachusetts, why he was so concerned about the problems of Springfield and what he planned to do about them.

From the first words she spoke, it was clear she was winning them. The women listened intently, murmuring approvingly when she told them how he wanted a better life for the elderly of the state, giggling at the remarks about her children, smiling when she tongue-twisted on a phrase and shook her head helplessly in a girlish manner, quite obviously *believing* her. One woman in the audience said: "She speaks like anybody, so natural, so sincere."

When it was over, Joan rushed up to Phoebe Dowd and whispered urgently: "How was I? Did I do all right?" Phoebe told her she had been great.

At 11:15, Don Dowd returned Joan and Sally to the West Springfield Motel and the fifteen-hour day was over. As he drove home, Don was elated. Later, he would say: "She was our secret weapon."

3. *"It Isn't My Bag"*

ONCE, WHEN IT was new, she enjoyed the excitement of campaigning. She looked forward to meeting important people, felt she was helping Ted advance his career. Her horizons widened too: in earlier days, when she was knocking on doors for John Kennedy and, on occasion, had gone through some of them and seen the inside of slum dwellings—the paint peeling from the walls and the damp seeping through cracks around the windows—she had gone away shocked. She hadn't ever come that close to the world of the poor, and she learned things she was never going to forget.

Joan Kennedy: "I remember one of the saddest things for me—because I'd never seen that side of life—I'd see women my age [she was twenty-six] with four or five children in such dilapidated surroundings. And they looked so tired, so sad. They had aged so fast. And there I was, ready with this big pitch about voting for my husband. And you know, most of them never had a chance to see a newspaper. And it was so sad."

Joan's social conscience was born during that campaign. Later, she would understand, as she had never understood earlier, some of the things her husband, as the liberal heir of the Kennedy tradition, was trying to do and say. Ted Kennedy himself had edged by short sideways shuffles toward the newer politics of the left. Standing just barely left of center as a youthful senator in 1962, he dipped cautiously into liberal issues, championing such uncontroversial ones as a reform of draft inequities, help for the tragic refugees of war and the upgrading of education. As the years passed he bided his time, cementing alliances, making strong friends, until he finally emerged, following the death of his brother Robert, as a full-blown left-of-center, post-cold-war liberal.

He has become increasingly involved in significant social legislation, which affects tens of millions: the poor and the dispossessed in the ghettos and in rural areas, the workingman, the aged and the helpless. He became deeply concerned about the growing distance between black and white America. He feared that the safeguards provided by the Constitution against incursions on personal liberty were in danger of being eroded. He took on foes no less politically formidable than the American Medical Association and the vast petroleum industry.

If Ted Kennedy's liberalism derived, in the beginning, not from personal experience so much as—his words—"the enormous influences" of his brothers, so too has Joan absorbed her husband's strong feelings, motivations and concerns. They have become hers by virtue of family association.

She *feels* now. Stupidities and injustices can outrage her, as they do Ted Kennedy. She can weep, as he did, when two million persons died in the Nigeria-Biafran war and believe, as he did, that the Nixon Administration's inhumanity was largely responsible. She is not, as some have said and many suspected, the same pretty blonde who hated her current events courses at college. She holds firm views and can build up a good head of liberal steam not unlike the Kennedys over the plight of the old, the poor, the sick, the jobless—the "voiceless ones," as Robert Kennedy called them.

But feeling keenly about issues, believing in her husband's programs, was one thing. Carrying on the game of politics in the Kennedy fashion was something else.

As the years went on, the physical act of campaigning became a drag. Rumors arose that she was being forced into a mold she no longer wanted, that she resented the merchandising. Shrewd observers such as Arthur C. Egan, Jr., a tough, ruddy Irishman who was an investigative reporter for the Springfield newspapers for eighteen years and watched her in action from her first appearance, saw a change from year to year and campaign to campaign.

"At the beginning," Egan says, "she grinned and bounced. She sparkled all over the place. You could tell, just looking at her, that her delight was genuine as she

In 1955 Joan Bennett, age 19, won a beauty contest in Bermuda and was crowned college queen. (Bermuda News Bureau Photo)

The next year, 1956, she was Queen of the Bermuda Floral Pageant, the highlight of the Easter season. (Bermuda News Bureau Photo)

The portrait submitted to model agency head Candy Jones by Joan Bennett's father, who thought his daughter had a modeling career potential.

The photo of Joan Bennett that was sent to advertising agencies by her modeling agency.

The press caption read: "Francis Cardinal Spellman celebrates the nuptial high mass as Edward M. Kennedy, son of the former U.S. Ambassador to Britain, weds post-debutante Joan Bennett at St. Joseph's R.C. Church in Bronxville, Nov. 29, 1958." (U.P.I.)

Ted Kennedy accepting the nomination for U.S. senator at the 1962 Massachusetts State Democratic Convention. (U.P.I.)

In July 1964, Joan talks to reporters outside New England Baptist Hospital after visiting her husband, who was injured in a plane crash. (U.P.I.)

With her sister, Mrs. Candace McMurrey, in November 1964, at the opening of the John F. Kennedy Memorial Library in Frankfort. (Wide World)

The Kennedys in 1965 after their return from a fact-finding mission to Southeast Asia. (U.P.I.)

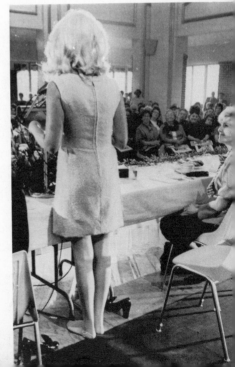

October 1968, campaigning in Indiana on behalf of Senator Birch Bayh. (U.P.I.)

With Mrs. Bayh. (Wide World)

At the December 1968 National Symphony Ball in Washington, wearing an Oscar de la Renta gown. (U.P.I.)

At the Corcoran Art Gallery's
Spring Ball, March 1969. (U.P.I.)

July 1969. At the funeral mass celebrated for Mary
Jo Kopechne in Plymouth, Pennsylvania (U.P.I.)

Reciting "Peter and the Wolf," at the Berkshire Festival at Tanglewood in August 1969. Arthur Fiedler conducts the Boston Pops Orchestra. (U.P.I.)

Making her first appearance after her miscarriage, Joan Kennedy at the September 1969 Symphony Hall reception for William Steinberg (left), the new conductor of the Boston Symphony. Arthur Fiedler is at the right. (U.P.I.)

went through the tough days, the rallies, the parades, the whole bit. But after 1964, the smile became too forced, the animation too obviously put on. Her heart was no longer in it. I could see that those hours on her feet, shaking hands with thousands of people on reception lines, left her exhausted. Afterward, she would collapse in a chair and say things like: 'I'm glad this one's under our belt' and 'I'm glad it was a short one tonight.' "

Joan herself finally admitted it. "It isn't my bag," she said.

She doesn't like being propelled through crowds by burly policemen. It makes her feel like a store mannequin, "so unreal and impersonal." Lately she has been telling her close friends how much she misses her children, how she resents the time she must be absent during their short growing-up years. In Massachusetts, when Kennedy was running for reelection in 1970, he began the day at six in the morning, an hour before Joan. They would meet at Boston headquarters or their Charles River Square home for coffee and sandwiches after ten P.M. To fortify herself for the sixteen-hour days, she would always eat enormous breakfasts and equally large lunches, and never gain an ounce.

There is no time during the day to rest or ease her aching muscles. And when she does try to steal a few moments, the sky can fall in. Once in Indiana for Birch Bayh, on a day when a huge rally was scheduled for the evening, she and Bayh's wife, Marvella, a beautiful, reddish-blonde young woman, had been running late all day long. They reached Indianapolis in the early evening and dashed to their hotel to change. In a few moments Marvella was ready and waiting for Joan in an adjoining room. Minutes passed and she did not appear. Marvella began pacing the floor. Finally, Marvella rapped on Joan's door. Calamity. Joan had decided to take a bath and made the same blunder as countless other travelers: Failing to notice that the tub faucet was turned to "shower," water had cascaded on her mane of hair. The two young women stared bleakly at each other. Joan was the evening's Big Attraction; reporters, photographers, TV crews would be there. Then Joan remembered—there was a fall tucked away somewhere in a suitcase. They rigged it up and the day was saved. But Joan never got to relax in the tub.

She is totally unlike Ethel, to whom political contests were like sporting events. ("Hooray for our side!" "Let's hear it for Bobby Kennedy." "We're underdogs but we'll beat 'em in the end.") Joan once said: "Ethel is the only Kennedy wife who enjoys politics." Jacqueline's distaste for the game and its practitioners has been well documented.

Nor does Joan have Ethel's show-must-go-on dedication when it comes to public and quasi-political appearances. Once Joan accepted an invitation to christen a ship in Massachusetts but shortly before the event asked to be excused, explaining that she was six months pregnant. Ethel agreed to pinch-hit. Afterward at a reception Ethel told some dignitaries: "My sister-in-law was supposed to be here, but she couldn't come. She's pregnant."

Ethel grinned as she said it. She herself was less than a month away from having her eighth child!

Still, Joan puts on an act good enough to deceive most newspeople and particularly all who watch her. Invariably, the reporters who cover her campaign travels write that she is having a glorious time and the photographs seem to prove it. They show her grinning as she dances with a seventy-nine-year-old man at a Senior Citizens Harvest Ball in Quincy, squealing in obvious delight as she tosses a strike at candle pins in an alley in Waltham, laughing, tossing her head, mothering babies. The dispatches go out to newspaper offices: "Mrs. Kennedy's delight in her role as campaigner was evident from the moment of her arrival at Barnes Airport in Westfield . . ." "Obviously Joan Kennedy finds most of the razzle-dazzle of public life and the responsibilities that go with it stimulating."

That is the image, nurtured by the Kennedy political technicians and by Joan herself. But the person behind the mask says in private: "If I weren't married to Ted, I'd be home with my children, leading a much more private life. I don't do that kind of thing for fun. I do it for Ted."

"That kind of thing" can involve some astonishing chores. Once, during Ted's first Senate race, campaign officials received a call from the Kennedy secretary in Pittsfield, one John McGarry. Joan, he said, must come out as soon as possible to see a patient in a hospital.

Several weeks earlier, the candidate, touring the town of Dalton a few miles east of Pittsfield, had asked a little blind boy if there was something he really wanted. There was, the boy replied—a dog. Kennedy instructed his staff to provide one and, soon after, the boy happily received a pet. Soon, however, the dog fell ill and was taken to a veterinarian in Pittsfield.

The gray-haired, ambassadorial-looking McGarry, who worked for the Crane Paper Company in the area, was a constant visitor. When he learned that Joan was making a swing through the section, he called and urged officials to take Joan to Pittsfield to pay a call on the dog. Don Dowd explained there was no room in the tight schedule, that even important meetings were being squeezed out, but McGarry insisted. It would, he said, be great public relations. The townsfolk would be enormously pleased and the boy would be delighted. Besides, it was a Kennedy dog and Joan had to follow through.

McGarry won. Joan, in a motorcade, had to make a long detour to visit an animal hospital in Pittsfield and comfort a small dog with a hernia.

During Robert Kennedy's drive for the Democratic presidential nomination, Joan flew around Indiana in a four-passenger, single-engine plane. In Vincennes, as the audience was trooping in for a rally, an official insisted that she go to the piano and thump out Bobby's campaign song, "This Land Is Your Land." Joan, aghast, explained that she didn't have the music. "Don't worry," came the hearty reply. "There's a band out there and that's the only song they can play. They'll help you out." Joan went out and dutifully played.

Joan was used not only to sway crowds but to convince individuals and she had her ways. When Abe Michaelson, a hard-nosed political columnist, didn't agree that Ted Kennedy, at the age of thirty, was the savior of Massachusetts, campaign officials suggested it would be "nice" if Joan paid a call on him. A key Kennedy staff member recalls:

"Abe was very hard on Ted Kennedy because he felt Ted didn't deserve to be a senator. He was very strong for Ed McCormack. The first one who came in to see him was Joan Kennedy, not Ted. She sat down with him, broke the ice and brought him around.

"She talked to him, saying she was there on behalf of her husband, that she felt he would make a good senator and she hoped he would feel that way too. Abe is one of our best friends today and I attribute that to Mrs. Kennedy.

"She charmed him. He was just won over by her."

Joan has been drafted for campaign duty on behalf of other Kennedys seeking office, and friends of the Kennedys, but she is not unleashed to all who ask. In 1968 she toured for Bobby and, two years before, she and her sister,

Candy, traveled to California to stump for John V. Tunney, who roomed with Ted at law school and is a close friend, and for Governor Pat Brown. Tunney won a Senate seat but Brown lost to Ronald Reagen. In 1968 she campaigned all across Indiana for the reelection of Senator Birch Bayh who, though injured himself, had dragged Ted Kennedy from the wreckage of a small plane that had crashed in Massachusetts four years before. She knew Bayh had risked his life to save her husband and there was a debt to pay. Bayh was the only Democrat to survive a Republican sweep.

The Kennedys, aware of the resource they possess in Joan, won't risk overexposure. Thus, when a number of politicians, some on the highest levels, hearing glowing reports of the crowds she drew and votes she garnered, asked for her services, they were turned down. Even Hubert Humphrey, who bid for her services when he ran against Richard Nixon in 1968, was refused.

She does her homework before each tour. Collecting batches of road maps, she pores over them carefully, studying the names of the towns and villages she will visit, getting pronunciations and locations just right.

The Kennedy clipping service supplies her with selected articles on political subjects from six daily newspapers to which the family subscribes. She stuffs them into her purse for reading on planes and trains. From these, and occasional special briefings by Kennedy aides, she keeps abreast of developments and is able to make knowledgeable replies to reporters' questions. Ted works closely with her, teaching and guiding. "He's a marvelous coach," she told the Boston *Record American*. "I report to Ted all the details of the previous day's activities, and then he gives me my orders for those upcoming."

While she dislikes large news conferences ("I'm used to

girly chats over coffee with a couple of reporters"), she has learned to handle the press deftly and rarely gets trapped. Once in 1968, during a session with more than 100 newsmen in Gary, Indiana, she fielded some of the toughest questions ever thrown at a Kennedy woman, who customarily aren't asked anything more politically explosive than to comment on the best age to start toilet training. Was she there, in a George C. Wallace stronghold, especially to campaign against the Alabama governor's primary bid? "I don't campaign *against* anybody, only *for* somebody." Had the recently concluded Democratic convention in Chicago, where a spectacle of violent confrontation unfolded before a shocked nation, hurt the party? "The Democrats have a wonderful way of reacting, of recovering. They look like they're going to come back to victory in November." Did Hubert Humphrey's sudden shift on Vietnam, from hawk while he was Lyndon Johnson's Vice President to dove as candidate for President, confuse her? Smoothly, she slid over to her husband's views. "Ted's position was different. It still is. Ted sent him a telegram congratulating him on the contribution made to the campaign and a step toward peace."

Whenever she appears at a rally, the band will strike up "A Pretty Girl Is Like a Melody," which pleases Joan but doesn't always enrapture the wives of other politicians who are not accorded the tribute. Toni Peabody, the wife of former Massachusetts Governor Endicott Peabody, who is herself an attractive blonde, remarks with some chagrin that Joan's theme song "makes me feel like Grandma Moses."

On a platform she still has not conquered her nervousness and doesn't believe she ever will. ("I have butterflies, just as I did when I had to get up and speak at Manhattanville. I did anything then to avoid giving an oral report.")

As she waits to be introduced, she studies her speech, typed on cards. Usually, a first draft has been written by one of her husband's aides, but she has cut it apart, rejiggered it and taped the pieces together with lengthy remarks of her own handwritten in the margins. Her speech-making voice is high, sweet, sometimes quavery, and she twists her wedding band as she talks. Occasionally she will stammer, stop, go back, and then she will break out in a giggle at a mistake and the whole performance takes on an endearing naturalness.

The press has been uniformly kind to her, often gushing. Wrote Nan Robertson in *The New York Times:* "With her blond lion's mane, dazzling blue-green eyes, clunky pilgrim shoes and mustard tights to match a shift that stopped four inches above her kneecaps, she looked as exotic as a butterfly . . ." Deedee Moore in *Cosmopolitan* magazine was even more rhapsodic, and anatomical, over her "well-shaped" shoulders, "firm and slender" arms, "dimpled cheeks, . . ." and "then there's this wow of a figure, with a cuddly bosom and an adorable bottom."

Joan has never learned one important trick of the professional campaigner. In a receiving line, when a hallful of people is snaking around the room to shake hands, there is a cardinal rule: Never ask questions. If you do, you'll have to wait for an answer and that takes time. The more people you meet, the more potential votes for your side.

Gerry Doherty: "The other Kennedy women were extremely skilled in receiving line technique. '*Nice to see you, thank you very much, nice to see you, glad you could come, thank you very much.*' Keep the line moving, moving. They knew that the line would move only as fast as they moved it, so they moved it fast. '*Glad to see you, so nice of you to come, thank you very much.*' Greet the people, pass them along and look the other way to the next one. An experienced campaigner knows that if you talk just two minutes to every single person, only thirty move through the lines in an hour and if you've got a few hundred people there that's awfully slow moving. Joan would rivet onto a person and really get interested in what he was saying and a lot of people got mad at her for doing this.

"But she has grown in lots of ways. She can spot a faker from a sincere guy in a moment. A senator, congressman, judge or anybody will come in and make all sorts of promises to help in the campaign. She'll listen to him and bat her eyes and, looking at her, you get the feeling that the whole conversation is going over her head. But she doesn't miss a thing. She'd have him pegged for a phony. She'll never say so in so many words, but she'll think, what a faker, all he wants are favors.

"Maybe she was once naïve, but she's not any more. She has everyone she talks to slotted in the right place, as workers, as real people, or as phonies.

"And she's gotten very good at smoothing out ruffled feathers. On the night of the Indiana primary in 1968, when she was out there helping Bobby, Senator Vance Hartke was in a pique because he hadn't been proclaimed as a rescuer, a champion, a savior, and if you know Hartke, he can pique pretty well. I was concerned about it because it had been my job to handle the primary for Bobby and I didn't want Hartke to go away angry.

"So I told Joan, 'Hartke is hurt.' Joan smiled and said: 'I'll go over and talk with him. Better than that, I'll tell you what I'll do if you're that nervous about it. I'll sit next to him all the way back tomorrow in the flight home to mollify his feelings.' And she did. She had become enough of a pro to be able to handle the situation."

The Kennedy political technicians were especially delighted with Joan because she never lost her femininity. Many candidates' wives undergo a kind of transference: stumping for the candidate, proclaiming his virtues, pleading his cause, they *become* the candidate. They adopt, not only his debating points, but his style and mannerisms. And—they come on too strong. [Says Don Bown:] "Toni Peabody would be great for Women's Lib because she's that *determined* type . . . she wasn't appealing. She was more or less demanding that you elect her husband, but Joan was *asking* for support."

Doherty: "They become imperious, too, some of these wives, throwing orders around to subordinates, and this gets tough to take. I've seen a lot of them order campaign workers to do this, do that, run errands, change things around to suit them. But not Joan. She was always the lady. She even picked up her own luggage.

"When I first met her in 1962, she knew little about politics, but she wasn't a dope to start with either and she learned, she learned.

"She has become enough of a pro."

The victory over George Lodge had been overwhelming. Ted and Joan Kennedy went to Washington in January 1963, he to occupy the Senate seat once held by John, she to start a new life in an enchanted setting.

6

Senator's Lady

1. Homemaker

SHE CAME TO Washington as the youngest wife of the youngest senator ever elected in the United States, wondering how she would cope with her new responsibilities and still give her small children care and attention. Kara was not quite three, as zesty and mischievous as her younger brother, Teddy, Jr., was big-eyed and quiet.

"I don't know anybody down there," Joan worried as she packed. She was facing, she knew, still another wrenching adjustment, not only to a new life but, as she soon discovered, to new kinds of people who were absorbed in this strange world of politics that she was barely beginning to understand, people with whom she had little in common. For the most part, they were twenty to thirty years older, wives of senators who looked upon her as their daughter, who had been through the political wars and were resigned to the pressures and uncertainties and who would pull out photo folders from their pocketbooks not of their children, but of their grandchildren, and show them off proudly.

But she did meet a few younger wives too and was grateful. At the swearing-in ceremonies for new members, held in the Senate chamber, she sat in the gallery near Marvella Bayh, who was proudly looking down at her husband, the dimpled Birch Bayh of Indiana, victor over the veteran Homer Capehart in a spectacular upset. Joan and Marvella, who was three years older than Joan and had a five-year-old son, became friends.

Marvella Bayh: "We talked about what our life would be like, the demands of our time, how we could be wives and mothers and still go to those official parties, luncheons and special events expected of us. Afterward, when we got into the swing of things, we told each other we felt like jugglers trying to hold four or five plates in the air at the same time."

Joan and Marvella became members of the Senate Ladies, an informal organization of senators' wives (the wife of the Vice President is always the president), and faithfully attended its Tuesday luncheon and bandage sewing and rolling sessions at the Capitol. The surgical dressings were sent to the Bethesda Naval Hospital. Joan sewed by hand and also operated a sewing machine, in the use of which she was still exceptionally adept. She was impressed with the history of the group, formed in 1917 during World War I to aid the Red Cross, and was grateful for the opportunity to meet informally with the other wives and chit-chat about common problems. (As the sixties progressed, however, Joan showed up less and less frequently; by the end of the decade, she almost never attended.)

She chauffeured constituents down from Boston on sight-seeing trips around the Capital. ("That way I do some sight-seeing that I might otherwise not have a chance to do.") She plunged energetically into as many activities as she could find time for: She was chairman of the Hope Ball and worked for the Joseph P. Kennedy, Jr., Foundation.

One thing she did not do: She did not become socially

involved with the young and rambunctious New Fron-
tiersmen who played as hard as they worked in those
early years of the Kennedy administration. Ted, whose
reputation as a lighthearted young man had preceded him
to Washington, was determined to remake his image; he
would be humble, hardworking and quietly efficient, and
he would listen to his elders. There would be no swinging
parties, no choice morsels for gossipy Washington to chew
upon. He and Joan would be a quiet, young senatorial
couple and make no waves.

Soon after the elections, Joan had flown down from
Boston to hunt for a house. With the help of Jackie and
Ethel, who had gone through the same chore when their
husbands came to Washington, she found a four-bedroom
red-brick home at 1336 31st Street in Georgetown, the
elegant residential section a few miles west of the White
House. A year later they were to rent a much larger house
at 1607 28th Street, so impressive that a taxi driver once
asked passengers alighting at the address: "Say, is that a
private house or some kind of institution?"

The contrast between the life-styles of Robert and Ethel
and Ted and Joan in Washington was striking.

The hijinks and low comedy at Hickory Hill, where
Bobby and Ethel lived with their rapidly multiplying
family and menagerie that proliferated even faster, have
been fully discussed, every practical joke on celebrities
described in detail, every pool dunking chronicled. The
big house on 28th Street, however, squatting sedately on
its quiet street, the vines climbing its brick walls and en-
circling its white-trimmed windows, was nothing like that
at all. If Hickory Hill had live animals in pens, corrals and,
likely as not, inside the Georgian house itself, Ted and
Joan had a farm, too, for their children, a toy one with

inanimate livestock. The only live quadruped around the premises was a poodle named Rusty who played quietly with the children in the privet-enclosed garden at the rear.

Inside was a huge drawing room, library, dining room and five bedrooms and baths. And all around, the special Kennedy touch in all their homes, photographs everywhere. There was a striking one downstairs of the three brothers in bathing trunks, each smiling broadly as they walked out of the waters of Nantucket Sound onto the beach at the compound. The staircase leading to the bedrooms was picture-filled. The master bedroom was beige-walled with a king-sized, pink-covered bed. Music from a small portable stereo played Mozart and Bach during the day when Joan was alone, show tunes and Irish melodies when Teddy was there. There was a governess for the children, a cook and, a new acquisition for Joan, a social secretary, a small, pretty blonde named Theresa Dubbs, who worked for the Kennedy organization out west in the 1960 campaign when Ted was coordinating the mountain states and "gravitated" into her job with the family.

In Washington they went to a few parties, choosing them carefully, and were big hits wherever they went. "These are two of the most dazzling kids in Washington," a woman reporter observed. "When they show up at a party the whole room lights up. Most nights, however, Joan was home. Ted was busy learning his trade—traveling to Vietnam to look into the plight of war refugees; staying late on assignments from the subcommittees on which he was placed, Labor, Veterans' Affairs, Aging, Judiciary; in the library reading reports. Joan would watch television with the children and put them to bed with prayers "for all the little children of the world who are sad," and then read or play the piano. She was getting accustomed to being alone.

2. Days of Innocence

SHE WAS UNPRETENTIOUS, often answering the doorbell herself for visitors, breathless from the dash down the steps, still adjusting the belt of her dress. ("Come in, *come in!* Please excuse the appearance of the place—it's a *dreadful mess*, but I've been *so busy* with the children.")

She was modest. Her head could easily have been turned by the compliments that came her way, but it wasn't. Comments about her attractiveness pleased her, of course, but they would embarrass her too. Once Art Buchwald, the humorist, was asked by *The Washingtonian*, a magazine published in the Capital, to name the city's ten most beautiful women. He put her name at the top of his list.* Ted preened, but a close friend said, "Joan wished Art hadn't done it. It singled her out for something she felt was hardly an accomplishment."

She was Joan in Wonderland. One winter she was packing for the trip back to Boston after a brief vacation at Rose and Joe's home in Palm Beach. John Kennedy, who

---

* Buchwald was nothing if not discreet. Far be it from him to hurt any woman's feelings! He named only nine, leaving the final one blank so that any woman who believed she merited a place on his list could add her name. His other eight selections were: Josefina de Coto Tejera-Paris, the wife of the Venezuelan ambassador; Rebecca Bell Rogers, the wife of Representative Paul G. Rogers of West Palm Beach, Florida; Bassima Al-Ghoussein, the wife of Ambassador Talaat Al-Ghoussein of Kuwait; Charlotte Collins Brooks, the wife of Representative Jack Brooks; Elizabeth Guest Stevens, the wife of film director George Stevens; Wendy Burden Morgan, the wife of news commentator Edward P. Morgan; Jewell Robinson Sheppard, the wife of Dr. James D. Sheppard; and Fiona Field Rust, the wife of David E. Rust, curator of the National Gallery of Art.

had been there too, offered her a hitch in Air Force One, the presidential plane, as far as Washington, where she could catch a shuttle. Entranced, Joan flew back with him, entering his helicopter at Andrews Air Force Base and stepping off on the lawn of the White House. The President went to his office, leaving Joan in the family quarters on the second floor.

"There was no one home," she says, "so one of the maids asked me in and showed me around. And there I was, like any tourist, rubbernecking in my very own sister-in-law's house."

She was thoughtful, uncommonly so in a town not noted for caring about other people's needs and feelings. One evening, at a dinner party preceding a charity fashion show, she spilled red wine over the front of her white gown. When several women sitting near her offered to swap dresses, Joan refused. She had promised a fashion reporter she would wear this particular dress to the show; and she knew the reporter had already written her article for the next day's newspaper. With a handkerchief dipped in cold water, she kept scrubbing away at the stain. Observed a guest at the dinner: "I don't know anyone else who would go off as she did in a stained and crumpled gown in order not to disappoint a reporter." One evening Ted telephoned from his office that he would be unable to get home in time to attend a performance of the National Symphony that evening. Promptly, she called the box office and said she was sending over Ted's ticket. Would they please give it, free, to a student?

She was ingenuous, sometimes to the point of creating political embarrassment. Late in 1962 she told an interviewer that she favors clothes designed by Oleg Cassini. "He gives me 50 percent off," she said, "which I think is terribly nice." Neither Mr. Cassini nor other designers

were especially enchanted by Joan's honest revelation that
she received a hefty discount to purchase (and of course
advertise) their creations.

To the same interviewer she talked disarmingly about
her life with Ted, and then she got on the subject of John
Kennedy and talked too much. "Ted's father loves to have
his grandchildren around him," she said. "In fact, all the
Kennedys love children. We've been married four years
and Ted can't understand why we don't have four children. He wants nine. He says if his mother hadn't had nine,
I wouldn't have him. Ted is the favorite uncle. He's so big
he can roughhouse with all the children.

"The President used to be the same way but now his
back is a problem. He can barely pick up his own son."

When he heard about Joan's announcement, Ted Kennedy held his head in his hands and moaned, "Oh, no!" In
the 1960 campaign there had been considerable talk about
John Kennedy's back: Plagued by serious problems since
football days at Harvard, he had almost died in 1954
following spinal surgery. The White House, exquisitely
sensitive to all matters relating to the health of the President, was screening all reports on his physical condition
with extraordinary care before releasing them. On May 16,
1961, he had wrenched his back while planting a tree in
front of Government House in Ottawa during a visit with
Canadian Prime Minister John Diefenbaker and had been
on crutches for several weeks. That June, during his sum-
mit conference with Soviet Premier Khrushchev in Vi-
enna, newsmen noted that he walked with obvious difficulty and speculation on the extent of his injury grew.

Kennedy was in agony much of the time; only the novo-
caine injections of Dr. Janet Travell, the President's physician, could give him relief. The White House was handling

the matter as though it was juggling a live grenade. And Joansie, in all her innocence, had blown the whole thing. She cried, appalled that "I might have hurt someone I love so much." The White House instructed Joan to issue a denial, which nobody really took seriously. Her remarks, she said, had been taken "out of context." She was also told, kindly, not to issue any more pronouncements about the health of anyone more important in the Administration than Caroline's pony or one of Bobby and Ethel's pets.

In her first full-dress interview she rattled on about Jackie: "Jackie," she said, "talked me into trying a wig. She has three of them and wears them a lot, especially for traveling. I tried one but just felt silly." She had not known that the First Lady was denying all over the place that she used wigs, though most alert fashion editors and women reporters were certain she did. When the White House aides gently pointed out that her remarks had been *infra dig*, she wept again and hurried to call the First Lady to say she had meant no harm. Jackie assured her she wasn't upset. It takes a while for a new celebrity to learn to give the proper non-responses to newsmen. A little while after the contretemps over the wig, Joan was asked if she was pregnant. She answered with an un-celebrity-like frankness: "I don't know for sure."

She was thrifty. Once Ted bought her a diamond pin worth many thousands of dollars, which she wore with pride to an embassy reception in Tokyo along with two strings of pearls she had purchased for $15 at Garfinckel's in Washington. "Everyone says they look so real," she said, "I don't think I'll bother buying the real McCoy." In contrast with her sister-in-law Jackie, who spent so much on her wardrobe that J.F.K. more than once howled in anguish, Joan frequently bought relatively inexpensive copies of famous designer's creations, spending $150 or less for an outfit.

One Thanksgiving she and Ted were hosts to Russia's Bolshoi Ballet troupe at the Squaw Island home on Cape Cod. She served them a luncheon of fish chowder but, not knowing how many to expect, she had had her cook prepare too much. Next day, when the other Kennedys came over for dinner, she gave them the leftovers.

Even Joe Kennedy recognized her thrift, and paid her and Ted a rare compliment, though at the same time driving one of her sisters-in-law to tears. At Hyannis Port, the old man got onto a discussion of money and how his children were spending it. "I don't know what's going to happen to this family when I die," he said. "There is no one in the entire family, except for Joan and Teddy, who is living within their means. No one appears to have the slightest concern for how much they spend." To one of the women he said: "And you, young lady, you are the worst. There isn't the slightest indication that you have any idea what you spend your money on. Bills come in from all over the country for every conceivable item. It is utterly ridiculous to display such disregard for money." The young woman thus blistered left the room in tears. Kennedy continued: "I just hope some of you girls try to live within your income or your children are going to live an entirely different type of life." President Kennedy broke the tension by remarking that "the only solution is to have Dad work harder."

Joan's clothing styles, naturally enough, received considerable attention in the press. Comparing her with Ethel, one commentator noted that both women liked "knacky or kinky clothes, dresses cut well above the knees and far-out jewelry. Each has a favorite gown for Washington's swinging parties. Ethel's is made of large squares of black and white vinyl with 'spaghetti' shoulder straps of rhinestones. Joan's is a very short shift of silver cloth with which she wears enormous plastic bubble earrings." The wives of other young legislators were also watching her for cues. On one occasion, the pretty young wife of a newly elected farm-belt senator was modeling a new dress which ended a considerable distance above her knees. "I know it's short," she said to her husband, "but really, not as short as Joan Kennedy's." The senator looked, turned red and pointed to the stairs. "You go right back upstairs and put on your pink chiffon," he told his wife. "What if a constituent sees you!"

Joan filled her closets with clothes by famous designers: Oleg Cassini was a favorite, but she also acquired gowns by Oscar de la Renta and Galanos; and she stocked up on Zuckerman suits and dresses by Mollie Parnis and Adele Simpson, all of which hung beautifully on her size eight figure.

If Joan's hemlines were escalating with the current fashions, her infrequent parties were sedate to the point of dullness. For the first few years she gave only small receptions, usually birthday and anniversary dinners and obligatory political functions, and turned over her home for a number of charity affairs, mostly on behalf of fine arts groups.

When she finally decided to have her first major social function it was a near-disaster, for she clashed head-on with the most formidable party-giver of them all, Mrs. Perle Mesta.

In May, 1965, Joan announced her plans. Bobby and Ethel would celebrate their fifteenth wedding anniversary on June 17 and she would give them a party on June 25. "We've never given a big party in Washington before," she said, "and we want it to be the best ever." She ordered a huge tent set up in her garden, a dance floor placed over the grass, pretty little pink-covered tables with gilt chairs, chairs of wrought-iron painted white for the shrubbed patio. A fountain, with lights playing upon the spraying water, would splash prettily atop a stepped-up terrace in the rear. Lester Lanin's orchestra was booked and a group of flamenco dancers engaged from the Spanish Pavilion at the New York World's Fair.

A few days before the party she discovered to her dismay that Mrs. Mesta had scheduled a function for the same evening and invited the same guests, most of whom had accepted both invitations! *The New York Times*, tongue firmly in cheek, nonetheless reported the story under a four-column headline: "Crisis in Capital: 2 Parties on the Same Night." There were also political overtones to the "ghastly social impasse." Mrs. Mesta's star had burned brightly during the Truman and Eisenhower years but had blinked out in the Kennedy Administration after she had strongly supported Richard Nixon in 1960.

Mrs. Mesta originally had set her dinner (honoring Senator Mike Mansfield of Montana, the majority leader) for June 24. At the last minute, however, a major Democratic fund-raising dinner in Chicago had been changed from June 3 to June 24 when it was learned that President Johnson would be in the city. Mansfield called Perle, who immediately sent out dozens of telegrams—her party was being moved a day ahead to June 25.

Washington wondered which of the two would end up being the hostess with the mostest. Many of the guests, trained as they were in the art of compromise, thought they had come up with a solution: Perle's was a dinner party, Joan's an after-dinner dance. Why not go to Mrs. Mesta's magnificent penthouse in Northwest Washington, have a cocktail or two, eat her fine dinner (filet of sole and guinea hen), take in the spectacular view of the Potomac from her two broad terraces, then go on to Georgetown for dancing and refreshments at the Kennedys'. But Perle didn't get where she was by giving quarter. She made it known that she too would have dancing after dinner. The guests were left on their own to solve the dilemma as best they could.

The final score: divided attendance. Joan, who had invited all one hundred senators, corraled sixteen, a good score since many were out of town and went to neither affair. She also got two Cabinet members and Mrs. Hervé Alphand, the wife of the French Ambassador and a mighty social gun, as well as a good sprinkling of judges and high administration officials. Perle had only twenty for dinner and another thirty arrived later, after attending pre-Kennedy-dance dinners given by Mr. and Mrs. Sargent Shriver, Ethel and Bobby and other close Kennedy friends. Like all hostesses disappointed when too few guests show up, both women had lots of food left over.

Joan had more luck, and a great deal more work, with her dinner parties at Cape Cod. Ted was given to informing his wife at the last possible moment that there would be guests for dinner. Around noon he would telephone to tell her there would be eight that evening; could she be ready? She would have a pad and pencil by the white phone on the terrace to scratch off quick notes; with the help of a cook and a young college girl hired for the summer to help care for the children, she would manage— somehow. She became so efficient that a party for three dozen Kennedys and their house guests wouldn't faze her: get a 24-pound rolled beef roast "like the side of a cow," send the mother's helper to the Big House to borrow Rose Kennedy's cutlery and dishes to supplement her own, have

pots of hot corn, vats of vegetables, a dozen deep-dish
pies and gallons of iced punch.

*Her days are fast-paced, exciting, "an absolutely last-
minute kind of life." Ted telephoning from Boston: A reception tomorrow, Joansie, come on up. She packs, calls
a taxi, leaves instructions for the governess and Theresa
Dubbs and is off to the airport. Next evening, beautiful in
a long gown, entering a ballroom filled with cigar smoke
and Democrats drinking rum punch and eating crackers
with cheese dip. Back in Washington, a great name in the
entertainment world is at her dinner table; the night following she sits next to a visiting head of state. Often she
dines upstairs in the private family quarters of the White
House—always promptly at eight—on china bearing the
Great Seal of the United States, and using silver engraved
with the words "The President's House" with the President himself at the head of the table, forking fettucini as
music from* CAMELOT *plays softly over the hi-fi. She chats
with Jackie about clothes, music, hairdos. Dinner many
times at the President's home on Irving Avenue at Hyannis
Port with the President and the First Lady; and over there,
at the other side of the large table, Bobby Kennedy, the
attorney general, whose wife Ethel had just raved about
her to an interviewer: "There isn't a toenail that isn't absolutely gorgeous." Afterward, being urged to the piano
by the family, playing accompaniment as Ted, in a baritone
more sincere than tuneful, belts out "Heart of My Heart"
and then the President himself, who always called her "the
dish," asking if she knows "September Song." And playing for him, for the* PRESIDENT OF THE UNITED STATES *as,
in a soft, unusually affecting tone he sings (prophetically,
though nobody guessed) of the days dwindling down to
a precious few. Trips abroad to Tokyo with Ted as guests*

*of the Japanese Council for International Understanding,
a private committee of leading Japanese citizens, and being
the star attraction at the reception in the American Embassy, outshining even Cary Grant. Receiving the unani-
mous adoration of the members of the women's press corps
in the Capital, astute journalists who do not give their approval easily or often to newcomers. Reading this about
herself: "Mrs. Edward M. Kennedy is so obviously in love
with her life and the future it offers that even Washington's crustiest political veterans are bound to be charmed.
All they have to do is hear her say, 'I adore Senator Dirk-
sen's voice. I've never met him, but he must be a nice man,'
see her wrinkle her nose, and they'll know it's so."*

*All these people and all these things. How glamorous
can life be?*

7

Square Peg

1. *Peter and Jackie and Ethel and Joan*

FEW WOMEN COULD successfully fulfill the role Joan accepted—membership in a family of tough-minded, domineering over-achievers, each one larger than life, quite possibly the most aggressive and able that modern America has produced.

Few women, or few men either. Peter Lawford, the British actor who married Patricia Kennedy and was divorced from her in 1966 after twelve years, was never accepted as a full-fledged member of the clan. He was liked because he was an easygoing fellow who made jokes and took neither himself nor them very seriously. Lawford cheerfully ran errands for the family. On election night, 1960, he padded shoeless through Bobby Kennedy's house at the compound, relaying messages from the executive staff to the press. He did perform one important service that earned a footnote in the histories of the times. At the nominating convention in Chicago that year he convinced the Nevada delegation to vote for Kennedy, a feat he was able to swing by virtue of membership in the Frank Sinatra "rat pack," which consisted of Dean Martin, Sammy Davis, Jr., and other star Las Vegas performers.

Lawford himself once quoted a Chicago politician's remark at the time J.F.K. was a promising presidential candidate: "When Jack gets to the White House, he'll make Bobby the attorney general, Teddy will run for Congress in

Massachusetts and Sarge Shriver will probably become governor of Illinois. But the big question is, what are they going to do with Peter Lawford?" Three of the four predictions came true, and they never did discover what to do with Peter, who called himself the "off-beat brother-in-law." The only child of Sir Sydney Lawford, a British lieutenant general, Peter was tutor-taught, shy and introverted in his youth, inoculated from birth with British reserve. He had never known a family like the Kennedys, much less understood how to act within its circle. "The rough and tumble of a large, gregarious family," he once said, "was completely foreign to me, and thus I became— by marriage—an outsider in an almost overwhelming situation." The bright red socks he wore with his ice-cream pants and blue blazer the first time he met Joe Kennedy (at Palm Beach during Christmas of 1954) didn't help. The patriarch kept staring at them all the time Peter was in his presence.

Before the marriage the following April, Mr. Kennedy, not given to tact, told Lawford: "If there's anything I think I'd hate worse than an actor as a son-in-law, it's an English actor." * The observation was not calculated to

* For her part, Lady Lawford wasn't enchanted by the Kennedys. "We would have liked Peter to pick a bride from court circles," she was quoted by *The New York Times*. When her acerbic remarks began appearing regularly in the newspapers, and after she had accepted a $50-a-week job (plus commissions) in a jewelry shop, *Hollywood Diary* reported Joe Kennedy had had enough. According to the trade publication, the elder Kennedy offered her a $1,000 monthly stipend and a chauffeured limousine on condition she leave the United States and cease giving press conferences. Lady Lawford, denying she had received such an offer, summed up their relationship: "I'm English and he's Irish and we don't see eye to eye and that's about that." She added a political comment: Had she been eligible to vote, her choice would have been Richard Nixon.

ease Lawford's entry into the family. Nor did the opulent life-style adopted by Peter and Pat delight old Joe. They lived like Hollywood royalty in a magnificent neo-Spanish beach home at Santa Monica, purchased from the estate of the late movie magnate Louis B. Mayer, who had spent $2,500,000 to build and gild it in the depths of the Depression. There was a marbled courtyard, a large swimming pool, a vast living room, a master bedroom of solid marble and a playhouse for the children (eventually there were four) reconverted from a greenhouse. In the living room, the paintings on one wall would slide away when a button was pressed, revealing two regulation-size motion picture projectors; at the same time, a large screen framed by a proscenium would rise from the floor.

After the marriage, Lawford became more at ease with the Kennedys. He golfed with the President, who genuinely liked him, although he proved to be such a distraction that the board of directors of the El Dorado Country Club in Palm Springs once called a special meeting to discuss his unorthodox playing technique. Peter golfed barefoot, upsetting the other members so badly that they complained to the management. The complaints reached the ears of the President, who took Lawford aside and, in the tradition of political compromise, made a suggestion: Wear shoes when you tee off, Peter, so that the players and guests around the clubhouse won't be annoyed, then when you stroll off onto the fairway out of sight, take off your blank-blank shoes and stockings if you wish. But remember, too, to put them back on when you approach the eighteenth hole. Lawford did and the members simmered down.

Nonetheless, Lawford was never a part of the family itself. He would sit at the dinner table, silent during the animated talk of political and world events. Nor was he up to the snap-snap way John Kennedy wanted things done. Once, when Lawford was visiting the President at the home he occupied briefly on top of Rattlesnake Mountain near Middleburg, Virginia, Kennedy wanted his opinion of a movie script based on Robert J. Donovan's book *PT 109*, an account of his heroic wartime adventures in the Pacific. (Warner Brothers was preparing a motion picture, which would star actor Cliff Robertson, chosen by the President himself, as the young Lt. John F. Kennedy who won a Navy and Marine Corps Medal for helping to rescue his crew after his PT boat was cut in half by a Japanese destroyer.) When he went to his bedroom that evening, Lawford found a copy of the script on his pillow and a note from the President: "Please read and be prepared to discuss at 8:30 A.M." Lawford tried manfully, but sleep overtook him midway into the script. In the morning, as a helicopter warmed up to take J.F.K. to Washington forty miles away, the President asked Lawford his opinion of the script. When the actor replied he had liked what he read but had zonked out for the last half, Kennedy grinned and left. The picture was made without any further assistance asked of, or contributed by, the only actor-member of the family.

Lawford appeared in dozens of movies but his star never rose high. His fame, such as it was, rested largely on his membership in Sinatra's inner circle where, for some obscure reason known only to the "rat packers," he was dubbed Charlie the Seal. The nickname hardly enhanced the prestige of his brother-in-law, who was actively seeking the Presidency, when it was bestowed and publicized in the movie gossip columns. After his election, the President became annoyed with Peter on at least two occasions. In August, 1963, Caroline Kennedy, then five years old, innocently recited a poem that had been taught to her, with equal innocence, by her cousin Christopher, several years older. The poem contained a word little girls should not use. It was, in fact, so filthy it made John Kennedy jump. He picked up the phone and chewed Peter out.

On another occasion, according to columnist Jack Anderson, J.F.K. gave Lawford a hitch in the presidential plane to Palm Beach. Lawford was sitting next to Kennedy until the President wanted to confer with an aide. "Peter," said J.F.K., "disappear." On landing, Anderson reported, Kennedy asked Lawford where he was staying.

"Where you stay," Peter replied.

"You're not staying with me. Let me know and I'll call you."

"I won't hold my breath," Lawford said.

"No, don't," the President advised him.

"This could have been good-natured banter," wrote Robert Curran in a 1964 book, *The Kennedy Women*, "but the word is that Peter would stay 'lost' during the 1964 campaign."

In the end, Lawford contributed little to the Kennedys except his four children, all of whom are being brought up as Catholics. Nor was he under an illusion that he could do more. Once he said that perhaps he might be able to help the President while he was in office—"if only by being around for laughs." Following the divorce, he has remained extraordinarily loyal to the family. He is on good terms with Pat and stays in close touch with her and the children, though he rarely attends family functions and social events. For him, Camelot is shining in the distance, receding year by year and, though he was never really a part of the glory he was close enough to cherish his days there and to feel "it's left a big void in my life."

her sisters-in-law were better equipped than Joan

to adapt to the Kennedy life-style. Ethel has an inner core of toughness formed layer upon layer during a rambunctious childhood in a wealthy, athletic, highly competitive family much like the Kennedys themselves, sheathed over with an additional protective covering of unshatterable religious faith. For Ethel, everything that happens on earth is God's will and must be endured. Jacqueline was closer than Joan to the world in which the rich and powerful move. Born in Southampton, molded at ultra-fashionable Miss Chapin's and Miss Porter's, summering in Newport, wintering in Europe, she knew far better than Joan the tribal customs of the rich and/or social. She could not be shocked by the cattiness, the intrigues, the casual relationships nor the infidelities that abounded there. She received the first, possibly the most traumatic blow of her life when she was only eleven, and thereafter became permanently hardened to further emotional assaults. Her adored father, the darkly handsome John Vernou Bouvier III, and her mother Janet were divorced amid overtones of scandal that could not escape the alert, extremely bright young Jacqueline. Janet charged her husband with misconduct with another woman; ultimately, she was to obtain a Nevada divorce but not before the richocheting gossip struck the ears of Jacqueline and her younger sister, Lee. At eleven, then, Jacqueline was living under the harsh strictures of "visitation rights," seeing her father one day out of seven, during half her vacations from school and six weeks in the summer. Shuttling between Janet and Jack, she had some of each but none of the family unity that, psychiatrists tell us, is the greatest benefit parents can confer upon their children. Her biographers, Gordon Langley Hall and Ann Pinchot, believe that Jacqueline's tendency to withdraw into "her private world" stemmed from the divorce. "She learned to participate, and yet remain an onlooker," they wrote. "It was perhaps a saving grace, enabling her to face what was unspeakably painful." With adolescence came loneliness, "a need for inner retreat and a search for self that was without satisfaction." And, with adolescence, came the development of that "private core that no one has since touched."

Beyond this, the personalities of Ethel and Jacqueline were from the beginning sharply different from Joan's. Ethel, literally without fear, was even as a small child able to withstand the most bruising blows with few if any tears, catapulting through her early years as though she were not mortal. Jacqueline, too, exhibited from childhood an extraordinary lack of fear; as a small girl, her nature was outgoing, breezy, even show-offy. She was imperious and demanding even then, something of an extrovert, a large handful to her governesses and teachers. Nor did she pay much mind to headmistresses either, not even the likes of Ethel Stringfellow who ruled iron-fisted at Miss Chapin's School in New York. When her mother learned that Jacqueline was being sent to Miss Stringfellow's office regularly for misbehavior, she was startled. "What happens when you're sent to Miss Stringfellow?" she asked. Jackie replied: "Well, I go to her office and Miss Stringfellow says, 'Jacqueline, sit down. I've heard bad reports about you.' I sit down. Then Miss Stringfellow says a lot of things—but I don't listen." Not Joan. *She* would have listened, had she ever been ordered to the principal's office. (She never was.) In John Parker's sixth-grade class, he remembers, she was "a goody-goody, too much so, always doing what the teachers asked. The other children didn't like it at all and so she wasn't very popular in the early years."

2. Trying to Fit In

THE OTHER KENNEDY women awed her and she tried to be as much like them as she could. She had taken tennis lessons at Charlottesville while Ted was a law student and, by appraisal of Mike Dolan, the pro at the Farmington Country Club, was playing a "really nice game" by the time she left. But it wasn't as good a game as the Kennedy girls played. She took more lessons and practiced a great deal. She tried to learn about boats and sailing and went waterskiing on Nantucket Sound. But she never could get the hang of sailing and she fell repeatedly from the water skis. One afternoon she came home and dejectedly told Luella Hennessey: "They do it so well. I'm a flop."

Her friend Marvella Bayh knew that Joan's ego was being battered because she, too, had faced a similar problem with her husband only a short time before. Birch Bayh is an excellent athlete but Marvella is as non-athletic as Joan. But she too went out on the playing fields with her husband and tried gamely to enjoy herself. She didn't, and began to feel that something had to be wrong with her.

One day when she visited her doctor for a checkup, he asked if she were getting enough rest and relaxation. The Bayhs had just gone through some busy months in Washington and Birch had planned a brief vacation. "My husband wants to go skiing," Marvella told the doctor. "I'm going with him and I'll get some relaxation then, I suppose."

She sounded unenthusiastic. "Don't you like skiing?" the doctor asked. "No," Marvella burst out, "I *hate* it." She told him how she despised those big clumsy things on her feet, how terrified she was of falling, that she much preferred to read a book or take long walks.

The doctor offered her sound advice. "You and your husband may be joined together in marriage," he told her, "but you are two different persons, with different physical and emotional makeups and different ways of expressing and enjoying yourselves. With so much common ground between you in other areas, why do you feel you must follow him in *all* the things he does? You have as much right *not* to like something as he has to choose what he wants."

From that time on, Marvella saw the sports and her marriage in a new light. Once she realized that her husband's enthusiasm for a sport put her under no compulsion to enjoy it too, her feelings of guilt and inferiority vanished.

Joan was unable to arrive at such acceptance and none saw this more clearly than Luella Hennessey. Because of a number of illnesses requiring extended periods of rest and recuperation, the Kennedy nurse became very close to Joan during her early years as a Senate wife.

Luella: "She admired the Kennedys so, their self-confidence, their poise, their physical strength. She knew she didn't have their stamina, that she hadn't been brought up for this kind of competition, but to please the family, especially her husband, she wanted with all her heart to be as good as all the others, and when she found, again and again, that she was not, she was terribly disheartened."

One afternoon, in the upstairs bedroom at Squaw Island, Luella tried to convince Joan to view herself and her relationship with the Kennedys in a new light.

"I've known the Kennedys since the 1930s," Luella told her, "and nobody knows better than I that they have many admirable qualities. Fine. But so do you. Yours are just as outstanding and they are very special; together, they make up *you*. So the one thing you can do, the *only* thing you *should* do, is to be yourself. There's no point in being a bad imitation of Ethel or Eunice or any of them.

"You must accept the fact that you are not one of the Kennedy girls. If you want to pursue athletics, fine, but do it for enjoyment and to feel better, not to win games and take home medals."

Joan stared out the window at the calm blue-green waters of Nantucket Sound as Luella talked.

"You must remember one crucial point," the nurse went on, "that Ted chose you because you were Joan, not someone like Ethel or Eunice or any of the others. If he had wanted a wife with their traits, consciously or unconsciously, he would have looked for such a person. Obviously he was seeking someone almost precisely the opposite.

"Why, then, would you want to change?"

Joan remained silent; Luella pursued her argument:

"Ted appears the big man, the strong man about town, but you know that deep inside he's soft as a grape, that he's a very gentle person too, who would weep if one of your children cut a finger." She reminded Joan that her husband was "a great big kid" with anybody's children, of the time in Palm Beach one recent Christmas when he gathered all the youngsters into a bedroom and rehearsed them in a play that he improvised, and how they had all trooped out and, with Ted coaching, given a performance for Rose and the paralyzed Joe Kennedy.

In this downward cycle of her emotional life, Joan was unreceptive to Luella's sensible argument. She accepted the maxim that, as she put it, "in this family you follow the crowd." She redoubled her efforts to compete against her athletic sisters-in-law and to match the sophistication of

Jackie, whom she admired enormously. She could not approach their mark and fell ever lower in her own self-esteem.

"I always used to say," she said at the time, "that Ted should have married my younger sister Candy. She was always the female athlete. She plays tennis and golf and rides beautifully, while I'm still allergic to horses." Of course, she didn't mean the words and hastened to make amends, but what emerged was even more pathetic: "But my tennis is getting better and so is my skiing. Anyway, I guess there's no going back now. Ted met me and not my sister."

The ability of the Kennedy women to bear more children than she could heightened her feelings of inadequacy, especially since Ted had announced exuberantly after their marriage that he wanted at least ten. "It was discouraging and depressing for Joan not to be able to see her way through her pregnancies like Ethel did," Nurse Hennessey says. (Ethel was having babies regularly, nearly at the rate of one a year. Eventually, she was to have eleven.) "Joan felt she wasn't as healthy as the others because she was unable to carry to full term. The problem lay in a hormonal deficiency, but there was no impairment whatever of physical health."

Joan was ordered to bed for most of the time she was pregnant with Teddy, Jr. In May, 1963, two years after he was born, she suffered her first miscarriage. In June the following year, she was rushed in the early morning hours to Georgetown University Medical Center but miscarried again at 3 A.M. Her physician, Dr. William J. Cusack, said she had been pregnant four months. Ted Kennedy, who had just returned from an eight-day European trip on behalf of the John F. Kennedy Memorial Library, canceled a speaking engagement in New England to hurry to her bedside. And once again, in late August of 1969, Joan lost a baby she was expecting in six months.

There were other medical problems, none serious but enough of them to strengthen Joan's feelings that her health was not as robust as that of the other Kennedy women. She had colds and sore throats and, finally, an operation to remove tonsils that had been taken out when she was a child but, somehow, had returned. Appendicitis and another operation. She had abdominal pains so prolonged and severe that she cried aloud. Exploratory surgery was performed to determine the cause. None was found. "It was probably some kind of intestinal virus," Luella says.

Like Luella, Ted too was aware that Joan was unsuccessfully trying to compete with the Kennedy women. She had gone to work for the Kennedy Foundation, as many of them were doing, but though the cause was admirable her interest was marginal. Ted encouraged her to find interests of her own and she tried. She became a member of the board of the National Symphony Orchestra. A short while later she was chatting with Robert Rogers, the orchestra's managing director, at a party. At the punch bowl, Rogers suggested that she narrate Sergei Prokofiev's musical fable, "Peter and the Wolf," with Arthur Fiedler conducting the National Symphony in Washington's Constitution Hall.

She accepted. When he heard about it, Fiedler, conductor of the famous Boston "Pops," was dubious. *Joan Kennedy?* But as rehearsals progressed, he was impressed. So was Rogers. "She threw herself into it as if she were Sarah Bernhardt doing a tragedy by Racine," he says. "She took coaching. She took advice. She participated in rewriting the script." She even had a sneak preview in a suburban theater, which was so successful that Ted promptly told Rogers he should consider a world tour.

"First I was timid," Joan recalls, "but by the time Ted got through encouraging me, I walked onto the stage before four thousand people, completely relaxed. The next day, my picture was in the papers instead of daddy's, and the children loved it."

After the debut, Joan was deluged with invitations from other symphony groups to recite "Peter," and she happily accepted a number, performing notably in Boston and at Tanglewood in the Berkshires. Her success was a spur to her ego, but it was hardly enough. She was still shy, still insecure and still "going along with everything" the family said and wanted. "I didn't dare to do otherwise," she said in 1971 in a backward look. Didn't dare to speak up and say what *she* thought or tell anyone what *she* wanted.

More than anything, she needed approval, most of all from the Kennedys and especially Rose. Marie Greene, a frail, white-haired but alert octogenarian who has been a close friend of Rose's since childhood and knows Joan well, sits in her memento-filled apartment in Brookline, Massachusetts, and recalls an illuminating incident.

One day Joan came up to Brookline High School to do her "Peter" narration with a student orchestra. Marie sat up front, watching, as Joan, in a dress inches above the knee, walked out on the stage and headed for a high stool in front.

Marie Greene: "I found myself wondering, 'How on earth was she going to perch on that stool in front of everyone with *that skirt?*' I almost held my breath as she began mounting it. With one swift motion, she deftly tucked the skirt under her thighs as she sat. 'How wonderfully professional!' I thought. And the narration was superb. Afterward I went backstage and told her how enormously impressed I had been by the way she handled the skirt problem and, of course, how thrilled I had been by her performance.

"She thanked me, then quickly she said: 'Would you write a letter to my mother-in-law and say I was good?' "

Marie understood at once and did better. Next day she telephoned Rose to say how well Joan had performed and how enthusiastically the audience had received her. Irrepressibly, Marie mimicked her old friend's flat Bostonian tones as she related her reply: "Why that's perfectly wonderful. I think it's darling of you to tell me."

She was a Kennedy, yet not quite. She was on the edge of the family, the last in the group photograph. As though symbolically: In mid-May of 1965, family members went to Runnymede, twenty-two miles southwest of London, for the dedication of a memorial to the late President, financed by contributions from British citizens. Photos published in British and American newspapers showed the lineup of world-famed personages at the ceremony: Queen Elizabeth and Prince Philip, Jackie Kennedy with Caroline and young John, Robert and Teddy, and, almost out of the picture, Joan.

She was a Kennedy, yet not quite. A member of the family, yet apart from them. One story told by Mary Van Rensselaer Thayer is sharply illustrative: The day after the President's funeral, Jackie sent for a well-known art collector to help the family choose a painting to be hung in the White House in Kennedy's memory. James W. Fosburgh, who had directed the selection of paintings for the renovation of the mansion the year before, went to New York and returned with about twenty paintings gathered from the galleries and dealers. He stacked them in the hallway in the family quarters between and atop the crates filled with personal belongings ready to be shipped out. Mrs. Kennedy, Fosburgh and four other Kennedys, Eunice Shriver, Patricia Lawford, Ted and Joan, narrowed them down to six.

Then Jackie called for the final vote. Fosburgh begged off: "You'll have to decide this without me," he said. But Joan, too, disqualified herself from the voting because, she explained, she had not been born a Kennedy.

She was a Kennedy, yet not quite, pushed from the magic circle by the clansmen who would clump together at large gatherings, excluding everyone from their midst but the full-blooded, like themselves. It would happen all the time, Rita Dallas, Joe Kennedy's nurse, reports in *The Kennedy Case*, her account of the patriarch's last illness. "Many times I've seen Teddy raise his head from the circle and look around the room for his wife, Joan," she writes. "When he found her he would flash her a smile and motion for her to join him. 'Come on over, Joansie,' he'd say, and occasionally she would, but it took courage to invade the Kennedy circle—for, united, they were a formidable group."

She was not, of course, ignored by the press, in America or abroad. In fact, there were incessant demands from newspapers and magazines for interviews, some granted but most refused, according to the Kennedy timetable of planned exposure. Her privacy was carefully guarded by the Kennedy aides and her social secretary. Once a reporter for the Women's News Service had to make three trips to Kennedy's Senate office for a few standard lines of bio-

* The family chose a painting of the River Seine in Paris on a beautiful morning by Claude Monet. It was hung in the Green Room.

graphical data on Joan. (Ted himself admitted in the late 1960s that Joan was being held under wraps. "I'm keeping her in the wings for 1970," he said—the year he was to come up for reelection.)

In the tight little social world in which she moved, Joan was admired for her truly generous and compassionate nature. Kennedy-watchers in the Capital pretty much agreed that Joan was the best-liked of all the Kennedy women. Jackie was the "cool cat," aloof, unfriendly. Ethel was outgoing, effervescent as Alka-Seltzer but, for many, too demanding. Eunice was bright and intelligent though reserved. Jean and Patricia were not in town long enough to be graded. Rose—was Rose; the indomitable grand-mère, the super-Kennedy. But Joan was your sorority sister who would listen to *your* troubles and *really* be interested. She was warm, friendly, a good companion, giggling a lot and always willing to do silly things for fun. "She doesn't act like a big shot," said Mrs. Peter H. Dominick, wife of the Colorado Republican senator. Mrs. Vance Hartke, whose husband is the Democratic senator from Indiana, said: "She's much easier to know than the other Kennedy women." And Barbara Howar, the Washington socialite, social maverick and journalist-author, called her "a sweet, lovely girl." Ted's staff, dedicated, hardworking young people most of them, adored her. Other Senate wives could be a nuisance, enlisting the staff for their own correspondence, badgering a press secretary to seek publicity for a party, but not Joan. Later, when she acquired the McLean mansion, she made the swimming pool and tennis courts available to the entire staff during the summer months when she moved her family to Hyannis Port.

Her closest friends in Washington as the sixties moved on were Mrs. Mieke Tunney, the lovely blonde wife of Senator John V. Tunney of California, whom she met when Ted and Joan were law school classmates; Marvella Bayh and Mrs. Ann Vanderpool, the wife of Wynant D. Vanderpool, a wealthy Washington architect.

There were moments of high excitement. In November of 1964, she and Candy toured Europe with an exhibition of the late President's memorabilia—his rocking chair and golf cart, the presidential seal, paintings, plaques and portraits from all over the world, the coconut shell on which Kennedy as a young lieutenant wrote a message asking for help after his PT-boat was sunk. It was a goodwill mission to offer the family's thanks to the people and nations for their outpouring of sympathy following the assassination.

Her first stop was Dublin. John Kennedy's visit to Ireland in 1963, he had said, had been "one of the most moving experiences" of his life. It had been a homecoming to the land of his forebears, a joyous, sentimental spree during which he was greeted by a nation almost in delirium. He had addressed a joint session of the Dail Eireann and Senate, the first outside statesman ever invited before the Irish Parliament; and he had eaten fine Scotch salmon and drunk strong tea at the home of his third cousin, Mary Kennedy Ryan, and met dozens of other relatives. A little more than a year later, forty thousand Dubliners lined the streets to see his sister-in-law, pressing into her hands small bouquets of country flowers with notes in them asking her to stay longer, and shouting *Cead Mile Failte*—"a hundred thousand welcomes"—as she passed. She lunched at Arus an Uachtarain with President Eamon de Valera who said the fog had been so thick it had taken him ninety minutes to get to the exhibition at the Municipal Art Gallery, but he had made it and spent many hours there. Thousands of

Dubliners stood four-deep in a line that stretched around the block; and so many kept coming that the exhibit was kept open long after the scheduled closing hour of 9 P.M. "It was almost as though they were in church," she remembered later, "the hush and the way they examined each of the objects." Another day, she drove south to Dunganstown and met Mary Ryan and her sister Josie and all the other relatives who had come to see John Kennedy the year before, and they wept a little after she had gone because she was a reminder of himself.

Then on to London, Paris and Frankfort, and finally to Berlin, where she saw the wall and cried when she saw a small wreath on the spot where a number of East Berliners had leaped to freedom. An exhilarating experience awaited her in the city. It was the night before November 22, the anniversary of the murder of John F. Kennedy on a Dallas street. Congress Hall in Berlin was filled with ticket-holders but the clamor to see a representative of the late President was so great that officials opened the doors to everyone. Every seat was taken, people jammed the aisles and backed up to the doors. They remembered what John Kennedy had said to them on his triumphant visit in June of the last year of his life when 60 percent of the population of West Berlin had flocked to see the President, who had come to inspect the Berlin Wall. Afterward, he had come out on a platform outside the City Hall and, looking out upon the largest mass of human faces he had ever seen in one place, he delivered the inspiring words:

> We . . . look forward to that day when this city will be joined as one—and this country, and this great continent of Europe—in a peaceful and hopeful globe. When that day finally comes, as it will, the people of West

Berlin can take sober satisfaction in the fact that they were in the front lines for almost two decades.

All free men, wherever they may live, are citizens of Berlin, and therefore, as a free man, I take pride in the words:

Ich bin ein Berliner!

The crowd had roared and wept. The human sea undulated; hundreds of thousands there were on the pinpoint of hysteria. The shouts, waves of deep-throated sound, swept over the President.

Now, a year and five months later, his golden-haired sister-in-law was standing in Congress Hall, talking to Berliners. In a small voice, husky, trembling at times, she spoke in English, as he had done, her remarks translated by a woman interpreter who stood at her side. It was a brief speech, telling of her pride in the accomplishments of the President and his ties to the free world. And at the end, she too spoke the words that had ignited those who had heard the President: *Ich bin ein Berliner!*

The crowd exploded. People rose in their seats, cheered her, wept. Joan, looking out at them, was profoundly moved. Candy's eyes were stung by tears. "I was so terribly proud," she was to say.

8

Showstopper

1. Minis and a See-Through Blouse

As she looked inward she began to understand more. She had been cheered by Berliners for words President Kennedy had spoken. She was the prime social catch of Washington because she was the beautiful wife of a Kennedy and the sister-in-law of another Kennedy who, they say, might one day be President too. But what was *she* contributing? How about her own life, her own accomplishments, her own worth as a human being?

Joan was ripe for what psychologists call a compensation syndrome. *Compensation*—"An attempt by an individual, consciously or unconsciously conceived, to make up for real or fancied defects"—Dr. James A. Brussel, M.D., former assistant commissioner of mental hygiene of the state of New York.

It can happen to a schoolboy who, despite all his efforts, finds he is unable to excel in sports. He will fix his attention upon another goal, perhaps to become a star academic performer or, if his emotional gears mesh that way, perhaps the class rowdy. It can happen to a schoolgirl, unpopular among her peers, less attractive than others in the class, who will resort to sexual activity to earn the popularity she wants so much. It can happen to a housewife who, convinced she is below the intellectual level of neighbors and friends, will concentrate upon excelling as a cook and a hostess.

And it can happen to a person who, like Joan, finds herself engulfed by an environment that is richer and fuller and far, far busier than the one in which she grew to maturity. Such an individual could become absorbed in the mass configuration and, for a while, enjoy a kind of prestige by association. But at the same time his sense of identity could be lost. Sooner or later, he will become increasingly aware that something of importance in his life is missing. He will become restless and unhappy. Ultimately, he will compensate for what he is convinced is an inadequacy by making a grand effort to stand out from the crowd in some other way.

To stand out, to be noticed, Joan struck out in an entirely different direction from that taken by the Kennedys. She chose a way that earned her the worst publicity of her life, including some scathing denunciations by prestigious commentators. Using the only assets she believed she had —her face and figure—she became a showstopper. Her hair became yellower and more free-flowing than ever, her skirts shorter, her clothing style "mod." She acquired clothes in wild patterns and vivid colors: hot pinks, passionate purples, maroons.

The girls in the senator's office, unaware of the deeper meaning, approved. "She's got the legs for it," one said. "If I had her legs, I'd wear those things too," said another. Around the country, the reaction to Joan's clothing explosion was decidedly mixed. Not surprisingly, men approved. To many women, she seemed the embodiment of the smart, swinging young matron from the glittering world of high-level Capital politics. To many others, she looked cheap, loud, garish. Fashion experts sided unanimously with the latter. Disgustedly, Kandy Stroud, Washington correspondent for *Women's Wear Daily* and an authority on what's in, out and proper in women's fashions, was aghast. "She looked like she bought her clothes in Gimbels bargain basement," Ms Stroud says, "her wardrobe was absolutely tasteless." *

Joan received consistently poor notices from *WWD*. Some of her close friends agreed privately that the criticisms were wholly justified, but none would risk hurting her by telling her what they thought or suggesting a change. Joan continued to pursue her course. Eventually, it culminated in two ghastly social blunders that made national headlines and set Washington tongues wagging.

Late in the afternoon of March 12, 1969, Joan hurried home from a trip to Washington, jumped into a shower and, from the long corridor of closets outside her bedroom, selected a glittering silver-sequined cocktail dress, cut low at the neck, which ended six inches above her knees. The invitation to the First Lady's annual reception for members of Congress and their wives read six o'clock and she had to hurry.

A few minutes before six she drove to the White House and joined the other guests in the Blue Room, lining up in twos and fours, moving forward a step at a time, chatting quietly as they shuffled beneath the great chandeliers until

* Because the Kennedys are recognized trend-setters, *Women's Wear Daily*, the industry's most important publication, faithfully records almost every item of clothing purchased and worn by the women in the family, not excluding young Caroline whose wardrobe was once reviewed thus: "Her smocked-to-the-waist dresses, her short white socks, her semi-fitted, velvet collared coats all point to another era. Today, ten-year-olds wear boldly striped knits, chain belts, bright tights."

they reached the President and First Lady at the head of the reception line. Mr. Nixon was in black-tie formal; Mrs. Nixon wore a floor-length, neck-high formal gown with white gloves to her elbows.

Joan, in her mini, shook up the White House and, it developed later, a good part of the country.* Pat Nixon, usually the model of rigid self-control, stared at her exposed thighs. The President shook her hand and, with admirable exercise of will power, looked at her face and said a few words of greeting. A marine in full dress uniform, standing behind the President, stood at attention, eyes straight ahead but, momentarily, lowered.

The other dignitaries and their ladies were not as restrained as the host and hostess. The documented comments at the reception:

"Wow!"—Robert Finch, then Secretary of Health, Education and Welfare.

"Her legs looked pretty good"—Rogers C. B. Morton, Republican National Chairman.

Senator Hugh Scott, Pennsylvania Republican, addressing Mrs. Ogden Reid, the wife of the representative from New York: "That dress comes up to Bryce Harlow's shoulder." Mr. Harlow, at the time a White House aide to President Nixon, is a small, slightly built man.

* Washington was shocked once again that year when Mrs. M. Robert Rogers, the wife of the managing director of the National Symphony Orchestra, wore a metal bra to the staid Symphony Ball. Constructed (forged?) of shiny little platelets, it topped a wide metal belt which girdled her tight, hip-hugging black skirt. Mrs. George Webster, a prominent resident of Georgetown, was prompted to cry out: "Her husband is a PAID employee and she had the nerve to upstage all the volunteers!" Mrs. Dale (Scooter) Miller, a close friend of President Johnson's, noted that Mr. Rogers must be planning to quit his post, which he did soon after.

"I only wish I had legs like that,"—Mrs. Melvin E. Laird, wife of the Secretary of Defense.

A dialogue in the East Room: Lady to Senator Scott: "Do you think Mrs. Kennedy is an exhibitionist?" Senator Scott: "I don't know, but she sure exhibits well."

A woman member of the White House staff: "What terrible taste."

The story (and, of course, pictures) hit front pages across the country and set off a clacking that didn't cease for months. The mail sacks in Kennedy's Senate office each day for the rest of the month contained more letters assailing (though defending too) Mrs. Kennedy's bombshell outfit than any other issue, including health insurance, crime and even Vietnam. Joan's enemies in Washington gloated. "She was incredibly gauche," one said. "What in the world did she think she was doing? This was a *White House reception*, not one of those uninhibited Kennedy wingdings." Carolyn Hagner Shaw, recognized as Washington's foremost authority on what's proper in social Washington, blistered Joan: "It was much shorter than it appeared in the pictures," she said. "Frankly, I was horrified." Joan's friends rallied to her defense: "Joan has the courage to wear what she's in the mood to wear," said Mieke Tunney. Some tried to pass off the incident as a lark. "Joan has a pixyish sense of humor," one close friend said. "She did this just for a joke to see what would happen. After all, she's young . . ." Bess Abel, a former White House social secretary, asserted that short skirts were becoming fashionable at black-tie affairs. "Besides," she said, "it was a very snappy dress and she has darn good-looking legs."

Joan herself, startled at the furor she caused, explained that she dresses for Ted who, gallantly, told her in private he did not object. Aware, nonetheless, of the thin lines between glamour that will attract votes and cheapness that can lose them, he confided to a friend: "I keep trying to pull those minis down."

Joan's mini was a conversation piece at many dinner tables in Washington that evening, not excluding the First Family's. In the upstairs family room at the White House, the President and Pat Nixon talked about it too and wondered *why*. Downstairs, Mrs. Nixon had been non-committal, telling reporters that women nowadays were wearing all sorts of things, but in the privacy of her own dining room, she told her husband that there *had* to be some reason because it was such an unusual thing to do. She was not angry nor was she critical; rather, she was sympathetic and understanding, her press aide, Helen N. Smith, told me in the White House as she recalled the incident.

Dr. Salvatore V. Didato, a clinical psychologist, adjunct professor of psychology at Iona College, who has established credentials as an analyst of personalities and news events for newspapers and radio networks: "Individuals with compensation syndromes often will develop a blind spot in their conscious minds to their actions. They become unable to view their behavior in its proper perspective, unable to subject it to their good judgment, unable to look upon what they are doing as self-defeating and, in the long run, destructive to their personalities. Not until, with the help of therapy, the individual can explore his unconscious conflicts and examine his transfer behavior objectively and unemotionally will he finally be able to 'see' its inappropriateness, understand the reasons for the actions he has been taking and set upon a new, constructive life course."

Joan continued to emphasize her appearance, making her striking appearances at parties, stealing the show wherever she went. Her reputation as a "mod" young matron soared. Three Sundays in a row she attended early mass at Holy Trinity Church in Georgetown, her family's parish, in a hot pink mini-skirted dress that took the minds of the worshippers off the text for the day. One January she went to a $100-a-plate dinner in Washington to raise funds to defray campaign expenses for the late Robert Kennedy. Joan and Ted arrived with Pat Lawford and Jean Smith, and not even the senator got as much attention from the crush of fans outside the hotel and the diners inside. They shoved and craned to see Joan, who swept in sheathed in a floor-length, figure-hugging silver dress slashed low in the neckline and back. One friend, who watched Joan inch through the gawking crowd surrounded by television and newspaper reporters, went away happy. "I got my money's worth just looking at her," he said.

2. Pizzazz and a President's Lady

As CONJECTURE MOUNTED about the possibility of a Democratic nomination for Edward Kennedy in 1972, talk about Joan as a First Lady gained momentum. Her credentials, possessed and lacking, were discussed at length in the press, and high on the list of topics was the question of her taste in matters related to living and especially in clothes. Nor was this a trivial matter. After Jacqueline Kennedy, America became sharply aware that a President's lady, though she may not set the nation's course nor leave a lasting imprint upon its history, can nonetheless put her stamp upon the tone and style of the country during the years she presides in the White House; and, no small thing, pour dollars into the economy by becoming a pacesetter in everything from hairdos to shoe styles, as Jackie had done. With her dark beauty, never before seen in the White House by any living person, her camellia-like elegance and superb taste in clothes, music, food and the gracious arts of living, Jackie had not only captivated the country but had opened new horizons for its citizens. At first suspicious of her, turned off by her hauteur and snobbishness toward split-level middle-America and all it represented, her countrymen made a strange and sudden turnabout. They came, and very quickly, to admire her for being true to herself and her tastes. They came to realize, as historian Arthur M. Schlesinger, Jr., wrote: "She represented all at once not a negation of her country but a possible fulfillment, a suggestion that America was not to be trapped forever in the bourgeois ideal, a dream of civilization and beauty."

But what dream of fulfillment did Joan, with her pizzazz, represent for America? The question was asked—screamed—in an eight-column headline over a nationally syndicated story: "HOW SWINGING SHOULD THE FIRST LADY BE?" Vera Glaser and Malvina Stephenson, respected newswomen, viewed the possible accession of Joan, given her attributes, with considerable alarm:

"The spectre of psychedelic art in the Lincoln bedroom or purple mobiles shimmying from the East Room chandeliers gives conservatives the shakes," they wrote. "A traditionalist might burst out in boils if Joan received the Queen of England in tights and a mini-skirt. Whether or not the 1972 campaign centers on youth vs. middle age, Joan's taste will be a factor if her husband is a candidate. By then voters under thirty will comprise more than one-fourth of the electorate. They may identify with Joansie.

"But if Ted's polls show that a majority seeks a more dignified image in their administration, Ted may have to tone down his wife's go-go appearance."

The blind spot persisted. On September 22, 1970, Joan

visited the White House once again as one of 117 guests honoring Mrs. Ferdinand Marcos, the wife of the Philippines president, at a luncheon in the elegant State Dining Room. Pat Nixon was hostess; present were Mamie Eisenhower, Virginia Knauer, special assistant to the President for consumer affairs; Dorothy Elston Kabis, treasurer of the United States; Marty Brooks, director of the Mint; Elizabeth D. Koonitz, director of the Labor Department's Women's Bureau; Rita E. Hauser, U.S. representative to the United Nations Human Rights Commission, and dozens more of the country's most politically distinguished women. Pat Nixon's staff of press secretaries, remembering what had happened the year before, buzzed for days about what Joan would wear. "It was such a notable company," says one. "We were really scared."

Their fears were justified: Joan created another sensation. Her knee-high shiny black boots, midi-length wet-look skirt and lacy see-through blouse with a baby blue brassiere visible beneath drew gasps from the other women most of whom, like Pat Nixon, wore conservative below-knee dresses.

Once again, Joan was blistered by the barbs. "Oh my God!" an executive of a major Seventh Avenue establishment burst out. "A Kennedy in a Barbarella outfit!" (Barbarella, a comic strip character, wears sexy space-age costumes.) Geoffrey Beene, one of Pat Nixon's favorite designers, said bluntly: "Mrs. Kennedy made a mistake. I hope people realize both fashion examples she set were in bad taste. Fashion is individualistic this year, but freedom can become too free." Reporter Marian Christy of the Boston *Globe* concluded that Joan, "who seems to be falling flat on her beautiful face," was being rated as the year's "biggest fashion bomb." She offered advice: It might help if Joan would equip her closets with locks, give the keys to a designer "who, from now on, will follow her around and daily give her the right clothes to wear." Mrs. Margaret Heckler, a Republican from Massachusetts and one of the most prominent women in the administration, was outraged. ("How do you like that!") and, apparently, had talked it over with the other women present who, she said, were similarly scandalized. "They didn't mind the wet look or the boots," she said. "They were just happy she wore her bra."

After a third incident, when she attended a luncheon of senators' wives at the White House in gaucho pants, a tight sweater with a bolero jacket of tie-dyed leather and suede boots, Harriet Van Horne, a syndicated columnist commented: "With her long blond wig, she looked like a faded film star on her way to a ranch cook-out. And one must, in all charity, wonder: Does this swinging young matron have any idea what she is telling the world by wearing such costumes to the White House?

"In her mode of dress, a woman is making a public statement. She is proclaiming her respect—or lack of it—for herself, her hosts, her husband and the milieu in which she lives. Naturally, she is also reflecting her time. But more obviously she is projecting her inner conflicts. One wishes, therefore, that pretty Mrs. Kennedy would discard those cheap novelties and hie herself off to the Paris couture—or to a good New York dressmaker. She can, one may assume, afford to dress well. Her mother-in-law, at eighty, looks elegant and womanly."

Dr. Didato: "With the help of therapy, solutions will offer themselves to individuals with compensation syndromes, and they will change, sometimes slowly, sometimes quite abruptly. They will no longer need to resort to bizarre or unacceptable behavior to compensate for any real or fancied defect."

Often a compensation syndrome is a healthy sign that the personality is seeking to reassert itself, trying to fight back, though frequently, as in Joan's case, at an immature level. Feeling herself unable to compete with the family on their level, she sought to glorify her appearance. The most healthy sign of all was that, by January of 1972, she was able to see clearly why she had acted the way she did.

She told me: "I wish I'd never done that. I wouldn't do it today or tomorrow, and I certainly won't do it this spring at the next annual affair at the White House. I didn't do it those times with a great deal of forethought. I feel a little ridiculous now that I wasn't able to foresee the stir it would cause. That was pretty naïve of me.

"I didn't realize it at the time, but I was trying to get some attention for myself. But I've gone beyond that now. I don't need to do that any more."

3. *The Loneliness of a Politician's Wife*

BUT THIS GROWTH, this feeling that Joan Kennedy had more to offer than a good figure cunningly draped, sometimes only partially, with cloth, was not to come until later. Meanwhile, her loneliness increased, a feeling not uncommon to most wives in her position. For loneliness is a built-in feature of any politician's household. To Marvella Bayh, marriage to a man in public life is worse in some ways than being wed to a traveling salesman, who at least comes home on weekends. "In politics," she says with a sigh, "sometimes the only way Birch can get to meet with these political organizations is on weekends. I don't mind him being away during the week, but Sundays are such a lonely time. I just try to keep busy, but it's hard when you're alone."

Both the sense of isolation and the pressure of political wifedom have affected government marriages for years in private, but in this age of increased campaigning, media coverage, and political complexities, the strain is beginning to show in public. In the past, politicians' families suffered in silence; today, marital problems are aired on television. When fifty-seven-year-old Governor Marvin Mandel of Maryland got up one morning and moved out of the executive mansion, declaring that he was leaving his wife for another woman, after thirty-two years, Barbara Overfield Mandel clung to the still warm marital bed and announced that she would stay as First Lady and, in fact, work for the governor's reelection. Events, as they unfolded, got more coverage than the state's budget: Barbara refuses to move out of the executive mansion. The governor goes to the Hilton Hotel in Annapolis. The governor, discovering that two were able to live more cheaply than one, finds he is unable to pay the rental on his new bachelor quarters, which cost $47 a day, and has to defer remittance of a $2,457 bill. Meanwhile, he moves into an apartment. Meanwhile, too, Jean Dorsey, the woman Mandel says he intends to wed, converts to Judaism, the governor's faith. No word on whether her four children will also convert. And from the executive mansion, where she plans to remain, Barbara Mandel issues a statement: "The pressure of this job must have gone to his head. I hope he gets some treatment." And all of it aired on prime time television.

Martha Mitchell kept the world informed about the state of her marriage (not good in 1972 when she gave her husband, John, then the head of the Committee to Re-elect the President, an ultimatum to give up politics or his wife. He chose his wife. The following year, when the consequences of Watergate began closing in, he left home, a fact duly announced by Martha). The year John Mitchell gave up politics to save his marriage, two congressmen made the same choice. Representatives William P. Curlin, Jr., of Kentucky and Patrick T. Caffrey, both Democrats, preferred their homes to the House, Curlin noting: "You pay a price in terms of family life if you pursue a Congressional career."

The price is heavy, for many political marriages, more than ever before in history, are coming apart. What's happening in Washington may well reflect the rising national divorce rate as well as new moral standards and the raising of the consciousness of women and their place in the world. It would seem, too, that divorce is becoming almost acceptable in Washington, a development that has not escaped the notice of politicians unhappy with their marriages. Whereas Adlai Stevenson's divorce seriously affected his presidential campaign, and Nelson Rockefeller of New York barely survived his marriage breakup and subsequent remarriage to Happy, divorce no longer jeopardizes a political career. But New Jersey's Harrison A. Williams, Jr.; South Carolina's Ernest F. Hollings; Kansas' Robert Dole; Wisconsin's William Proxmire and California's John V. Tunney, senators recently divorced or separated, will most likely survive in their chosen calling, though for some, different wives may be pouring the tea for constituents. Their marital problems have been recorded in the media, eyebrows were raised, tongues wagged; but no cries have come for their political scalps.

Michigan Representative Donald W. Riegle, Jr., a Republican, whose marriage ended after thirteen years, worried about the public reaction but got little. "There has been a radical shift in the country's attitude toward divorce," he says. Dole is confident he will be judged in 1974, when he seeks reelection, on his record and not on the basis of his personal problems. Note what happened to Andrew Jacobs, Jr., a Democratic representative from Indiana, who won his seat in 1964, won a bride during his term and was voted back into office in 1966. Afterward, however, he lost his bride through divorce, ran once more in 1968—and won. He won once more in 1970; he is still in Congress. "People," he says, "accept a candidate on his merits."

Last year, when the handsome baby of Congress, John Tunney, and his lovely Dutch-born wife, Mieke, filed for divorce after thirteen years of marriage and three children, Washington was shocked, but mostly because, like the Kennedys, the Tunneys were a beautiful young Washington couple. Tunney, son of boxer Gene Tunney, admitted candidly that Mieke "just couldn't take the life. Sometimes I get home at 10, sometimes 8:30, rarely before 7." Like Joan Kennedy, Mieke Tunney is a very private person. When she was not campaigning for John, she would go off by herself to New York to escape the hubbub of the hub of government. The twenty-three-year marriage of Phyllis Dole and her husband Robert, the Republican National Chairman, could not survive the demands of political life. "He got so involved with his job," says Phyllis, "that he let family fall into the background . . ." He has succeeded at everything he's done . . . except his marriage. Ambition breeds separation. He was with us less and less."

But if a marital crackup no longer endangers a political career, it is the nature of a political career that it endangers a marriage. Nowhere else are the strains so great. As Nelly Connally, the wife of former Texas Governor John Connally, says: "Togetherness is impossible in politics. It's passing in airports, communicating by note and no privacy. Your life is not your own." For Ellen Proxmire, former wife of Wisconsin Senator William Proxmire, "goldfish in a bowl are much better off than the public figures they resemble. Though the fish's every move can be scrutinized from every angle, people observe them only as things of beauty or objects of scientific interest," she says. "Those who study their silky movements from outside the glass don't criticize what they are wearing, what they do, what they say, what they mean; nor do they ask the fish lots of questions, or expect them to do much more than entertain. For political fish, life is truly lived in a glass bowl, but with all the necessary human results added."

With television cameras probing every aspect of political life, public figures are on instant, constant view, expected to perform accordingly. Politicians and their families are being subjected to the movie star syndrome of a decade ago. The fact that they are merely human beings who are under pressure in terms of financial and energy expenditures, torn between two homes, separated often from friends and family with obvious effects on family and sex life, is rarely taken into account. They are in the limelight and they are expected to behave in a manner above reproach. The men are supposed to be strong and powerful, guiding the country and speaking the ultimate truth. Their women are supposed to support their men's views, help their campaigns, care for them, raise their children, and oversee their homes, smiling all the while, being ever gracious and well-groomed.

To promote this attitude, the National Republican Congressional Committee issues a ten-page booklet, "Wives Manual," for candidates' wives to follow. The idea is that the wives are supposed to become 100 percent immersed in their husbands' campaigns and that, therefore, they are also supposed to act like ladies. The advice is in the form of dos and don'ts: Applaud as though you mean it. Don't chew gum. Bow your head during the invocation. Never talk loud or argue about your husband or his political positions with anyone. When sitting on a stage or at the head table, either cross your ankles or keep your knees together. Never let your picture be taken while holding a cocktail glass or a cigarette. Discriminating women never smoke on the street or when dancing; they never let a cigarette dangle from the lips or exhale through the nose. The cover of the manual shows a beribboned smiling female elephant wearing a pantsuit and bright red lipstick.

The Republicans, never especially alert to new times and attitudes, were stingingly rebuked for this one by several individual political wives and by the Capitol Hill Chapter of the Women's Political Caucus. The committee was reminded sharply that a new age had dawned for women, and that the etiquette advised in its white-glove booklet was designed to submerge the candidates' wives in their husbands' identities, and this is what the women were rebelling about in the first place.

Even when they're born to politics, the young, beautiful couples seem to have problems. Sharon Percy Rockefeller, wife of Jay Rockefeller, the young West Virginia Democrat who was defeated for the governorship in 1972 by Arch A. Moore, Jr., is no stranger to the life. As the daughter of Senator Charles Percy of Illinois, Sharon says that she was well aware of what she was marrying into. "I've been in politics a long time," she noted. "When I married Jay, I knew what our life would be." Well, life is a lovely home decorated by society's Sister Parrish, piles of money and two magnificent children; still, Sharon Rockefeller feels lonely. "In election years Jay keeps an eighteen-hour day six or seven days a week," she has said. "I cry and get angry. He can count on one major blow-up a month. People forget that just because you grew up in politics, you're just as human as anyone else. I finally told Jay if he'll just come home on Sundays, I'll campaign for him three days a week." To accommodate her husband's schedule, Sharon planned both babies for off-election years.

The pressures on the children can be just as horrendous. Abigail McCarthy, the former wife of Senator Eugene McCarthy, the Minnesota Democrat, has sensitively recognized their unique problems: "Ours were Congressional children. They were born into a life of moves and campaigns in which organized family life suffered, tension necessarily mounted and into a life in which I feared all too often they were made conscious that whatever they did might reflect on their father."

Politics has been no less hard on Senator George McGovern's children. The senator admits that his thirty-year marriage has required sacrifices from the whole family; in 1958 alone, he was away twenty-two weekends because he was running for reelection to Congress. In 1961, when he lost his first Senate race, he moved his family back to South Dakota, and when President Kennedy named him Food for Peace Administrator, McGovern's oldest daughter, Ann, refused to be uprooted again; McGovern moved to Washington but his family remained in South Dakota. Of that period, Eleanor McGovern says: "When the children felt they weren't seeing enough of their father, I would tell them he was trying to provide a better future for them."

That's not so easy to explain to youngsters who simply want love and a daddy at home. Nancy Riegle, Don Riegle's former wife, says: "The trouble is these guys think that what they're doing is so important they lose perspective. They think they're being unselfish worrying about the kids in Vietnam and the poor in the ghettos, but that's a bunch of crap. All they want to do is see their name in print. It's all for their own aggrandizement. When it comes to being a daddy or a husband, there is no time."

Some wives, unwittingly, even use their children as reinforcements. "The most difficult part of our marriage was when we first came to Washington," says Betty Ford, the wife of Vice-President Gerald Ford. "We had just been married. Gerry was invited to everything, night after night, as Representative Gerald Ford. I was not included. I was sitting at home without a child or a chick to look after and was beginning to blow sparks. I finally said, 'I didn't come to Washington to sit in an apartment.' There's no doubt about it, it's a lonely life. I've managed to keep quite busy since, with four children: three boys and a girl."

The two oldest McGovern daughters are married now and both sons-in-law campaigned actively for presidential candidate McGovern in 1972; but, the lone McGovern son, Steve, then twenty, stayed away from the campaign. "I think he's terrified about my getting the Presidency," said McGovern at the time. "It would mean the end of privacy, and there's the awesomeness of the office. Steve's a very private person." Steve quit college before the campaign. "He didn't do well in high school," McGovern said. "He was bored. But his native intelligence is incredible. I guess he needed some kind of association with me that apparently was not there. I find it hard to converse with him. He may be the principal casualty of my campaign."

Another near-casualty in the McGovern household was Terry. When she was campaigning for her father in 1968 she was arrested for possession of marijuana. The jolt to the family was certainly worse in 1968 than it would be

today, considering the number of children of public figures—including the Agnews and the Kennedys—who have
been arrested on pot charges since then. But, at the time,
McGovern considered giving up his campaign. "At first,"
he said, "I thought Terry's trouble was a reason not to
run. Then I thought it was a reason TO run. I remember
telling Eleanor, 'If the country is so mixed up that even
our daughter is playing with drugs, maybe I ought to do
it.' " Whether his reasoning was correct or not, the incident drew the family closer together as they supported
Terry, whose case was dismissed on a technicality. According to Eleanor McGovern, "It enhanced George's
awareness that the kids needed more of his time. Afterward, although he was, if anything, busier than ever, he
made a greater effort to be with them."

Joan Mondale, the wife of Senator Walter F. Mondale
of Minnesota, one of the wives who does not complain
(she prefers handling the house and bills herself, plus writ-
ing children's books, putting out a newsletter, and
campaigning for her husband with a slide show-talk she
presents called Politics in Art), finds that now that they
are settled in Washington, her husband is home more than
ever before—four nights a week—so the children actually
have closer communication with him.

Certainly it is no easy task for any one parent in any
walk of life to take full responsibility for the children.
But it is even harder when the wife is expected not only to
take care of the household, but also to campaign and appear with her husband at political functions. Ellen
Proxmire, no political novice when she married Bill (she
was executive secretary of the Wisconsin Democratic
Party), loved it all at first; then, like most of the others,
began to loathe it. Now she looks back upon campaigning
as a nightmare: "You start off planning on a very low

level. The pace picks up and the demands increase. The
fatigue is cumulative, and in the last month, like the Sorcerer's Apprentice, you can't stop it. Then there's a horrible letdown and you wonder, was it all worth it? Politics is a great strain for every family." After her divorce,
Ellen Proxmire was involved in two businesses, one a
wedding consulting firm, Wonderful Wedding, another
called Washington Whirlaround, which arranges convention activities.

California Congressman Pete McCloskey spent seven out
of twelve months in 1972 campaigning against President
Nixon's stand on Vietnam. His wife did not campaign
with him. In fact, he came home to find that his
wife, Caroline, nicknamed Cubby, was leaving him after
twenty-three years to marry another. Single-handedly she
had raised the four McCloskey children, painted and pa-
pered the family home (even to pouring concrete for a
patio), worked on community projects, and become a
real estate agent.

It had been twenty-three years of hard work; but, after
seven months of being left constantly alone, Cubby finally decided to get out. Pete McCloskey has regretted
his focus. "You know," he says, "a friend once said about
me, 'Pete's a great guy. He'll do anything for his country,
his friends, and his family—in that order—which is not
very good for his family.' He was right. I put Cubby
second when I should have put her first. I took her for
granted. I thought she'd put up with it. She never asked
for anything much except that I put her first when she
needed it. But I didn't even do that. You get so involved
with the cause you lose your sensitivity to people. And
it's all goddam cocktail parties where you have to do half
your business, so you're never home."

According to Washington psychiatrist Dr. Frank Caprio, two out of three politicians' wives are unhappy with their marriages and particularly with their sex lives, a startling figure. Add to that the fact that because of their power, politicians often attract what Dr. Caprio thinks is a special kind of rich, intelligent, attractive woman who gets into politics because she enjoys associating with dynamic, attractive males. The idea that political wives are expected to put up with such situations for the good of the party is almost overwhelming.

Even the wifely function of being a hostess is attacked by Betty Beale, a columnist for Washington's *Evening Star*. "Women," she says, "count for very little in Washington. The biggest pretense of all is that Capital society is dominated by great hostesses who have ruled the social roost since Dolley Madison's day. This is a monstrous myth perpetrated by the men with power who are loath to be seen as social stars. They may not get as much publicity as Truman Capote, but men toss all the wingdings of note."

Perhaps it is Betty Talmadge, the wife of Georgia Senator Herman Talmadge, who has hit upon the best solution for keeping a political marriage intact: Make your own life, do as little politicking as you can get away with and rarely see either your husband or his associates.

"I never made a political speech in my life," Betty says. "In the campaign, I went along with him, and I shook hands but I never made a speech. I've got something going all the time, but not that." What she has going is a thriving meat business, begun in 1951, which grosses $3,500,000 a year; Talmadge Farms pork products are sold all through the southeast.

The senator rises at 3 A.M. every morning, reads the newspapers, makes phone calls and leaves for the office.

He is in bed by 7:30 P.M. And he does this seven days a week. Meanwhile, Betty Talmadge, once named Atlanta's Businesswoman of the Year, works at selling ham hocks and sausages. In her spare time in 1972 she took a course in accountancy to help her handle her investments. She gets big kicks out of her grades and her earnings statements, while he sat on the Senate committee investigating the Watergate scandals and helps make laws. The arrangement works.

9

The Tragedies

1. "Contemplation of Violence . . ."

JOAN REACTED IN sharply different ways to the five hammerblows that struck the Kennedy family in the six years between 1963 and 1969.

In August of 1963, when Patrick Bouvier Kennedy, the President's infant son, died in a Boston hospital of hyaline membrane disease less than two days after his birth, she reached out to John Kennedy, simply and spontaneously. He listened and was comforted by her genuineness and artless sincerity; having been exposed to the artful kind so long, he had developed a bank teller's feel for the authenticity of an item handed to him and was not often fooled.

After the baby's funeral, Kennedy, more deeply grieved than the nation knew at the time, secluded himself in a small house near his brother's Squaw Island residence. Joan and Ted came over every evening.

Dave Powers, former White House aide, who has known the President and his family since shortly after World War II: "The first night, she sat with him for a long, long time and just talked. There was none of the orthodoxy you might expect, no talk about how Patrick was in heaven and happy, but just warm, human, simple talk. She said nothing, really, yet she said everything. The President listened and was deeply moved. They left at

eleven that night and the President walked with them out
to the driveway. 'You know,' he told me when he returned to the house, 'she's a great girl.' She was there the
next night and the next, and the President was grateful.
She did a great deal for him.''

Three months later, when Kennedy was killed, she almost went to pieces.

Nothing in anyone's life prepares one for the assassination of a President. Little wonder that eight persons out of
every nine in the country were physically affected by the
murder of John F. Kennedy, according to a University
of Chicago study soon after the tragedy. Joan was part
of the overwhelming majority. She was prostrated.

Once more underscoring the difference, she was the
only Kennedy woman to be so affected. Ethel bucked up
Robert at Hickory Hill; when he recovered from the first
horror and she knew he was in command, she drove off
to Stone Ridge Country Day School in Bethesda, Maryland, to tell her children, Kathleen and Mary Courtney,
and take them home. Eunice Kennedy knelt in prayer in
her husband's Washington office at Peace Corps headquarters, then went to the White House where she consoled
members of the staff. Pat Lawford, in Los Angeles, arranged for a flight to Washington where she joined the
family to help with arrangements for the funeral. Jacqueline and Rose, despite moments of private anguish, never
faltered: the widow, crisp and firm in her decisions; the
mother hiking over the sodden sands at Hyannis Port to
keep from collapse, returning strengthened to comfort her
sobbing husband. Only Joan took to her bed, felled.

Kara, then almost four, and Teddy, Jr., two, had gone as
usual to the kindergarten set up in the White House by
Jacqueline Kennedy for Caroline and John and a few
special children of friends and government officials. After

lunching with their cousins, they would soon be back at the 28th Street house in Georgetown. When the children had gone off to school, Joan had taken a taxi to the posh seven-story Elizabeth Arden salon at 1147 Connecticut Avenue to have her hair done. She had planned a catered dinner party that evening to celebrate her fifth wedding anniversary—one week early because all the Kennedys would be going to Hyannis Port for the Thanksgiving holidays. The next day, Ted and Joan were to take a group of friends to the Harvard-Yale football classic and remain at the Cape over Saturday night and Sunday. Candy and her husband, Robert McMurrey, were flying in from Texas for the party and, by coincidence, had taken off two hours earlier from Love Field outside Dallas where Kennedy's body was being removed from Parkland Hospital and Lyndon Johnson was being sworn in as President.

Barbara Brown, manager of the hair salon, heard the news at lunch and rushed back to the fourth floor where, in a cubicle, Marguerite Muguet and an assistant were doing Joan's hair. Barbara told Marguerite and the two women held a whispered conference, wondering what to do.

Barbara Brown: "We didn't want Mrs. Kennedy to get into her car and hear it over the radio. But we didn't feel that we were the ones who ought to tell her either. As we talked, the White House got through to us and said they were sending someone. I told Marguerite to rush her through as quickly as possible and we'd get her downstairs in time for the White House representative. They finished her up and we got her into the elevator, still not telling her, and expressed her down to the main floor. She had been in a wonderful mood when she came in, laughing and joking, and she still was. We walked with her through the lobby to the entrance, just as a man ran in."

It was Milton Gwirtzman, an aide of Senator Ken-

nedy's, who had rushed with the senator to the Georgetown house where a maid had told them that Joan had gone
to Elizabeth Arden's.* Kennedy remained behind, trying
to get through to the White House, while Gwirtzman
raced the several miles to Connecticut Avenue.

In the car heading homeward, he told Joan. Ted was
on the doorstep, having been unable to find a working
phone because all telephone circuits in the Capital were
overloaded. Frightened, Joan wondered aloud if there
could be a "national reason" why the phones were dead.

Suddenly exhausted, she went inside as Ted and Gwirtzman returned to the White House where, at last, they
found live phones. At 3:30, her sister Candy telephoned
from the airport. They felt that Bob should return by the
next plane to Texas to do whatever he could. Joan pleaded
with them to remain in Washington; there would be
dozens and dozens of callers for they were the closest
Kennedys in the Capital. Bobby and Ethel were in Mc-
Lean and the Sargent Shrivers were in Maryland. The
house would be thronged in no time. The McMurreys
assented and came over. So, too, did the caterers; despite
the news, a vanload of food and supplies for the dinner
party pulled up at the door. It was sent back. Joan was
upstairs in her bed, prostrated by the events.

All that day and the next, she remained in bed, secluded,
the only Kennedy mother so affected. "Like Montaigne,"
William Manchester wrote, "Joan found the mere con-
templation of violence crippling." She was barely able to
be present at the funeral. It had all been too overwhelming.

---

* William Manchester, in his monumental *The Death of a
President,* writes that Gwirtzman met her as she was preparing to
pay her bill. Kennedy women never pay bills in beauty parlors;
bills are sent home monthly.

2. The Lone Campaigner

IF JOAN WAS shattered by her first Kennedy tragedy, she
rose to almost noble heights of performance by a close
brush with another only seven months later.

She had gone to Springfield a few days early the following June for the first really good thing since the assassination: She would watch her husband win the nomination
for senator at the State Democratic Convention and accept it triumphantly. All signs pointed to an overwhelming victory. Ted had filled the two unexpired years of
his brother's term well, made no enemies, won new friends
and the grief over his brother's death had washed away
most traces of the bitterness of the earlier battle with Ed
McCormack.

Joan, driven by Jack Crimmins, the Kennedy's gray-
haired, middle-aged chauffeur and family retainer, was
taken in hand by Phoebe Dowd, a slender blonde state
committeewoman, the wife of Don Dowd, the Kennedy
campaign coordinator for western Massachusetts. Phoebe,
correctly reasoning that Joan would be besieged by newsmen and everyone else eager to see a Kennedy close up,
found a hideaway for her—a seven-room blue and white
house at 180 Poplar Avenue, recessed 100 feet behind tall
shrubs and white birches. It belonged to Alan and Ann
Biardi, old friends of the Dowds, who were on vacation.
"Stay here," Phoebe told Joan. "It's quiet and only a
couple of miles to the convention hall. Nobody will bother
you."

There was the usual pre-convention hoopla—receptions
for the delegates, a house party or two, a big dinner the
night before at which Joan, stunning in pink, had said
something sweetly unimportant and brought down the

house. Phoebe was right. Nobody bothered her there in the quiet house on the elm-lined street until close to 1 A.M. on June 20, a drizzly, fog-shrouded night. And then it was with news that her husband had crashed in an airplane.

Ted Kennedy was flying up from Washington in a small twin-engined Aero Commander, flying through the gloom with Birch Bayh, who was to deliver the keynote speech, and Birch's wife, Marvella. With them was hulking Edward Moss of Andover, Massachusetts, Kennedy's administrative aide.

Just after midnight on this Saturday, the 20th of June, Gerry Doherty, Ted's campaign chairman, stood by himself near the edge of the platform in the steaming Coliseum in West Springfield. An eerie silence had settled over the huge bowl where, moments before, there had been a pulsing roar, rising and falling like the sea smashing against a cliffside. Like the 1,857 delegates, Gerry had been confused by three announcements from the podium just after midnight: Kennedy's plane had crashed. And quickly afterward: No, it had not been Kennedy's plane at all. But once again: Yes, it was the Kennedy plane and he was being rushed to Cooley Dickinson Hospital in Northampton.

Doherty, up since seven to fight the challenge to the renomination of Governor Endicott Peabody by Lieutenant Governor Francis X. Bellotti, felt no special weariness, just a deep feeling in his gut that another tragedy had come to the Kennedys. He thought of Joan in her hideaway on Poplar Street. She had to be brought to the hospital, to see a husband or a corpse. Who knew?

Gerry leaned far over the edge of the platform, shading his eyes, searching for Phoebe Dowd in the crush. He spotted her and waved. She caught his sign and elbowed her way through to him for his urgent message: "Tell Joan. Quickly. Take her to the hospital." Watching her go, Doherty, his eyes now clouding behind the light horn-rimmed glasses, stopped to utter a quick silent prayer, then looked across the floor for Phoebe's husband, Don.

Don Dowd knew the roads from Springfield to North-ampton like the palm of his hand and the night was a bad one for driving the twenty-six miles. Don had gone to Barnes Airport in Westfield where the Kennedy plane had been scheduled to land, but there had been no news. He was told the Aero Commander left National Airport in Washington well before 9 P.M., but the soupy weather made slow going. He decided to return to the convention to await further news. Entering through a side door near the platform, he saw Gerry Doherty waving. Doherty sent him after Phoebe to get Joan.

Phoebe, an athletic young woman, had bolted through the crowd of sweating, shirt-sleeved delegates, weaving through them like a broken field runner, spinning around those who stood in her way, earning curses. She had raced to the parking lot of the Eastern States Exposition Grounds, leaped into her Chevy convertible and sped to Poplar Street and into the house, so excited she left her car lights burning all night.

Joan had taken off her pink dress and, in a matching slip, was resting in an upstairs bedroom, eyes closed but not sleeping. As soon as Ted arrived, she would meet him at the convention for the acceptance and the tumultuous greeting. She had turned off the television and the radio. Crimmins was waiting in the living room downstairs.

Crimmins heard the news on a portable radio. He sat up, listening hard; then, when there was no longer any doubt, he went upstairs and knocked on Joan's door. *She heard the knock and answered. Time to go. Time to look*

into the faces and hear the roars. Time to be applauded
and waved at, time to wave back and smile.

But it wasn't that at all. "There's been an accident,"
Crimmins told her as gently as he could. He could tell
her no more than he knew, sketchy news that Ted's plane
had gone down "somewhere near Springfield" and that
the senator had been rushed to a hospital.

Joan dressed rapidly. Crimmins went downstairs to start
up the car and met Phoebe Dowd rushing in. Less than
a minute later, Don Dowd drove up. Joan, her face dead
white, came down the stairs, went to the driveway and
climbed into Dowd's car. Phoebe caught Joan's eye. "Hi,
Phoebe," Joan said, her voice almost inaudible but calm,
"isn't this terrible?"

But she did not weep, not then nor during the long
agonizing ride to the hospital over the dark wet roads,
through the fog that settled over them like a yellow gauze
tent. Don hunched over the wheel, peering into the road-
way; his lights, low beam, high beam, whatever he
switched on, were almost useless, shooting back clouds
of mist into his eyes. Joan, in the front seat, began chatter-
ing half to herself—just "nervous talk," Phoebe remembered, saying things over and over to reassure herself.

"I hope they'll be all right," she was saying, "Birch and
Marvella and everyone on the plane . . . Sometimes they
say a plane has crashed when it's really landed, don't
they? Or they say there's been a crash when only something minor has happened, like maybe a tire blew out or it
skidded on the runway. Sometimes they say it's bad when
it might not even be bad . . ."

Don remained silent, watching the road. Phoebe agreed
with Joan; it might not be bad at all. Silently, Phoebe
was praying Joan was right and praying that Don, who was

doing sixty on the perilous roads, would get them all safely to Cooley Dick.

At the hospital, Joan rushed past the throng of newsmen and was taken immediately to see her husband. Crimmins leaped out of the back seat and, in his haste and excitement, slammed the door on Phoebe's face, which remained bruised and swollen for days. Later, in a room next to Ted's, Phoebe helped Joan undress and got her into bed.

The hospital sent in coffee and, to the Dowds and a handful of other visitors, Joan said: "I spoke to him and he talked to me. He told me he'd be all right." It was no longer nervous talk, Phoebe was noticing, not any more a hope in the darkness, but confidence that Ted would survive.

If there is a turning point in human existence, this was one for Joan Kennedy. She had no notion of the extent of Ted's injuries (which, at the time, were thought by the doctors to be life-threatening), but something had happened between the moment in bed at Poplar Street when she heard of the accident and the time she saw him, his back broken in three places and hemorrhaging inside from nobody knew where. From somewhere during that hour and a half had come an infusion of strength, and only later would she realize what it meant.

Man needs desperately to be needed. "The need to carry one's own weight is at once the great need of mankind and of man," writes Dr. Howard Lane of San Francisco State College. Frustrate this basic need and man feels diminished, unimportant to the life around him. He weakens, becomes demoralized, functions less and less ably, turns his thoughts inward and broods upon his uselessness.

It is there on all levels and at all ages. Children who are not permitted to use and demonstrate their abilities and talents, slight though they are, to perform a task or service, may never develop into secure adults. Alert, healthy senior citizens, important one day and suddenly unneeded the next when they retire, languish and fade and even die long before they otherwise would.

Back there, in the dazzle of Camelot, Joan Kennedy had been busy, but she knew, as she whirled through the day's activities, that she was accomplishing little of substance. Was being an adjunct to Ted Kennedy's career, keeping the homes and caring for the children, enough? *"What was I doing? What was I contributing?"* Not even when the tragedies came could she feel truly needed. John Kennedy lying dead, his head shattered by an assassin; his baby unable to draw breath into his immature lungs after thirty-nine hours of life—these were terrible things she could only cry over and say how sorry she was. But her husband, broken in an accident, was another matter. She could reach out to him, comfort him, help him survive, carry on for him.

Like Jacqueline in her anguished moments two years before, Joan's face was impassive as she moved through the crowds of news reporters, television crews and the curious crowding near the entrance to the hospital. Later, she sat silently at the funeral of Ed Moss who had been killed in the crash, along with the pilot, walking through the throngs as regally as Jackie had done. And there was, too, a touch that was pure Jackie: On Sunday evening, she asked Mrs. Jacqueline Brown, the hospital's night supervisor, to show her the chapel. She remained inside for about ten minutes; the next morning, she sent three dozen long-stemmed roses, which were placed near the altar. The flowers and the candy that kept arriving by the vanloads she sent to the patients at Cooley Dick and, when still more arrived, to other hospitals in the area. Later, she would send personal replies to everyone who sent a card, letter or telegram.

The accident had happened on a Friday. After the numbness of the first hours, she had been terrified that Ted too would die, a fear heightened by the sight of him in the emergency room of Cooley Dick, inside an oxygen tent, tubes sticking out of both nostrils, the blood flowing into his veins from the transfusing bottles and his dreadful pallor. She was trembling when she emerged. He had recognized her and spoken her name, but he looked terrible and she said so.

It was touch and go that night and all day Saturday, but by Sunday the surgeons could assure her, after a six-hour operation on his spine, that he would live and walk again. After the dread of losing him, that had been worrying her the most. "A broken back can mean a wheelchair forever," she said.

She didn't stop to think that weekend and can remember very little as the hours of day and night blurred into each other. "You do all the things required of you automatically," she says. "You take the call from President Johnson, you talk to Lady Bird. You reassure Ted's friends as best you can. And, mercifully, you are rarely alone."

By Sunday the whole clan had gathered from all over, tiptoeing in and out of Ted's room. Joan kept a vigil there most of the day, sleeping fitfully next door at night. She found time, then and later in the week, to visit Birch Bayh and Marvella who were miraculously uninjured, except for bruises. Marvella is a courageous girl, reared on a farm in Indiana, and no stranger to trouble. She was almost killed a few years before in an automobile crash; in 1971, she would undergo surgery for breast cancer.

Marvella Bayh: "She couldn't have been nicer to us. Here we were, up in Massachusetts, in a strange town where we knew absolutely nobody. She came in to see us daily. I had only planned to be gone two nights, but we were up there in the hospital ten days. I had been out there in this apple orchard when we crashed in the drizzly rain and my hair looked awful, like I had been standing in a shower and it was bothering me. She went out and came back with some hair clips, went out and got them herself from someplace, and this at a time when Ted Kennedy's condition was so, so serious."

By Monday Joan was sitting down with Gerry Doherty, Ed Boland, the Democratic congressman from Springfield, and Ed Martin, Kennedy's press aide, for emergency political planning. It was obvious that Ted would be out of action at least six months, perhaps longer; it was equally clear that he would not withdraw from the race. Joan would have to stump for him.

And she did. Only three weeks out of the hospital after her second miscarriage, she launched nearly five months of campaigning. She was the ingenue thrust suddenly into the lead by the star's illness. Her part had been all planned out for her by the Kennedy people: She was to be the icing, the role she had performed superbly the last time, but she turned out to be the whole cake. She was the phenomenon of the 1964 campaign in Massachusetts and she did it all herself, while her husband, prone in a hospital, filmed a few television spots, read many books and watched her, flushed with excitement, come and go.

She would drive up daily from Squaw Island, where she was staying to be with the children, chauffeured by Tommy Joyce, a husky young campaign worker who would be outside the house soon after 8 A.M. An hour and a half later, she would be at New England Baptist Hospital in Boston seventy-five miles away, where Kennedy had been moved three weeks after the accident. She would confer with him over the speeches she would make that day and night, bending low over the orthopedic frame to which he was strapped to catch his words.

She installed herself in an office next to his suite where, with Angelique Voutselas, his personal secretary, she would screen the hundreds of visitors who asked to see her husband, deciding who could come and who could not. Then, after brisk conferences with the nurses, a last look in at Ted, she would be off campaigning, and it would still be well before noon.

Nobody could figure out how she did it, shaking as many as 5,800 hands every day at the meetings, receptions, luncheons, dinners, teas and garden parties from early July to election eve. In the first ten weeks alone, she visited 39 cities and 312 towns, making eight and nine stops every day. Dave Powers, the statistician of the New Frontier, who can cite you the vote from every ward in every election since John Kennedy first ran for Congress in 1956, rattles off the stops: "The first day she campaigned in Chelsea, Revere, Lynn, Salem, Peabody and Marblehead. The next day she went through Charlestown, East Boston, Somerville, Cambridge, Dorchester, Mattapan and Roxbury. On the third day they took her to and through Medford, Malden, Wakefield, Arlington, Winchester and Belmont. On the fourth day . . ." He clicks off the places and one's admiration for Joan grows.

She was no polished performer this time either. En route to a reception, yakking with Tommy, she would suddenly grow quiet a few miles from the hall. Tommy knew the sign: She was tensing up, beginning to tremble a little, especially when there would be a large crowd. She would mumble the words of her speech to herself, rehearsing them. Later, on the floor, her voice would quaver, but the smile would be dazzling and the gestures natural and winning. Always she would tie the audience at once to Ted. *At the block-square Statler-Hilton on Park Square, before the annual convention of the AFL-CIO:* "I just came from the hospital and Ted asked me to give you a message. He wants to thank you for your support. He's coming along very well. I guess he's just about the busiest patient New England Baptist Hospital has ever had. He's keeping up with his mail, with office work that's sent to him from Washington and running the campaign." They loved her.

Six days a week she did all this. On overnight trips, hating to rise early, she would nonetheless be up at dawn and away, sometimes alone, often accompanied by Sally Fitzgerald. Once again there were the grueling days standing in front of banks, at factory entrances, in the shopping centers, smiling and shaking hands and telling the people all about Ted, gobbling hamburgers, being stared at and shaken up by the crowds, grabbed by the office seekers in the small towns who wanted their pictures in the papers with their arms around Joan Kennedy's pretty bare back. The smile never came off as she showed, time after endless time, the same campaign movie made for Teddy, and as she whirled around the hall of the Kosciuzko Veterans Association Building with State Comptroller Joseph Alecks in a fast polka at the Pulaski Day banquet.

Sometimes, when she found the hour and she was close, she would stop in at the hospital to report to Ted. If nothing was scheduled for the evening, she would remain with him until nine-thirty or ten, then be driven to the Cape, dozing on the way.

Senator Kennedy expresses pain while being hugged by a woman who broke ranks during the St. Patrick's Day parade in 1970 in South Boston, as Mrs. Kennedy looks close to tears. (U.P.I.)

June 1970. Senator Kennedy announces he will stand for reelection. The children are (left to right) Kara, 10, Ted Jr., 8, and Patrick, 2½. (U.P.I)

The Kennedy women at a dinner dance that raised money for Ted's reelection campaign: (left to right) Ethel Kennedy, Patricia Kennedy Lawford, Eunice Kennedy Shriver, Jean Kennedy Smith, Joan Kennedy. (Wide World)

Making her debut as a concert pianist with the Philadelphia Orchestra at the Academy of Music, October 1970. (Wide World)

At a bowling alley in Waltham, Massachusetts, while
campaigning for her husband. (U.P.I.)

Outside the Charles Street polling place in Boston
with Kara and Ted Jr., November 3, 1970. (Wide
World)

Wearing a brocade mini-dress over matching bikini hot pants, Joan Kennedy chats with conductor Michael Tilson Thomas in March 1971. (Wide World)

In April 1971, at London's Heathrow Airport, en route to Bonn where she narrated "Peter and the Wolf" with the Boston Symphony, Joan Kennedy was quoted as saying she did not want to be the First Lady. (Wide World)

Ted Kennedy escorts his mother and wife to the premier of Leonard Bernstein's *Mass* at the John F. Kennedy Center for the Performing Arts in September 1971. (U.P.I.)

With Alan King at the Telethon during the July
1972 Democratic Convention in Miami. (U.P.I.)

November 1973. Taking Ted Jr.
home from the Georgetown Hospital after his operation. (Wide
World)

At White House functions over the years: 1969, Mrs. Nixon's luncheon for the wives of congressmen (U.P.I.); 1970, luncheon for Mrs. Ferdinand Marcos (U.P.I.); 1971 and 1973, luncheons for senators' wives. (U.P.I. and Wide World)

A series of portraits taken in 1964, 1969 and 1971. (Wide World, Wide World, U.P.I.)

The work was exhausting, but Joan was exhilarated by it. At the hospital she radiated confidence, beaming at the children as they scuttled around their father lying prone in his Stryker orthopedic frame, listening to Ted reading Irish poems from a book Rose brought from home and, as fall came and Ted grew stronger, having long whispered conferences with Angelique about a big party she would give for him the day, not long off, when he would take his first step.

The victory was tremendous, a defeat of the Republican Howard Whitmore, Jr., by a majority of 1,129,245 or 76.5 percent of the vote, the highest ever recorded in Massachusetts. In New York, Bobby Kennedy, in the Senate race watched more closely than any other in the nation, defeated the incumbent Kenneth Keating by a significantly lesser margin, a majority of 719,693 or 54 percent of the votes cast.

It was a wonderful party the day Ted, his back heavily braced, walked for the first time in nearly six months. The hospital suite was filled with old friends and political associates, the Claude Hootens, the John Tunneys, Eddie Martin, Andy Vitali, Jack Crimmins and, of course, the family. The nurses were there, including the pretty young one who, a month before, had put an Irish reel on the record player and danced an exuberant jig while a physiotherapist exercised Ted's legs. There was champagne, mountains of food, a huge cake and the jokes and laughter went on into the night.

Joan's glow continued. In the VIP Senate gallery one month later, where she and the other Kennedys watched Ted and Bobby sworn into office, the pleasure shone in her face. She had helped put him there and she knew it.

No other Kennedy woman sitting beside her had done

what she had done, conduct an entire campaign in place of an incapacitated husband. (None has done it since, either.)

Everyone praised her. Tens of thousands of letters poured in to Ted from all over Massachusetts, telling him how lucky he had been to have her help. Every member of the Kennedy organization privately thanked and congratulated her. James King, who headed the campaign in Boston, needled his boss for years thereafter: "You didn't win in 1964; Joan won in 1964."

But the most cherished were the compliments from those whose approval she wanted most, the Kennedys. Bobby pointed out to Ted that with Joan campaigning the vote had been five times greater than when he had campaigned for himself two years before. Only half-jokingly, Bobby kept telling his friends: "His wife won the election for him." Eunice and Jean said she had performed fabulously. Jackie said she had been great and—most important of all to Joan—Rose was impressed. Rose, shrewd and observant at seventy-five, who had been watching her and receiving reports in the daily telephone chats with her daughters and the family, complimented her warmly and gave out interviews saying that Joan had met the issues squarely and charmed her audiences. And, of course, Ted had told her many times how well she was doing and, at the end, that he could not have won without her.

She grew measurably that year and many people noticed, even Harry Bennett. "Joan," he said, "is becoming more and more like Candy. Ted has brought her out of herself, helped her to be more outgoing, to participate in things more easily." He was only partly right. Ted was responsible, but not for reasons Harry believed. He had needed her and she had responded.

3. Worst Summer

FOUR YEARS LATER, his need of her was even more crucial.

Ted Kennedy, devastated by the murder of Robert in that greasy little hotel pantry in California, was in the gravest emotional crisis of his life. He had been as close to Bobby as Bobby had been to John and was affected as deeply. When the President was killed, Bobby suffered a nervous breakdown, that catch-all non-psychiatric term that defines a severe emotional storm, and there had been fears for a while among his intimate friends that he might not emerge from his depression. Ethel, with patience, tact and love, helped sustain him in his grief during the healing process. Joan, who had known what Ethel had done in those months when Bobby, sunk in gloom and apathy, would sit for long hours, staring vacantly at nothing, must have realized on that early June day, as she flew across the Atlantic, that it was now her turn.

She had been in Paris as a guest of Eunice and Sargent Shriver. Her brother-in-law had replaced Charles E. Bohlen as Ambassador to France three months earlier and Eunice was scheduled to pay a courtesy call on Mme. Charles de Gaulle that afternoon. Joan had just arrived from London after performing another ceremonial chore for the family, dedicating a John F. Kennedy Memorial Forest in Ireland. It was dawn in Paris when Bobby, victor in the California presidential primary, fell mortally wounded at the Los Angeles Ambassador.

Joan, awakened, could not cry. "None of us cried," she said. "We were too numb." With Eunice, she went to the Elysée Palace for the brief appointment with the French President's wife. Then, still dry-eyed, she drove to the airport for the flight to New York.

Later, though, she cried, at the funeral in St. Patrick's Cathedral in New York, on the long train ride that bore Bobby's body to Washington and, in the weeks that followed, when she saw what was happening to Teddy.

"The flight to New York, six hours to think, that was the worst thing," she said. "I thought of Ted more than anyone else, and his family burdens." She arrived in New York in time to meet the Air Force 707 that was sent by President Johnson to bring Bobby's body home. There she joined other members of the family on the hydraulic lift that was raised at the front end of the aircraft to lower the coffin. Alongside her were Eunice and Sargent Shriver. Ted, Ethel Kennedy, Jackie and two of Bobby's children, Joseph and Bobby, Jr., emerged from the plane. She went at once to Ted's side and rarely left it during the hard days that followed.

Ted and the family members went at once to Steve and Jean Smith's lavishly furnished Fifth Avenue apartment to make the extensive arrangements for the funeral. She said almost nothing; she sat with him, brought him coffee, listened. As she watched, the thought struck her: He was the only one left now. A few weeks later, after the funeral in St. Patrick's Cathedral, after the long train ride that bore Bobby's body to Washington and burial in Arlington Cemetery, she was to say with some bitterness: "What is that monolith of Kennedy power now? Just Teddy and me. All the others are either dead or old."

Working on the thousand details that needed to be planned for the funeral, Ted remained awake for two nights. Joan catnapped as she stayed with him. When he insisted on delivering the eulogy, she sat with him as he went over the text, line by line, in the Smith apartment, not saying much, bringing him the hot coffee and trying to make him eat. She kept her eyes upon him during the service at St. Patrick's Cathedral and, when his voice broke at the beginning, she started suddenly and leaned forward almost imperceptibly in the front pew behind the coffin, as though she would leap up and help him if he needed it.

It was Joan, not Ted, who told their children, one of the hardest tasks she has had to face. For in addition to their great loss—they had loved their Uncle Bobby dearly—she knew the children would now be looking inward and asking terrible questions: Their cousins' daddies, who had been in politics, were killed. Would their daddy be killed too?

When the news came, Joan had telephoned home and talked to Ursula, the governess. She did not want to inform the children by transatlantic phone that their uncle had been murdered. She asked Ursula to keep as much of the news as possible from Kara and Teddy until she got home. Ursula kept the children at home but, fearing that they might hear explicit descriptions over the radio or television, she told them gently and with no detail. Neither Teddy, Jr., nor Kara was taken to the funeral services in New York, but both stood in the moonlight at Arlington as Bobby's coffin was lowered into the grave.

A week later, when Ted, Joan and the children were in seclusion at Squaw Island, she told them what had happened. "Ted couldn't do it," she said. "It was still too painful for him."

She saw him grieve and grieved with him and for him. And watching him, his eyes staring out to the sea, unshaven, refusing to eat, she wondered how he managed to stay sane. "Why must it be my husband?" she asked the few intimate friends who, with the family, were the only ones she and Ted wanted around them during that

mourning period. "Why *my* husband? Why must he be
the man to carry these terrible problems of the world on
his shoulders?"

She looked after him as completely as Ethel had looked
after Bobby in his anguish after the murder of John, talking to him quietly and comfortingly as she had talked to
the President five years earlier when baby Patrick had
died; she was at his side when he wanted her, walked on
the beach with him or let him work out his grief in solitude
when he wanted that.

Only one month afterward, a new chill swept through
the family compound. The Democrats, about to meet in
August to nominate a candidate for President, were talking about Ted Kennedy. The talk grew louder; the calls
became insistent, and the fears enlarged daily. The family
and the friends all knew and some even said it aloud: He
was the last of three and perhaps a final target. Said Joan as
she recalled the weeks: "I can't say I urged him to run."
Ted considered the offers seriously but, at last, said no. "It
was the wrong time and under the wrong circumstances,"
he said. The chief reason for the refusal then, just as it was
the No. 1 consideration in his mind in 1972 and will be as
1976 approaches, was his family's concern for his safety
and his own sense of responsibility to them.

Now, in the summer of 1968, Joan knew and could
verbalize what she had only felt inwardly before, that Ted
needed her. We can only surmise the point at which
awakening came: perhaps the first real look at his haggard,
tear-stained face at the Cape where he had gone after
Bobby's funeral, the lips drawn down at the corners, the
unshaven chin, the slump of his shoulders. A part of the
mystique grown up around the Kennedys is the belief that
"Kennedys don't cry." Joe Kennedy would say this
sternly to his children when their tears started to come:

"Kennedys don't cry!" And, manfully, they would try to choke down the sobs. Bobby said it to his children, too. Ethel will still tell a young visitor who has hurt himself in a fall and given vent to tears: "This is my house. You can't cry here." But Kennedys *do* cry, and it is nonsense to believe otherwise. Rose and Joe Kennedy wept inconsolably many times after their tragedies. Jacqueline Kennedy cried into her pillow when she finally went to bed after that long, terrible day and night in 1963. After Bobby's murder, Jacqueline was so overcome she had to be given a sedative at the hospital; and Ethel wept, her children wept, and Ted Kennedy wept too. At Cape Cod, where he remained for two and a half months that summer, he broke down a number of times after despair had replaced rage.

"I realized that summer," Joan told me, "that Ted needed *me*." There it was, put into words, and with a stress on the *me*. Of course, she went on, he had his sisters and mother and brothers-in-law to consult with and rely upon, but the father whom he admired was paralyzed and speechless, following his stroke in 1961, and his two brothers, with whom he had been so deeply involved, were now gone.

"Nobody is as close to a man as his wife," she said, "and this was something I had not really understood or felt until that time. It was the very beginning of a new closeness between us, a closeness that came from the knowledge that Ted needed a loyal wife and a loyal friend."

Who can put a measuring stick on the therapeutic value of a human being engaged in the process of helping to heal another human's bruised emotions? Who can even gauge the value of a professional healer of the mind, since one third of all emotional storms eventually pass without

their intervention? Perhaps Ted would have emerged from
his despair just as quickly whether Joan was there minister-
ing to him or not. The timetable of recovery or the means
employed to bring it about doesn't really matter here.
What *was* important was the strengthening of Joan,
through the awakening of her importance to her husband.

And then came the incident at the bridge on Chappaquiddick Island.

10

On Her High Horse

1. "Sour Smell of Scandal"

JOAN KENNEDY HEARD about the midnight episode on the isolated island when they were taking the body of Mary Jo Kopechne, packed in a carrying bag, to the Martha's Vineyard Funeral Home in Edgartown. Ted Kennedy called her at Squaw Island, rousing her from sleep. He told her that the story of what he had gone through that night would soon be black headlines and big television news.

Three months pregnant that July 19, not sick but not well either, she waited for him to arrive home. Long before he flew in that afternoon, the news had hit the TV and radio; next day the Boston *Sunday Globe* would carry ten separate articles on the incident, giving it more space and prominence than one of man's greatest adventures since history was recorded, the first landing on the moon. He had gone over the side of the wooden bridge in the big black Oldsmobile, plunging into twelve feet of cold swirling water. With him went the blonde, twenty-eight-year-old Washington secretary whose body was recovered from Poucha Pond hours afterward when morning had come. He had dived repeatedly but vainly to save the girl, he had told police, then walked back to the cottage, half out of his mind, to get help, the rented cottage stocked with food and liquor where the six men and six girls had had their cookout following the yacht races that afternoon in the waters off the Vineyard. He had returned to the bridge with two of the men and once more tried to find Mary Jo but failed. Then he had driven to the landing where the little ferry plied between the island and the mainland and, impulsively, dived into the water and swam the 500-foot channel to Edgartown. He reached his motel room at 2 A.M. and, finally, at 9:25 A.M., nearly eleven hours after he had plunged into the water, Ted Kennedy, his cousin Joseph F. Gargan and his friend Paul Markham showed up at the police station on Martha's Vineyard and told the husky, six-foot-three police chief of Edgartown, Dominick "Jim" Arena, that there had been an accident out there on the Dike Bridge on the sandy, sparsely populated Chappaquiddick Island. Then he had made his phone calls, one to the family of Mary Jo in Berkeley Heights, New Jersey, one to Rose Kennedy at the compound, the one to Joan.

How does a wife react in a crisis like this one? Her husband was driving a pretty girl to her motel along a paved road leading to a ferry. Instead of veering left and remaining on the paved road leading to the ferry he had turned right along a bumpy dirt road to a narrow hump-backed bridge. On the other side was a beach where, just that afternoon, he had gone swimming with a group of the men and girls. Later, he explained that he was un-familiar with the road back to the ferry and had turned right instead of bearing to the left. But could any driver, even someone who had never driven that way, mistake a rutted road for a paved one? The conclusion—that Kennedy had planned a romantic interlude on the de-serted beach that night—appeared inescapable.

How does a wife react to this? Stiff upper lip and suf-fer in silence? Weep and carry on, brush it off, run to a lawyer? There had been a human tragedy: The only

child of a middle-aged suburban couple was dead; a shining political career may have been wrecked. Was a marriage
shattered too? In Boston, Washington, New York and other
capitals the rumors grew. Kandy Stroud, *Woman's Wear
Daily*'s saucy Washington correspondent, wrote bluntly in
a national magazine that "the marriage could be over . . .
there had been too many tragedies. Too many disappoint-
ments. And now, on top of everything else, the stunning
accident on Chappaquiddick Island . . . It was a great
shock for Joan, close friends say. She seemed a shattered
woman: furious and deeply disappointed that this could
happen to her. Joan felt like a woman betrayed, and this
is a bitter cup of tea for any woman to swallow."

The article was quoted widely, adding to the swelling
chorus of gossip that Joan had had it with Teddy. For,
the whispers said, it had not been the first time that the
handsome senator had been involved with women, liquor
or both. The newsweeklies were among the first to bring
into the open what had been talked about in the inner
circles of the press but never discussed in print. Wrote
Newsweek on July 28, ". . . the senator's closest associates
are known to have been powerfully concerned over his in-
dulgent drinking habits, his daredevil driving, and his
ever-ready eye for a pretty face . . ." On August 1, *Time*
wrote: "As for women, there are countless rumors in
Washington, many of them conveyed with a ring of con-
viction. Some who have long watched the Kennedys can
say with certainty that he often flirts with pretty girls in
situations indiscreet for someone named Ted Kennedy. At
the same time, he and his wife Joan are rumored to have
had their troubles. There is no question that they are often
separated. On one journey alone last summer, he was seen
in the company of another lovely blonde on Aristotle
Onassis' yacht. Such incidents might be recounted about

innumerable people in Washington and elsewhere; it is only the Martha's Vineyard tragedy that suddenly makes them seem pertinent." In the same issue, the magazine wrote that "Kennedy has been drinking more heavily since his brother was murdered last year, but he is far from being a drunkard." His driving habits came in for close scrutiny: newsmen recalled the four violations since 1958, once for speeding ninety miles an hour through a residential district in Charlottesville, and his tendency to jam his foot on the accelerator whenever he got behind a wheel.

Once the unspoken ban on mentioning the unmentionable was lifted, the outpourings about the youngest Kennedy became a deluge. Nearly everyone with access to print or a microphone had something to say about his life-style. Finally, they said, all three factors—the drinking, the driving, the eye for a pretty face—had all come together and culminated in a tragedy. "As the sour smell of scandal drifted over the land," Ms. Stroud wrote, "Joan Kennedy's friends began to wonder if her marriage could survive this latest tragedy. The public wondered if any woman could forgive and forget such a cruel betrayal."

The friends of Joan, Ted and the other Kennedys divided sharply into two camps. Many of Joan's woman friends, until recently starry-eyed in admiration of her handsome husband, turned bitterly against him. They added up the published facts: There had been six girls, all young, pretty and unmarried, and six married men at a little cottage on a quiet island with few people around; there had been great quantities of vodka, scotch and rum along with the food; it was Regatta time in Edgartown, an occasion always followed by gay parties that ran on until dawn. The sum of all this: What else but an orgy?

Then there were the Kennedy loyalists, men like lanky,

crag-faced Lem Billings who had been John Kennedy's roommate at the fancy Choate School and has been at the family's side in all their trials ever since. Lem is one of the few persons all the Kennedys trust and he honors their confidence. Jackie, who zealously guards the privacy of Caroline and John, allows them to walk over from their Fifth Avenue apartment to visit with the bachelor Billings who lives nearby and listen to his endless stories about their father's adventures in prep school. She knows that he will never discuss the children with the press. Lem Billings has a little treasure trove of private letters from John Kennedy, written in student days, which historians would love to study, but he will not allow them to be published; they are locked in a bank vault and won't see the light of day until after his death. More than most so-called "close friends," Lem is aware of what goes on inside the clan and says little about what he knows. To me he said: "She never for a moment considered leaving Ted. I know that for a fact. She stuck by him and she believed him, as we all did. There was no problem there at all as far as Joan was concerned, no confusion in her mind, no doubt. I know exactly how she felt because I was there all through the period."

The rumors were false. She was his loyal friend and fierce defender all through the aftermath of the messy affair. She told me this. Knowing her character, background and reputation; listening to her talk and watching her; bringing into the judgment instincts developed during thirty-five years of interviewing persons of high and low degree in all sorts of human crises, I believed her. Lem was right and the "close friends" were expressing their views and perhaps their wishes, not Joan's. I asked her if she had felt betrayed or thought about ending the marriage because of the Chappaquiddick incident. "I never said that or felt that way," she replied. "It's absolutely untrue. Absolutely."

She grew angry as she discussed the stories that she had doubted her husband. "I believe anybody who did doubt has never really looked at the situation, hasn't talked to the eleven or twelve people who were involved. They made such a mountain out of a molehill, except that it ended in a terrible tragedy. I felt very badly for the girl's parents and her friends. It was a very, very, very tragic thing. But I see it just as that, an accident."

There was another thing her friends misunderstood totally about Joan Kennedy: She wanted no sympathy, not from them, not from anybody. But they gave it to her, great gobs of commiseration for her plight conveyed in whispers as they leaned toward her, touching her arm. They were astounded by her reaction. Instead of choking down a sob and thanking them for their understanding, she lashed out at them, tight-lipped, in a cold, hard voice.

"It takes me a long time to have things jell in my mind," she told me. "Things occur to me almost like after the fact and I start thinking about them. As time went on, I got fiercely loyal to Ted. And if people would say anything derogatory or insinuating anything, that was the only time I'd show any kind of—well, maybe anger isn't the word but I'd get kind of mad at people for making little comments like, 'Oh, poor Joan,' or 'You poor thing.' You know people love to think that you love sympathy. 'Oh, you poor thing' [mimicking] 'You must have gone through hell.' And I'd say to them, 'You know, I don't need, I don't want your sympathy. Don't feel sorry for me. Don't feel sorry for either of us.'

"When I said that, people would be startled. They kept giving me all this, 'you poor thing' and 'how can you

live through all this' and a lot of other things I won't
say. They kept insinuating that my life must have been
pretty miserable because . . . and then they would give me
all the rumors that were going around.

"And I'd find that absolutely repulsive. And some of
these people were some of my good friends. I told them
where to go. I said, 'Don't tell me that!' It was kind of like
I got up on my high horse for the first time in my life. Not
that I was being defensive, but I just said, 'Look, that's
not the way I feel at all. Not at all!' That was the first time
since I was married to Ted that I felt so strong a feeling."

2. Aftershock

Sickish, worried about her pregnancy, anguished by the
tragedy, Joan remained in virtual seclusion at Squaw Island
through the summer. Remembering her two previous miscarriages, she had been taking every precaution. "She
knew she had difficulty holding a baby in early pregnancy," says Luella Hennessey. "And so this time she was
being very, very careful. She rested a lot each day, stayed
close to the house, gave up tennis and swimming and other
sports that required exertion, exercised only by walking.
She wanted this baby very much, and so did Ted, who had
always wanted a large family."

The third month of pregnancy is one of the most critical
times for a woman prone to miscarriage. Joan knew she
should have gone with Ted to the 46th annual Edgartown
Yacht Club Regatta, the highlight of the season, in which
Kennedys had participated for years. They had talked
about her going but dismissed it almost at once: However
she traveled, by car down Route 28, then the steamer to
Martha's Vineyard, by plane to Edgartown or by boat
across Nantucket Sound, there would be risk. He went

down alone, flying to Martha's Vineyard, coming in a poor ninth in the race.

Four days after the accident, Joan accompanied Ted to Barnstable Airport and, with a large group of family members and friends, went aboard a twin-engined DC-3 owned by the Great Lakes Carbon Company, a corporation owned by Ethel's family. An hour later, at 8:50 in the morning, the plane landed at the Wilkes-Barre Airport.

The ride to Plymouth, a poor, worked-out mining community, took less than fifteen minutes. Shortly after nine, Ted and Joan, who was wearing a simple white dress, had slipped into the rectory of St. Vincent's Roman Catholic Church to face Mary Jo's parents, Joseph and Gwen Jennings Kopechne. They were alone with the bereaved couple for a few moments, then emerged and pressed through a crowd of several hundred persons at the church door. Ted took Joan's arm and led her to a fourth row pew, across the aisle from the Kopechnes and only a few feet from the bronze coffin. Joan's face was impassive, Ted's grim and pale above the soft nylon brace he had been ordered to wear by Dr. Robert D. Watt of Hyannis, who had examined him after the accident. (Many newsmen at the time scornfully referred to the collar as an affectation; few knew that X-rays had disclosed an acute cervical strain.) All of the girls were there, sitting near the Kennedy party, the "boiler room" girls who, because they were the brightest and most dedicated of the Kennedy staff workers, had been given the sensitive task of keeping track of delegates in Indiana, Pennsylvania, Kentucky and the District of Columbia. Mary Jo, who had first worked for Senator George Smathers of Florida, and then for Bobby Kennedy, had worked her way up to this assignment.

Gwen Kopechne sobbed aloud as Monsignor William

E. Burchill began the Requiem Mass. Kennedy looked one time at the coffin in the aisle to his right, then kept his eyes averted. "Do not hand her over to the powers of the enemy," the priest intoned, "and do not forget her, but command that this soul be taken up by the bold angels and brought home to paradise." When the services ended, the Kennedys walked down the aisle, he looking straight ahead, she nodded to several friends. At the entrance, they pushed through the crowds, hearing the gasps and shouts —"there they are, there are the Kennedys!" "Kennedy in 1972!"

They entered a limousine and crawled through heavy traffic along a winding road to Larksville Cemetery on the edge of the town where an open tent had been erected over the freshly dug grave. Ted Kennedy kept his eyes lowered throughout the short service at the graveside, lifting them only after Monsignor Burchill had commended the girl's soul to God. When he raised his eyes, they were filled with tears. Once more, Ted and Joan spoke privately with the Kopechnes, then left for home. They reached Squaw Island about two in the afternoon and Joan went straight up to bed.

Despite all the precautions, Joan lost her baby. On Thursday, August 28, Ted, Kara and young Teddy had gone on a camping trip to Nantucket Island. Joan, feeling poorly, had remained behind to rest. At eight that night, ominous signs developed. She telephoned Ethel and, with Jean Smith and Luella, went to Cape Cod Hospital in Hyannis. Ted, reached on Nantucket, flew back to Hyannis.

After Chappaquiddick, Ted needed her once again and again she responded, though this time weakened by the recent miscarriage. Nurse Hennessey, watching her closely, knew that the emotional blow that follows the loss of a baby for which a woman has been preparing herself can be more severe than the physical aftereffects. It was two months before Joan was over both traumas.

Ted looked terrible. "The massive body had grown thin," Sylvia Wright wrote in *Life*, "the jowls which had always made him look a caricature of himself were barely noticeable. The ashen face was melted down, leaving a bone structure so visible that one could only think that there, under all that cheek and baby fat, had been the face of his brother Bobby all the time. The tortured eyes looked out tentatively, seeking signs of loyalty or defection, then were cast down again. He walked and move more softly, more slowly."

Joan tried to maintain as normal a home routine as possible during the trying period. In the morning, after breakfast on a tray in her room, she would play with the children as much as her strength permitted, send them over to the compound or have their friends and cousins at the house. She would insist on a punctual all-family dinner, 6:30 on the dot, during which she would make small talk —was young Teddy getting the hang of the crawl, how was the birthday party Kara attended, would they all like a barbecue the next night. Ted, listening to the chatter, joined in, as Joan doubtless knew he would.

One would assume that, when the family gathered in the evening, Chappaquiddick and its ramifications would occupy most of the conversation. Not so. They discussed everything but the accident.

Nurse Hennessey: "The tragedy was never brought up. Among themselves, the family rarely talks about any of their tragedies. There was never any 'isn't it awful?' and 'what do you think?' and all that. They went on trying to live as normal lives as they could."

But it could not be forgotten. There were the incessant reminders on the news programs, the headlines in the newspapers, the sacks of hate mail that poured into the compound and the Kennedy Senate office. Luella told Joan: "You just have to ride with it. We won't bother listening to the news. You can't do anything to stop it, so we'll play some records or we'll talk about something else." Joan replied: "How cruel they are. They say things they don't know anything about."

Joan Kennedy: "It seemed to drag on and on. It went on for months. I remember being up with Ted at the Cape in January when he had to go to the courthouse for the inquest and I was pretty blue. It was very cold and windy . . ."

She awoke early that Monday morning on January 5 and dressed warmly against the cold in a dark belted coat buttoned to the neck. Bill Barry, the tall, broad-shouldered former security chief for Robert Kennedy, had flown up from New York to accompany them to the Dukes County Courthouse in Edgartown for the inquest. He drove Joan and Ted to the Barnstable Airport where the three boarded a single-engine plane for the short flight. At 9:15 they landed at the Martha's Vineyard Airport and Barry drove them to the century-old courthouse.

Ted, gazing out the windows of the car and plane, said little on the way down. Barry did most of the talking. In Edgartown, on the way to the courthouse, the sun broke through the clouds. "Hey," Barry exclaimed. "Looks like we're going to have a great day." Ted replied glumly: "We could use a good day."

That remark sticks in Barry's mind, that and one other thing. Ted and Joan held hands all the way down and back by car and plane, her face close to his.

Crowded on the steps were the newsmen, stamping their feet to keep the blood flowing. Twenty minutes before the Kennedys arrived, the five surviving "boiler room" girls had driven up, followed by Gargan, Markham, Crimmins and the other guests at the cookout. They said nothing as they pushed past the reporters and cameramen. Nor could the newsmen get a word from a grim-faced Ted who walked up the courthouse steps at 9:45. Joan, not permitted in the inquest room, remained in a small white cottage nearby. Ted told his story, picked up Joan at the cottage at 2:30 and, with Barry, drove back to the airport and flew home.*

After the new flare of publicity occasioned by the judge's report had died down, Joan thought the incident would at last be forgotten. As the months went on, she be-

---

* To refresh the reader's memory of the events: The inquest, which was not a trial but an investigation to determine the facts of a case, lasted three days. In his report dated February 18, 1970, Judge James A. Boyle of the Edgartown District Court stated his belief that Kennedy and Mary Jo "did *not* intend to return to Edgartown at that time" as Kennedy stated; that Kennedy's turn onto the dirt road leading to the bridge was "intentional." Dyke Bridge, said the judge, constitutes a traffic hazard and must be approached with extreme caution. He wrote: "A speed of even twenty miles per hour, as Kennedy testified to, operating a car as large as this Oldsmobile, would at least be negligent and, possibly, reckless. If Kennedy knew of this hazard, his operation of the vehicle constituted criminal conduct . . . I believe it probable that Kennedy knew of the hazard that lay ahead of him on Dyke Road but that, for some reason not apparent from the testimony, he failed to exercise due care as he approached the bridge. I, therefore find there is probable cause to believe that Edward M. Kennedy operated his motor vehicle negligently on a way or in a place to which the public have a right of access and that such operation appears to have contributed to the death of Mary Jo Kopechne."

came convinced that it was in truth a "dead issue," that "even with people who don't like Ted particularly" it was over and done with.

But the sorry story would not fade. Almost four years later it was still making headlines. In 1973 Kennedy journeyed to Decatur, Alabama, to join Governor George C. Wallace in his state's big Fourth of July celebration where Wallace received the Audie Murphy Award for patriotism, Kennedy made the principal Independence Day speech and both watched beauty contests, sack races and arm wrestling and hooted and hollered as country boys tried to catch a greased pig. The astonishing political flirtation of the extreme right wing of the Democratic Party with its left was a bold stroke—Wallace seeking to show he was acceptable as a national party leader and Kennedy wanting to demonstrate that he could head the main ticket without alienating the southland and turning it all over to the Republicans.

Things happened fast:

■ The move immediately raised speculation about 1976 and at once Chappaquiddick was pulled into the picture. Barry Goldwater, the G.O.P. standard-bearer in 1964 and now back in the Senate, invaded the South too with all the details of the plunge into the pond fresh in his mind. In the Decatur speech, Kennedy had attacked President Nixon and his administration for abuses uncovered in the Watergate scandal. Goldwater, addressing Atlanta Young Republicans, indicated that the senator from Massachusetts had a hell of a nerve talking about morality, that he should be "the last person in the world to lecture us" about Watergate. Then he made the point that would be uttered many times afterward: "Until all the facts involving the Chappaquiddick tragedy are made known, the American people can do without moralizing from the Massachusetts Democrat." Once again, the Kennedy staff had to resurrect the same replies: There are five volumes of inquest testimony, and the distinguished senator from Arizona was welcome to the lot if he wished. Kennedy had told all he knew for the record. "If people have questions about it," an aide said, "they ought to study that record."

■ Hate mail, which had decreased but never stopped, rose sharply. A letter from Albany, New York: "If you aren't the most contemptible and most despicable creature alive. Your recent trip to Alabama to see Gov. Wallace tops just about everything you have done, except Mary Jo's death." From Edina, Minnesota: "How dare you! For shame! We'll never forget . . ." From Los Angeles, California: "I thought Gov. Wallace had more character than to be seen on the same platform with you." From Cranford, New Jersey: "Lest we forget. July 19. Chappaquiddick. Just heard your speech from Alabama. Need I say more?"

■ A nationwide telephone poll conducted by Sindlinger & Co. of Swarthmore, Pennsylvania, appeared to echo the Goldwater attitude. A total of 2,239 persons were asked: "Which action do you yourself feel is the more morally reprehensible—which is worse—the drowning of Mary Jo Kopechne at Chappaquiddick or the bugging of the Democratic National Committee?" Thirty-eight percent cited Watergate, but 44 percent rated Chappaquiddick worse, while the rest declined to answer or had no opinion.

■ And once again, Joseph and Gwen Kopechne were sought out by the press and prodded for their reactions. In Berkeley Heights, Kopechne, now sixty years old, said he had no bitter feelings but a "cordial, friendly and understanding relationship with Senator Kennedy. We wish him well."

■ An astonishing report was published in the Washington *Post* by Bob Woodward and Carl Bernstein, the two young reporters who had broken the Watergate story. Senior White House aides, they wrote, had ordered secret investigations into the lives of their "enemies," among them Senator Kennedy. An apartment has been rented in midtown Manhattan, furnished elegantly. A handsome young stud would be hired to meet one or more of the "boiler room" girls, take them to this pad, seduce them. A hidden camera would take pictures, which would be used to blackmail the young women into telling all they knew about the events at Chappaquiddick.

Joan was wrong. The ripples from the plunge into Poucha Pond keep widening.

11

To Find Herself

1. Psychiatry

WHATEVER IT WAS that had given Joan a glimpse of identity and an infusion of inner strength in the 1960s, it was not enough to create more than a fragile confidence that soon collapsed, and once again she was assailed by a sense of her own unimportance.

Her very real achievement during the Senate campaign was quickly forgotten by the Kennedys as Ted and Bobby took their seats. The family and the rest of the country watched the brothers and compared their performances as senators, ignoring Joan, who returned to her duties as a Senate wife. Soon she too forgot.

No surprise, this. "Feelings of accomplishment are . . . weakened and destroyed by a general feeling of low esteem," Dr. Theodore Isaac Rubin, a New York practicing psychiatrist, wrote in *The Winner's Notebook*. Even major victories that earn genuine admiration from others mean little to those who rate themselves low. Secretly, they are convinced their victories are frauds, flukes or not really significant at all. Thus it takes no special exercise of the imagination to tune into her thoughts as the 1970s opened: "If *I*, lowly little me, was able to do any of these things, just how important could they be after all? So none of the other Kennedy women had conducted a campaign all by herself for her man. But *Ethel* could have done it if she had to. *Eunice* could have done it. Certainly *Rose* could have done it too. So what was so special about *me* doing it? And if I did help Teddy get over his emotional problems, what was so special about *that*? Wouldn't any wife do the same thing?"

She told me candidly:

"I had really lost my self-confidence. The only thing I knew, that I was sure of, was that I was a very attractive young woman and that I had a pretty good figure."

Soon after the decade turned, she went for consultations with a Washington psychiatrist to sort out her feelings about herself, her conflicts, her personal attitudes toward the Kennedy family and especially her relationship with her famous husband. She had wanted to go for a long time, having recognized the need, but Teddy had objected and, besides, she feared the exposure of family "skeletons." She revealed her plans to Luella Hennessey, who agreed it was an excellent idea. She had been trying to make herself what she was not, and never could become, Luella told her, saying: "First, last and always you must be true to yourself."

After several years, she finally got Ted to agree. But still she kept the matter secret until the accident on Chappaquiddick Island. After rumors had been circulating for more than a year, she agreed to let me publish the story in a national magazine. The news commanded attention throughout the world, a strange and depressing thing. Public figures are not supposed to suffer the inner torments of lesser individuals; when they do, and seek help for their troubles, the news is headlined and announced on radio and television.

Yet perhaps a case could be made for the newsworthiness of Joan's decision to talk out her problems with a psychiatrist. She was the first Kennedy to seek such treat-

ment voluntarily.* None in the family had ever gone or
put much stock in psychotherapy. John Kennedy once
brushed it all off with: "I don't go for that couch stuff."
In their deepest emotional turmoil, neither Bobby nor
Ted turned to a doctor who treats mental and emotional
illness. Joe Kennedy hovered close to a breakdown after
his eldest son, Joe, Jr., was killed during World War II.
For months he sat alone in a dark room, listening to
somber symphonic music and weeping inconsolably, but
no psychiatrist was called. Rose, unable to sleep at night,
weeping alone when her tragedies came one after the
other, never asked for a psychiatrist's help.

Little wonder, for as recently as the 1920s and early
'30s, when the devout Rose was rearing her children, religion and psychiatry were still implacable foes, joined in
battle ever since the father of the mind healers, Dr. Sigmund Freud, wrote that all religion was "a universal obsessional neurosis." The assertion that faith is only the
manifestation of a personality swinging out of balance
alarmed and outraged churchmen. There were other reasons for conflict: Freud taught that man is swayed by
unconscious urges, therefore he could not always be held
to account for his actions; but many religious groups
teach that man is born in sin but has the free will to choose
between good and evil. Religion objected strongly to the
stress psychiatry placed on "pan-sexualism," the idea that
all of man's actions stem from his sexual drives. Churchmen, too, felt that psychiatry was attempting to remove
all feelings of guilt from individuals, leaving them with no
restraints. Psychiatry replied it sought to eliminate only

---

* Rose Kennedy consulted with psychologists at Harvard
when it became evident that her eldest daughter, Rosemary, was
retarded.

unconscious guilt, often a leftover from early childhood, which was creating anxiety that, in turn, produced illness.

While some suspicion and hostility still exist, many of the differences have been healed. Freud's concept of religion as an obsessional neurosis has long since been discarded by many analysts, and a number of schools of scientific thought no longer believe sex rules our every thought and action. On the other hand, today's clergy is scarcely embarrassed by, nor does it sidestep, sexual problems. And compromises are being made in the crucial "sin versus sickness" conflict.

But not in Rose's time, and it was Rose who was largely responsible for bringing up the children. The Kennedys believed in good doctoring for the body and got the best; the children were taken regularly for inoculations and checkups and nothing that looked serious was ignored: The doctor was called. Old Joe, himself, was nothing if not loyal to American medicine and used its services often. When he was Ambassador to the Court of St. James's and a problem arose, he sent samples of his stool in the diplomatic pouch to Dr. Sara Jordan, the famed gastroenterologist of the Lahey Clinic in Boston, for examination.

Psychiatry, however, was something else. Joe probably coupled it with the contents of the pouch and it remained for Joan to blaze a trail.

She had no notion of it, nor can it be documented, yet judging by the waves she made by her admission, Joan may have helped psychotherapy as much as the treatments were to help her. For despite all that has been said and written about the science, millions of Americans still look with distrust upon the experts in human behavior who treat mental and emotional problems. Many still believe only "crazy folks" and "weirdos" go to psychologists and psychiatrists, that anyone who admits needing a "shrink" has got to be "nuts" or "soft in the head." Dr. Karl A. Menninger wrote in 1929 that "to most people dietetics is still more important than psychometrics and appendicitis more interesting than neurasthenia." Some thirty-five years later, the Joint Commission on Mental Illness and Health, mandated by Congress to survey U.S. resources and make recommendations to combat mental illness in the country, discovered that a significant percentage of Americans (one in seven) who needed help for emotional problems failed to get help out of a sense of shame or feeling of stigma.

Letters came by the hundreds to newspaper and magazine offices and to the author, thankful that Joan had found the courage to admit her need for help and had sought it. Joan herself had told friends she had been worried lest the admission hurt Ted; afterward, she was buoyed by the response.

And it was, in many instances, heartwarming. In Orchard Lake, Michigan, Joan King, a forty-four-year-old housewife and mother, afflicted with serious emotional problems, wrote her a letter from a Holiday Inn in Sarnia, Ontario, where she was vacationing:

"I must tell you how much your words meant to me at a very difficult time of my life. So many of your fears have been my fears and your struggle for identity, my struggle. Your courage in revealing your fears has brought me from the depths of despair and I am going home today with peace of mind and knowing the challenge I face will not end in disaster."

Like millions of others in middle America, Joan King had two beliefs, both wrong, both potentially harmful, which Joan's admission helped to change: She mistrusted psychotherapy and was ashamed of having problems. She told me one year later: "I always thought we had to

fight our way out of our fears by ourselves, that no outsider could really understand those funny little fears inside us, much less help us get rid of them. Mrs. Kennedy's
frank admission was a revelation, almost an instant one.
Suddenly, in that motel room, I realized that if she,
with all her tremendous advantages of money and position, was able to admit, not only to herself but to the
world, that she had problems she was unable to solve, what
was so wrong about *me* having them and going for help?"

Certainly many other wives of political leaders have
sought psychiatric help and some are now willing to admit it. Betty Ford, the wife of the Vice-President, visited
a psychiatrist in 1972. The tension of being alone most of
the time, worsened by the pain of a pinched nerve in her
neck, ultimately prompted her to seek help. The psychiatrist also asked to see her husband, who went for
several sessions. "But it had nothing to do with Gerry,"
Betty Ford says. "It was just his dumb wife." She is glad
she went: "It was helpful talking over the problems of
being here alone quite a bit of the time and having to make
decisions about the children at a crucial stage in their
growing up. I had been assuming the role of both mother
and father."

Barbara Howar believes Joan may have pioneered a
trail for the wives of officials in Washington and elsewhere
around the country. "At the very least," Ms Howar wrote,
"she shed some needed light into the darkness that sur-
rounds the emotional problems of political personalities."

2. The Concert

IN THE EARLY summer of 1970, while Joan was still trying
to persuade Teddy to agree to her psychiatric treatment,
she received an invitation to appear as piano soloist at a

fund-raising function for Governor Milton Shapp of Pennsylvania the following October. She had entertained at family gatherings and thumped out tunes at campaign rallies, but this would be her concert debut before twenty-five hundred persons at the historic Academy of Music in Philadelphia, accompanied by sixty members of the Philadelphia Orchestra, one of the world's most distinguished musical organizations.

Awed, frightened at the prospect (she knew the publicity the event would doubtless generate), she accepted. Without the prompting of a therapist, she must have recognized that this would be therapy of the very best kind. What motivations, conscious or not, could have led her to the decision to play? This must hit close to target: If she could appear in America's great concert hall and opera house and really pull it off, wouldn't it prove something to the world, to the Kennedys and, most important of all, to herself?

Not since the campaign of 1964 had she been so busy as that summer and early fall. Ted was up for reelection and Joan once again had her role to play. She darted off on campaign tours wearing her huge "I'M FOR TED" button, showing her home movies about the family, explaining to afternoon television interviewers that she often shampoos her own hair, *"rolling it up on rollers, brushing it out when it's dry and that's it,"* telling women audiences who ask her that she's making *"no commitments"* about the midi or longuette look but *"just waiting to see what happens,"* answering questions about women's lib with the observations that *"women should stick up for their rights but never, never become so aggressive that they lose their femininity,"* speaking glowingly about Rose Kennedy, remembering John and Bobby, and finishing every little breathy speech by saying how proud she was of her husband and how much *"real good"* he has done and will do for the state of Massachusetts.

In between, whenever she could and wherever there was a piano, she practiced. She had selected the second movement of Mozart's Piano Concerto No. 21 in C major, more popularly known to modern audiences as the theme from the motion picture "Elvira Madigan," which she would play with the full orchestra, followed by Debussy's "Arabesque No. 1," a piece she had known since college days. She had taken a long time to make the choices, finally deciding that "it was easier for an amateur to play eighteenth-century music than the more complex modern pieces."

A week before the concert William Smith, assistant conductor of the Philadelphia Orchestra * who was to wield the baton that night, came down to McLean to go through the music with her. Joan had just returned from five days of campaigning during which she had tried to protect her hands from enthusiastic hand-shakers; she had not been too successful—her fingers were tired and sore.

It was the oddest concert rehearsal in Smith's memory, a "friendly family afternoon, with a little music." Smith's wife, Deborah, a flutist, was there; Rosalie Helm came in and the Kennedy children, impressed, sat and listened. Smith was struck at once by Joan's careful attention to detail.

Smith: "She wanted everything just right. She was far more fussy than many professionals, concerned about how she would react to the public and how they would react

---

* Technically, Joan did not appear with the Philadelphia Orchestra. Because of the nature of the occasion, the orchestra association did not have any official part in it. However, some sixty members of the orchestra agreed to play as individuals.

to her, but most of all concerned about her playing. Her
music had been meticulously marked, the fingering and
phrasings, the passages that were to be played *crescendo*
and *diminuendo*, every indication. The music had become a graph."

She went through the pieces, Smith at her side, stop-
ping her now and then with suggestions ("The oboe comes
in here . . . now the clarinet") to make her aware that, at
performance time, there would be sounds other than the
music of the piano that she had been hearing when she
rehearsed alone. Smith was pleased with her playing and
told her so. She beamed with gratitude.

The conductor, a pianist and teacher himself who has
had considerable experience with young musicians,* noted
her nervousness:

Smith: "She struck me as a very unconfident young lady
who had to do this to prove she could do something on
her own. She did not feel confident as a Kennedy woman.
It showed clearly in her demeanor, in the way she had of
wringing her hands every now and then. She had the feeling of filling very large shoes in that royal family atmosphere, where she had to prove herself or be submerged.
But she was determined to do it. It was her grit that impressed me. She certainly proved a great deal to herself
that night just a few days away, and she proved a
great deal to those of us who observed her. We admired her
tremendously."

Joan's tension mounted. Her playing had to be as good

---

* Smith conducts the orchestra at the Curtis Institute of Music
in Philadelphia and each season, teaching the complexities of
orchestral literature to students, supervises the presentation of
younger musicians at the Philadelphia Orchestra's Music at the
Museum series.

as she could make it: She rehearsed longer and longer hours. She had to know everything about her appearance: A few days later, Smith received a letter from Joan containing a long typewritten list of questions. At what point did she go onstage? Whom did she acknowledge? When did she bow? How did she get off? Who would take care of her music? Smith wrote the detailed replies she requested.

There were still two more days of campaigning with Ted up in Massachusetts before the concert, with the risk that some enthusiastic supporter would grab her hand and squeeze it too hard. Someone asked her what would happen in this eventuality, not unknown to politicians; she grimaced and replied: "Oh, please, I hope not!" When she returned, hand intact, her practice sessions lengthened. The children were kept out of the living room when Mommy was in there bent over the Steinway baby grand in front of the great window-doors, the piano Ted had given her for her birthday. She would play the selections until late at night, then begin early in the morning— over and over and over.

The Academy of Music in Philadelphia ignores the modern city around it the way an aged mastiff disregards a playful pup. It sits stolidly at the corner of Locust and Broad, a square building in the style of Italian Byzantine, gas lamps * burning at its five great doors which are topped with symbolic heads of Poetry, Music, Dance, Comedy and Tragedy. Completed in 1857, it is the oldest auditorium in the country still in use in its original form for its original purpose.

* Not the originals, alas, but replicas donated by the Philadelphia Gas Works.

If the first audience, which came to see *Il Trovatore*, could return, little would seem different: The crimson, gold and green colors have been retained in the proscenium arch, the great curtain, the parquet and tiers; the ornate ceiling, with its immense chandelier holding 240 gas burners (electrified now but looking the same), seems unchanged. Mozart in bas relief still looks down from atop the proscenium architrave. Sixteen-year-old Adelina Patti, newly arrived from Madrid, sang her first Lucia here, the baby fat still in her cheeks but the voice already glorious. Tchaikovsky conducted part of a concert in the hall on May 18, 1891; Edwin Booth played the malevolent Iago here and returned many times with his Hamlet; Paderewski and Fritz Kreisler played here, Caruso and Jean de Reszke sang here, Arturo Toscanini conducted here, and almost every President from James Buchanan to Dwight Eisenhower spoke here.

There was enough history and tradition in the old house to give any young performer the quakes, and it did no less to Joan when she saw it on her arrival in Philadelphia. She had come in the night before, alone except for a friend, publicist Pat Newcomb. Ted Kennedy, on this night before her appearance, was busy in Washington.

Pat Newcomb: "I had never seen her so nervous. She desperately wanted to be good. We checked into the Sheraton Hotel in adjoining rooms. There was a piano in Joan's and she went to it almost as soon as she arrived. She practiced—and practiced, from early evening until far, far into the night. Next door, the music kept me awake hour after hour. I still don't care if I never hear that Elvira Madigan again!"

The next day Joan went to the theater for a rehearsal with the full orchestra, which went well, returning to her hotel with Pat for a brief rest. At seven she was back, entering the building through the tall black doors on the Locust Street side, walking through the tiled green room to the backstage area, past the huge lights and the wardrobe trunks in which the orchestra members transport their instruments, to dressing room No. 2, which had been assigned to her. It was the most elaborate in the dressing room corridor, fifteen-feet square, air-conditioned, and red-carpeted, with beige walls, a private bath and an eight-foot long mirror above a dressing table. A small piano stood against one wall.

Ted Kennedy, arriving from Washington a half hour before the concert, came to the dressing room and remained with her until the concert was ready to begin. Deborah Smith, the wife of the conductor, came backstage and knocked on her door. Ted answered and she introduced herself. Joan was silent, ashen-faced. ("She was shaking and wasn't saying much, so I wished her luck and told her I'd be thinking of her," Mrs. Smith says.)

By eight, the hall had begun to fill up. Some twenty-five hundred persons, many of them socialites and high-ranking politicians, had paid from $4 to $100 for their tickets, contributing more than $40,000 to the Democratic Party coffers. Mayor James H. J. Tate of Philadelphia, tall and white-haired, received a round of applause when he entered his box.

Tenor Jan Peerce was backstage with Milton Shapp and Shapp's son, Richard, a twenty-two-year-old Temple University music major. Peerce was to sing a duet with young Shapp, and the gubernatorial candidate was to bring the evening to a close by accompanying Peerce on the violin in his famous "Bluebird of Happiness" number.

For Shapp and Peerce, the evening would be a romp, a fun night not to be taken seriously. Milton Shapp had not played the violin in public since he was sixteen, some forty years back, and, a member of the orchestra confided, his rehearsal that day had confirmed the melancholy fact that he was woefully out of practice. No matter; nobody would hold him to account for the quality of his tone or his fingering. Backstage, the quips flew. Shapp twitted William Smith, wagging a finger at him as he said: "You weren't following me at rehearsal." Smith made a joking rejoinder and Peerce, hearing the talk, popped out of his dressing room. "If you can't stay in tune," he warned the candidate, "we're going to have mud instead of a chord."

There was more joshing and laughing. Inside her dressing room, Joan might have heard, but she did not emerge to join in the fun. Ted had left to watch the concert from a box. She was alone; and for her the evening was deadly serious business.

The houselights dimmed and the concert began. Smith conducted the orchestra in the overture to Mozart's *The Magic Flute*. Joan was scheduled to appear just prior to the intermission. The sounds came through the door of her dressing room where she waited for her call. Five minutes before her appearance, there was a knock and a stage-hand's voice with the traditional: "Five minutes, Mrs. Kennedy."

She opened the door and went out, lovely in a black lace Valentino gown with a scalloped neckline cut low and long sleeves. She walked fifty feet to a closed door where William Smith awaited her. He had come off to applause to re-enter with Joan. Onstage, the orchestra was seated in a shell, a solid hardwood box shaped to enhance the acoustics of the magnificent old house.

"I'm so very, very nervous," Joan whispered to Smith. "What should I do?"

"Just relax," he told her. "Relax and think only of the music you're going to play. That'll keep you busy."

A hush.

The door opened and Joan walked out on the stage to the black Steinway in front of the shell. Smith followed her out and mounted the podium.

The violins began with the long slow melody. Joan's hands poised on the keys, weaved into the melodic line of the delicate dreamlike movement. Was there something here that Joan was communicating through Mozart? There is an unmistakable anguish in the andante, an emotional depth that the composer, at the height of his genius, expressed not in passionate terms but in delicate, pastel shades. It is a movement for a pianist who would convey some inner longing intensely, yet quietly. It is introspective, not outgoing; contemplative, not physical. There are no flourishes, no opportunities to show off virtuosity. There is grace and nobility. And it ends on soft, quiet notes, fading away like a reverie, gently, as the daylight slips away on a summer evening.

After the Debussy, her second and final piece, the audience rose to its feet, cheering and applauding. It was, of course, a friendly crowd, all Democrats, all loving the Kennedys and especially Joan, but nevertheless, it was a standing ovation for her piano playing and she glowed with happiness up there, one hand on the Steinway, bowing and smiling. She left the stage, but they called her back for three curtain calls. The last time, an usher mounted the stage and handed her a bouquet of red roses and again she smiled radiantly at the audience.

It was a moment of supreme triumph, and yet no Kennedy woman had been there to see any of it, the playing in this great hall with musicians from one of the world's foremost orchestras, the wild ovation, the traditional bouquet handed an artist.

During the applause, Ted Kennedy left his box and

made his way backstage, flashing his campaign smile. In the wings, Joan saw him approaching. Her face took on an extra glow, as though some switch had turned it to its highest voltage. Cradling the bouquet, she reached out her arms to him.

Ted put his arm around her shoulder and said: "Well done, Mommy, well done."

She had climbed a mountain. She had done well and she knew it; she had proven what she set out to prove. And from the man whose praise she wanted above all others she had earned a "well done, Mommy."

Reporter Tom Fox of the Philadelphia *Daily News*, watching the encounter, was astounded. "This is the way the Irish talk when they have made it to the drawing room," he wrote next morning. "Well done, Mommy, for God's sake!" Fox drew a sharp contrast between Ted's response and that of Milton Shapp.

"Shapp was not afraid to show his emotion," he wrote. "The kid is only twenty-two years old and he's not sure if he's a tenor or a baritone, but he sang this duet with Jan Peerce and he brought down the house.

"And when the kid was finished, his old man . . . walked out onto the stage and he kissed the kid. He kissed the kid in front of a couple thousand Democrats and the place came apart."

There was no sign from Joan that she considered her husband's response perfunctory. She linked her arm in his and went to her dressing room, emerging in a few minutes to go outside and watch the rest of the concert with him from their box.

Afterward, when she returned backstage, crowds gathered around her, heaping praise. By this time, the glow had vanished and her body sagged visibly. Smith recalls: "She'd gotten through it and she hadn't failed. She had met a great challenge and she had succeeded. You could see the tremendous relief on her face. She was one happy little girl."

The reviews were good. One, by Daniel Webster in the Philadelphia *Inquirer*, she read over and over, and filed it away in a buff-colored folder, marking it in purple ink: "One of my favorite clips!"

"Joan Kennedy was the decoration on the concert Tuesday at the Academy of Music," Webster wrote. "The wife of Sen. Edward M. Kennedy was making her first appearance as a pianist with an orchestra, although she has used the piano as a means of making politics sing in Massachusetts.

"She is in music what she appears to be in other fields; deft and engaging, and she has what every pianist wishes for—instant charisma. She had everyone hanging on each note as she faced a battery of cameras in box one and started through the slow movement of the Mozart Concerto No. 21.

"The piece is familiar . . . and the visual effect of this pianist with this music had theatrical impact. The long line of the music was not very profoundly sustained and her nervousness showed in the blocky way the melodic line progressed.

"The simplicity of this music requires a very great stylist, quality an amateur pianist cannot supply.

"Her playing in an unaccompanied Debussy work was better. She was less tense, and the sound she drew from the piano was more appealing. In this 'Deux Arabesques No. 1' it was apparent that she has a good deal of musical polish and sense of proportion. It was apparent, too, that she was beginning to enjoy what she was doing and this communicated in her playing."

Conductor Smith evaluates Joan's musicianship thus:

"She's a talented amateur who plays within her technical limitations. She has neither the time, talent nor dedication it takes to make a performing artist. Specifically, her limitations are digital. Her fingers only move in certain ways; if, for example, she were practicing the pole vault, she is perfectly capable of clearing the bar at ten feet but is unable to make sixteen or eighteen. For professional musicianship of high caliber, the musical equivalent of sixteen or eighteen is essential. One must discipline one's self to put in long hours to achieve this sort of technical professionalism. As for her talent, it has never been fostered; what talent she possesses is just a bud that hasn't blossomed. To be a musician, as in politics, one must devote all one's time to the task. It cannot be an avocation.

"I cannot praise her enough for what she accomplished that evening. To make your first appearance as an amateur with such a prestigious group of musicians on such a stage before such an audience is a very daunting thing."

But, of course, her musicianship was not the central point of her appearance, and Smith recognized this clearly. What mattered was her psychological victory.

"Everybody proves something when he does something worthwhile in public," Smith says. "She struck me as being very diffident about herself and her accomplishments. An act such as this, successfully accomplished, helps to build one's personality, helps to create self-confidence."

She became increasingly involved with her music. In March the following year, she appeared on the nationally televised Andy Williams variety show, playing the Debussy Arabesque and accompanying Williams on the theme of "Love Story." For four minutes of playing and some banter exchanged with the TV star and conductor Henry Mancini, she received a fee of $7,500.

Unbelievingly she gushed: "To think that they actually paid me for my work, a guest star's fee, that they thought I was worth it, that they really wanted me and that I contributed something—I can't tell you what it's done for my ego!

"To accompany Andy Williams on the piano, to follow Henry Mancini's conducting, to be treated like a regular pro—it's given me self-confidence and enthusiasm. I start thinking, 'Maybe I can have a musical career of my own? Maybe I can be more than Ted Kennedy's wife?' It's sort of like coming out of the shadows."

Two months later she played an impromptu piano duet with Peter Duchin, the society bandleader, at the preview opening of the John F. Kennedy Center for the Performing Arts in Washington. This time, three Kennedy women were among the one thousand onlookers—Ethel, Eunice and Pat. Ethel, crowding close, applauded and cheered her on. She and Duchin played for twenty minutes, responding to requests yelled out by the throng and, as Duchin said afterward, "having a ball." In April she flew to Bonn to narrate "Peter and the Wolf" with the Boston Pops Orchestra and the following January she played at the third annual ball of the Washington Performing Arts Society before a distinguished audience at the Shoreham Hotel. Henry Mancini, observing her, says, "She plays exceeding well, with feeling and with understanding. She knows what she's doing at the keyboard."

There were more appearances, and later she would be able to say that her music played a large part in her search for what Norman Mailer has called the "obsession" of identity. ("We search for it," he wrote in *Marilyn*, "because the private sensation when we are in our own identity is that we feel sincere as we speak, we feel *real*, and this little phenomenon of good feeling conceals an existential mystery as important to psychology as the *cogito ergo sum* . . .")

But she had not yet attained that precious goal of good feeling, and the worst of times was yet to come.

12

Sex and the Married Senator

1. Congressional Pairing

IN THE SUITES of United States senators, buzzers summon
the legislators to the chamber for roll-call votes. Early
one afternoon, when the door to a distinguished member's
private office remained closed after a vote-alert, one of
his aides knocked gently, remembering that his boss had
recently taken to napping after lunch. When he got no
response, he opened the door, then quickly shut it again.
The senator was on the couch, but wide awake, in am-
orous dalliance with a new clerk-typist.

Not many members of Congress are discovered *fla-
grante delicto* in a Senate office building prior to a vote
in important legislation, but liaisons elsewhere in non-
official surroundings aren't uncommon either. While leaks
about government matters of consequence have been
everyday stuff for years, until recently hijinks among lawmakers has been, not surprisingly, one of the best kept
secrets in Washington. There has always been gossip, but
little of it has ever found its way into reputable print.

Chappaquiddick may have done more than becloud the
political future of a rising star: It also marked the water-
shed that altered the reporting by print media (radio and
television are less forthright though coming along nicely)
about members of Congress. Once either cloyingly chatty

or stupefyingly dull, the reportage has become considerably more spicy, frequently X-rated.

Thus we find Warren Weaver, Jr., the Supreme Court correspondent of *The New York Times*, who once covered Capital doings, discussing swingers and swinging on the Hill in his book about Congress, *Both Your Houses.* Pointing out that lawmakers in heat do not always employ the politician's art of subtle suasion, he writes:

"One of the Senate's most effective leaders had a long-standing affair with his secretary that he made little effort to conceal. In fact, at a stag party with a group of newspapermen one night, he absorbed a considerable amount of Scotch and decided to telephone her. 'Sally Sue,' he bellowed into the phone, 'come on over to Bob Black's place. We all want to fuck you.' To the relief of his uneasy companions, the lady declined."

If Washington women, understandably enough, will generally decline sex with this kind of ad hoc group, many are not reluctant to participate on a one-to-one basis, a fact that leads Weaver (and other observers of the Capital scene) to conclude that "Congress swings as almost no other part of the Federal establishment. Any halfway attractive female newcomer to the Hill—member, staff aide or reporter—discovers in short order that invitations from lawmakers for varying degrees of social involvement are rapidly forthcoming."

One cannot blame any young congressman who ascends Capitol Hill for the first time for assuming that a great deal of this sexual activity is performed with high-priced call girls provided by lobbyists seeking favors in return. Don Riegle, the youthful representative from Michigan, whose marital problems were discussed earlier, discovered this was "one of the prevailing myths about the House." It may happen occasionally, but he neither heard nor saw, nor was he approached. "Members," he found, "—even elderly members—who want girls usually don't have to rely on anybody to get them. The life that congressmen lead brings them into contact with large numbers of people, including women."

Why is there so much sexual activity in Congress? For one thing, largely because of television, the charismatic and physically magnetic qualities of would-be candidates play a significant role in their selection by political organizations. Some of the men now being sent to Congress by their constituencies are as rugged and handsome as movie stars. Naturally enough, they attract women who, Washington social life being what it is, shower them with invitations to parties and personal attentions. Some accept both.

But this would scarcely account for all the swinging going on. Some members of Congress who would never be asked to pose for centerfolds in the new women's magazines also lead active extra-marital lives. Some, in fact, are senior citizens. A story is told on Capitol Hill of a visitor who asked a representative, "Why is it that, in the Senate, one of the important committees is called the Senate Committee on Foreign Relations while in the House it is the Committee on Foreign Affairs?" The congressman replied: "We in the House are too young to have relations, while over there they are too old to have affairs." The joke is funnier than it is accurate; actually, no one is too young or too old in either House, for sexual activity is not only widespread but a status symbol, somewhat like in college fraternities. Weaver writes: "Senators like to pretend they're never too old. Carl Hayden of Arizona, who was ninety-one when he finally retired, used to shuffle slowly into the Senate each morning, a tall, gaunt figure barely in motion. Senator Thomas Kuchel of

California, the Republican Whip, would regularly call over to him, 'Hey, Don Carlos, did you get laid last night?' Hayden would reply with a ponderous wink, so slow and comprehensive that observers swore it put him out of breath for a moment."

Congressmen are as vulnerable to a pretty face and figure as any other group of normal males: They, too, will stop their work to ogle. Once a colleague dug Don Riegle in the ribs and wagged his head toward the gallery where a lovely young redhead in a green mini-dress sat, one thigh fully exposed. The word got around faster than Capital gossip. Within minutes, the business of legislation all but halted as the House members cast glances upward, some distinguished legislators even moving to more advantageous locations. Short-skirted visitors to the House gallery should thus be warned: "Thigh-watching," says Representative Riegle, "is one of the most popular diversions of the House."

But, of course, sex is more than a spectator sport among the members. Obviously, part of the reason for the high-octane sex in Congress lies in the personalities of the individuals. Some men, whether legislators, accountants or insurance adjusters by trade, will plunge into affairs indiscriminately, urged on by an underlying emotional illness. (Dr. Phillip Polatin, a professor of clinical psychiatry at the College of Physicians and Surgeons, Columbia University, and a practicing psychoanalyst: "Such indiscriminate sexuality usually represents a pathological drive. . . . Satisfaction cannot be found with any one person; therefore it must be sought with all. The endless quest is really an endless running away from self, wherein lie the roots of dissatisfaction.")

All this notwithstanding, we must look for another reason. Congress is something special. Its members are important people, engaged in shaping the great issues that directly affect the lives and well-being of Americans. This is awesome power, and power of any kind endows a man with sexual appeal. Thousands of government girls, starry-eyed and breathless at finding themselves close to the scene of the action, soon come even closer than they had anticipated, because the invitations to parties come quickly; should they be shapely and attractive, as many are, the lawmaker is attracted. Add to the mix a certain heady feeling in the Washington air, a sense of un-reality, a here-today-who-the-hell-knows-where-we'll-be-tomorrow attitude, close to that of an army installation in wartime. A romance that ordinarily would not blossom in another city and another atmosphere for months or even at all can reach full flower in a single afternoon and wither by nightfall.

Secretary of State Henry A. Kissinger once remarked that "power is the ultimate aphrodisiac." Rather portly, with over-sized ears and a prominent nose, Dr. Kissinger attracted an impressive collection of lovely women prior to his marriage to Nancy Maginnes in the spring of 1974. When he was not tete-a-tete with actress Jill St. John, he dined with Liv Ullmann, Marlo Thomas, or television producer Margaret Osmer. Not for nothing was he called the "Playboy of the Western Wing," though he knew full well the fount from whence the attraction flows. "I am no fool," he once said. "I realize the game. I am their celebrity of the hour, the new man in town. I don't kid myself."

Some politicians, lacking Dr. Kissinger's astuteness, are carried away by their newly acquired appeal for women; they will make demands and turn surly when refused. Sally Quinn, an attractive blonde reporter and former CBS newscaster, recently disclosed that a senator once offered her a ride home from a party. "It was raining and so I accepted," she said. "On the way he mentioned that his wife was out of town and put his hand on my head, then on my neck and pulled me close. I pulled away from him. 'I thought you were offering me a ride home,' I said. He looked at me and said, "What do you think I'm running, a taxi service?' "

There is a strong *esprit* in the office of a United States senator or representative, measurably greater than can be found in the typing pool at IBM. Dedicated young people become attached to their legislator whom they come to invest with the gallantry of a St. George sallying forth to smite a dragon. They cheer when he wins a point and many have been known to weep when a measure he is sponsoring loses. As one young woman who had a brief affair with her boss points out: "Working together on legislation that will affect millions of human beings can bring you a lot closer to someone than if you prepare an estimate for construction of a one-story taxpayer."

Which isn't to say that the relations that can ensue are necessarily enduring. Most last no longer than summer romances, some are weekend affairs and others are zam-bam thank you ma'am. Sometimes, too, disillusionment can come fast. One representative, quiet after a dalliance, was asked by his still romantic partner what he was thinking. He shattered the glow, and the romance, with his reply: "Are you sure you sent the final copy of that pollution speech to the press room?"

2. *The Virile Kennedys*

HE IS, AFTER all, a virile Kennedy male. From Joseph, Sr., on through sons Joseph, Jr., John, Bobby and Ted, susceptibility to women has been handed down along with the spirit of competitiveness and old sailboats. Pearl Buck wrote in *The Kennedy Women,* "The Kennedy men were never celebrated for faithfulness to their wives. . . . Faithful in heart though they usually are to the essential women who are their wives, the need for the diversion of play is very real. They are not so much tempted by the other women as they are flattered, amused, and easily aroused sexually." For feminists, the Kennedy *machismo* is an infuriating thing. Thus Ms. Cornelia Noland, selecting Washington's "biggest male chauvinist pigs" for the *Washingtonian* magazine, finds the three Kennedy brothers were just about the leading sexists in town. "All the Kennedy men from the patriarch Joseph P. to Teddy," Ms. Noland wrote, "have had a roving eye and have lived the double standard that women's groups find so hypocritical and galling. The Kennedy males were brought up as victims of the 'madonna complex,' according to a friend of Jack's. The wives were expected to have children, involve themselves in religious and charitable pursuits, and keep up appearances, while the men pursued their *machismo.*"

Speculation continues about what the Kennedy wives truly think and feel about all this. Naturally enough, none has ever spoken out on the subject except to attribute the "rumors" to scandal-mongers and political enemies and to reaffirm their faith in their men. Rose Kennedy breathes not a word in her lengthy memoirs about her husband's reputed long-standing affairs with Gloria Swanson and other film stars during his years as a movie magnate,*

* Recognizing the start of a booming industry, Joe Kennedy leaped into the movie business in the 1920s. He gained control of a chain of New England motion picture houses and was board chairman of five movie, vaudeville and radio companies, including Paramount, First National and Keith-Albee-Orpheum. Naturally, this meant he had to spend considerable time in Hollywood.

though many others have spoken and written amply about
his adventures. Thus, psycho-historian Nancy Gager
Clinch, co-director of the Center for Women Policy Studies in Washington, who has examined the psychological
forces that moved the family and its individual members
in *The Kennedy Neurosis:* "The senior Kennedy became
fairly notorious as a successful womanizer, especially after
his connection with Hollywood queen Gloria Swanson.
. . . The mystique of masculine sexual conquest seems to
be an integral part of the Hemingwayesque Kennedy
ethos as practiced by Joseph Kennedy and his sons. This
belief says, in effect, that to be a tough guy, one must
also be a ruler of women and a possessor of many
women." Pearl Buck commends Rose Kennedy for her
"steadfast loyalty to her husband while he continued a
long relationship with a beautiful film actress. Outwardly,
she maintained a proud silence. But the inner struggle must
have left a mark upon the children. Perhaps no word was
ever spoken, yet none needed to be spoken." One can assume that Rose knew, since the reports of Joe Kennedy's
romances came to the attention of President Franklin D.
Roosevelt, who had named Kennedy chairman of the Se-
curities and Exchange Commission. Roosevelt reportedly
asked Kennedy to end one of his affairs, to which Old Joe
was said to reply that he would provided the President
end *his* relationship with his secretary, Marguerite (Missy)
LeHand.†

———

† It has come to light in recent literature that Franklin D.
Roosevelt, despite his confinement to a wheelchair, had at least
two deep affairs. Of course, he and Eleanor were at a disadvan-
tage—they had the Victorian era to contend with. Their son Elliott
says in his book *An Untold Story* that "she [Eleanor] went into
marriage with exactly the same feeling that Granny [F.D.R.'s
mother] expressed: sex is a wife's duty, never a source of joy or,

(Some of the older residents of Bronxville appear to remember the financier's much talked-about womanizing above his other accomplishments and do not regard him highly for it. One elderly gentleman pointed out that the town's coat of arms bears the Latin inscription "Ne Cede Malis"—Do not yield to evil.)

All his adult life, John Kennedy had a roving eye, which did not cease its wandering when he ascended to the Presidency. Norman Mailer believes that his thousand days in office "might yet be equally famous for its nights." Ms. Clinch writes there is "strong evidence that J.F.K. was frequently faithless to his wife and that she knew it," both apparently having reached an understanding to submerge their private feelings "for the sake of their ambitions."

For some reason, John and his father had a weakness for

---

as it can be at its best, of ecstasy. She had, in her own words, 'an almost exaggerated idea of the necessity of keeping all of one's desires under complete subjugation.' That thought would be completely alien to Father, who was beginning to develop a lusty love of life in all its rich variety." Consequently, after Eleanor Roosevelt performed her marital duty of providing five healthy children, and because she knew of no other way (or consulted no one on the subject) of limiting her brood, Elliott Roosevelt says that his mother cut off her sex life completely.

The obvious choice for F.D.R.'s lust for life centered on Lucy Mercer, Eleanor's social secretary. The affair was broken off when Eleanor found Lucy's letters to her husband and threatened divorce. According to Elliott, Granny intervened by threatening to cut off her son's finances, so a compromise was reached—F.D.R. would give up Lucy and Eleanor would remain his titular wife. Soon after, Eleanor Roosevelt channeled her energy into her own determined career in politics and diplomacy. By the time Missy LeHand entered his life in 1920, Eleanor apparently was beyond objecting. Missy became the true hostess of the White House; it was Eleanor who visited.

airline stewardesses. Once, during his Senate years, John drove with a chauffeur to the small apartment he kept on Bowdoin Street. He looked around the cheerless place and turned to the driver. "Say, cahn't you get us a stewardess up here to cook dinner for us?" The driver could. Up to the time he suffered his stroke in 1961 at the age of seventy-one, Joe was also eyeing the stewardesses—and all other pretty girls. One day he met a young employee who was escorting an exceptionally beautiful girl. "I'd like you to meet Alma, Mr. Kennedy," the young man said. Joe, talking to his employee but never taking his eyes off the girl, said: "Why don't you come up to the Cape this weekend? Oh, and bring Alma." The couple arrived; Joe barely noticed the employee, but his attentiveness to the girl was exceptional.

Bobby was the least active of the Kennedys in this form of athleticism. His reputed affair with Marilyn Monroe has now been raked over thoroughly, most recently by Mailer in his "novel biography" of the star. Mailer does not believe there was an affair, though the two were often together in the last summer of her life; nor does this author, who sifted through all the "evidence" in his biography of Ethel Kennedy, published in 1971. However, Max Lerner, commenting on Bobby's virtues and faults, observes: "Nor was he by any means a saint. He shared with his brothers the human failings of mortal flesh. At a time when sexual codes were changing, the Kennedys—father and brothers—were part of the change, and not part of the resistance."

Of the three, Teddy apparently has been the least restrained and restrainable. At Harvard, he would waste little time with preliminaries or circumlocution: He would tell girls straight out what he had in mind and expect a prompt decision. Judging by the stories circulated about him in Washington, there is little evidence that he has altered his approach.

There are many stories going the rounds, none, of course, documented, but all juicy gossip. A few samples:

He sits next to a pretty girl on a plane from New York to Washington and makes a dinner date. Afterward, he goes to her hotel room . . . he asks an aide to arrange a luncheon date with a former beauty contest winner he meets at a fund-raising meeting in New York . . . he escorts the daughter of a famous black show business personality through the family quarters of the White House while his brother is the President and makes a pass in, of all places, the Lincoln bedroom.

At a banquet in New York City, he met the beautiful brunette wife of a correspondent for a popular magazine and was so smitten he followed her to her apartment. The young woman, at first flattered by the attention, finally became angry and told the doorman not to allow him upstairs.

One afternoon in Washington he sat next to an attractive young delegate at a convention of a national woman's civic organization. When she took out a matchbook to light a cigarette, he asked if she were staying at the hotel whose name was imprinted thereon. She said yes. He lit her cigarette and slipped the matches in his pocket. Later, there was a telephone call, but she had already gone home. Still later, there was a guardedly written note telling her how much he enjoyed chatting with her and that he would be in her city soon. She never answered. Relating the story, she says there is no doubt in her mind that "the man is a rake."

Ted and Joan were hosts to a large group of friends at a dinner-dance in a Washington hall, each seated at different tables. It grew late and most of the people at the other tables had left, but Teddy was still raring to go. He got up on the dance floor with the blonde married daughter of one of the country's most famous industrialists and performed an erotic dance. Joan was sitting with her back to the floor, chatting and trying to ignore the whole thing.

He met a British musical comedy star at a party and was so turned on he propositioned her on the spot. She refused him and he got very angry. He kept calling her so often that his friends quietly asked her to leave town.

On a plane to New York from Paris, Teddy met a French actress, who introduced the man beside her as her fiancé. Ted ignored him and invited her to a party his sister and brother-in-law, the Stephen E. Smiths, were having that evening at their Fifth Avenue home. Later, he called for her in the lobby of her hotel, but she was accompanied by the young man. Ted hadn't counted on the male escort. "What's he doing here?" he demanded. "I'm not taking him to any party!" And off he went, leaving them staring after him.

At a skiing lodge in Stowe, Vermont, he met a young woman, chatted with her for ten minutes, then disappeared with her into a room, emerging forty minutes later.

He met an attractive girl at a cocktail party in New York and said: "I'd like to see you later." She gave him neither an answer nor her address, and the two drifted apart. Hours later, when she was in bed, her doorbell rang. *He* was outside. He had obtained her address, got past the doorman of her Park Avenue building and found her apartment. "You didn't take me seriously," he said to her. He remained all night.

These stories, and others like them, have not escaped the notice of political enemies as well as his friends. Seymour K. Freidin writes in *A Sense of the Senate:* "Once regarded, as his late brothers were not, as a man of the Senate, Kennedy haters nurtured grievances and circulated all the gamy stories they could to do him discredit. A regular Republican crack that always made the rounds: 'Teddy can't keep his pants buttoned.' * Another—more bipartisan—had him closely nuzzling a young Eskimo girl when he was in Alaska inquiring into local injustices."

"Even as Teddy's presidential star rose in 1971 and 1972," Ms. Clinch wrote in the *Washingtonian*, "the prodigal senator couldn't stop womanizing." How much womanizing; and, if any, how much was real, how much the invention of a scandal-hungry press? One cannot look up a legislator's romantic score like his voting record, so it must be underscored that much of the talk about Teddy and women is in the realm of speculation. Following the accident at the bridge, Teddy was big game for the press. Almost every time he was seen with a woman not his wife there was gossip and, not infrequently, headlines, especially in the less reputable publications. The occasion could be innocent and probably was in many instances, but no matter: If the woman was attractive and she invariably was, it made a good photograph and a good story.

No senator performing even a minimum of his duties could possibly have the time, let alone the durability, to give attention to as many women as Ted Kennedy was credited with in the post-Chappaquiddick period. At the same time, however, the plunge into the cold, dark water apparently did not immobilize his roving eye nor, presumably, dictate a change in the philosophy he had once

* One of America's most distinguished women utters a remark that many Democratic politicians, in their heart of hearts, would probably echo: "If they could only cut out that part of him and leave the politician, wouldn't it be wonderful?"

expressed: "The Kennedys can afford one playboy—why not me?"

In the spring of 1972, rumors about Teddy and his stepped-up girl-chasing began returning again and again to beautiful twenty-eight-year-old Amanda Burden, the estranged wife of a New York City councilman, Carter Burden, himself a blueblood descendant of Commodore Cornelius Vanderbilt. Burden was formerly a legislative assistant to Senator Robert Kennedy and New York co-ordinator in Bobby's presidential campaign. Amanda, the daughter of William S. Paley, chairman of the board of the Columbia Broadcasting System, had been married to the thirty-one-year-old Carter for eight years.

The breakup of the Burden marriage, ironically, was apparently another political casualty. When they were wed, Carter was still studying at Columbia. They lived in an expensively decorated co-op in the Dakota where they entertained lavishly. Between terms Carter studied at home in a green velvet smoking jacket and $75 needle-pointed slippers. In 1964 the Burdens were titled the Fun Couple of New York. They moved to posh River House overlooking the East River before his political career be-gan to take shape. Then they moved again so he could campaign in East Harlem. Since then it has been a social whirl of handshakes at the local bodega and tramping through pizzerias to gain the votes of the people. By 1971 Amanda confided to a *New York Times* reporter that because Carter was doing what he most wanted to do, she didn't mind being the wife of a politician. She did ad-mit that she never knew when there would be a crisis in East Harlem that would keep him from getting home for dinner or a first night at the theater and that many nights she sat home alone reading. On their eighth anniversary,

Amanda announced she was seeking a divorce. It would seem she got tired of sitting home and being lonely.

The gossip-hungry Capital pounced on the report of Teddy's involvement with Amanda and bounced it around like a table-tennis ball. Even Kennedy himself heard and took the extraordinary step of issuing a public statement, the second time in three years he had been forced to deny rumors of an extra-marital relationship. (After Chappaquiddick, he said of Mary Jo Kopechne in a nationally televised broadcast: "There has never been a private relationship between us of any kind.") Characterizing the reports of a romance with Amanda as "nonsense," he said that "people write this sort of thing about me all the time."

A month later, a reporter wrote it once again, this time in a story that ran six columns long under two lines of 96-point type:

TEDDY SAILS OFF MAINE
WITH TUNNEY, 2 WOMEN

Arthur C. Egan, Jr., an investigative reporter for the Manchester *Union Leader* and the New Hampshire *Sunday News*, tracked down a tip that the two senators were on a holiday sail without their wives. (John Tunney, Kennedy's roommate at the University of Virginia Law School, was having marital problems; his wife, Mieke, had filed for divorce in May.) Egan drove out to Rockland, at the mouth of Penobscot Bay and sent back a dispatch, which appeared September 3 in the *News* and the following day in the *Union Leader:*

> Two high-stepping, playboy U.S. senators, taking advantage of a Congressional recess, spent a pre-Labor Day

holiday sailing around Penobscot Bay with "two lovely females" who were definitely not their wives.

U.S. Sen. Edward M. Kennedy of Massachusetts and John R. Tunney of California spent at least four days aboard the *Curragh*, Kennedy's power sloop, with the two young women. The only other person aboard the Kennedy craft was a negro crewman acting as captain of the sloop.

One of the women with the two Democratic senators has been identified as Mrs. Amanda Burden. . . . The second woman remains unidentified other than "being a lovely young thing in her late twenties" . . .

Kennedy and Mrs. Burden have been linked romantically by articles in *Newsweek* magazine, the Washington *Post*, the New York *Daily News* and *Women's Wear Daily*, a national trade publication. However, Kennedy has denied any romantic interest in Mrs. Burden, saying the two have been "in each other's company a total of three times at various gatherings."

The Rockland four-day holiday is the first time Kennedy and Mrs. Burden have been reported together in what could be termed a "romantic setting," that of being alone with only another couple present.

The "apparently romantic holiday," the lengthy story continues, began on August 29 when Kennedy arrived with the two women at the Down East Air Line Terminal in Boston and flew to Rockland. Tunney reached Rockland later in the day and the four set out aboard the *Curragh* in midafternoon. Egan wrote: "The driver of the cab which transported Kennedy and his female companions to town, Harold Harvey, in a telephone conversation on Thursday, identified one of Kennedy's companions as 'Mrs. Burden—her picture was in the New York [*Daily*] *News* today.' Three days later, however, the cab-driver was hedging. This time he wasn't certain the woman was Amanda. "Look," he told Egan, "I've thought it over and I don't want to get into trouble about this. I've had all the trouble from the Kennedys I need for a lifetime." Egan said, "Harvey explained this statement saying, 'Some years ago, Bobby [Kennedy] came in here just like that—with women—and I told about it and I got into a lot of trouble. So now I don't need that kind of trouble.' However," Egan wrote, "Harvey would not deny that one of the women was Mrs. Burden and although asked specifically to deny the woman's identity, Harvey would only say, 'I'm not getting involved.' "

Mrs. Frances Mills, a secretary in the Rockland Chamber of Commerce whose office is on the municipal dock, saw the women board a tender for the *Curragh* but would not identify one as Amanda, telling Egan: "We Mainers mind our own business. Lots of important people take friends out to their boats from here . . ." The pilot of the Down East plane also refused to confirm or deny that Mrs. Burden was aboard the flight to Rockland, saying: "Man, you're asking me to twist Senator Kennedy's tail. I'd not only get fired but I'd probably never get a flying job again. No sir, I'm not getting involved. Kennedy's too powerful for me."

A swift response came from Kennedy's office. On Monday, September 4, the Boston *Globe* quoted a spokesman who confirmed that Kennedy and Tunney, with several members of the Kennedy family, were sailing on Penobscot Bay, but that Mrs. Burden was not aboard.* Later,

---

* At the time of the sailing trip, Mrs. Burden was fulfilling the six-week residency required under Idaho law of divorce petitioners. She had gone to Sun Valley early in August and was granted a decree on September 20. (Noting this point, Tunney denounced the story as "scurrilous journalism." "Look," he said, "the Manchester paper called Reno and confirmed that Amanda

at a party in New York, Kennedy himself told the Washington *Star-News* that the sailing trip had been "a family affair," during which they had sailed southward and put in at Cushing, where they were guests of the artist Andrew Wyeth at his summer home. Joan and their three children had joined the sailing party for four days, Kennedy said, adding: "The rest of the time I was stuck with my two sisters [Pat Lawford and Jean Smith]. Can you imagine anything worse than being stuck off the coast of Maine with those two?"

All right, Kennedy did (did not) go on a romantic sail along the rockbound coast of Maine with a beautiful socialite in the late summer. All right, we can believe or disbelieve one member of the family by marriage who expressed amusement at what he called the "current rumble" about Ted and Amanda. ("God, this has been going on for years. The Kennedy family has known about it for several years—including Joan. And nobody can deter him from his pursuit of Amanda. Even Rose is aware of it and the jeopardy in which it places him politically.")

The reader can make whatever judgment he wishes or shrug and say that the senator's private life, colorful though it might appear to be, is really no concern of his and what does it matter, really? History offers numerous examples of high-achieving statesmen whose personal lives

---

was there. Yet they ran the story anyway.") How could Mrs. Burden be in Idaho and, at the same time, in a yacht with Teddy Kennedy?

Egan insists he telephoned Amanda's hotel in Sun Valley (not Reno), some fifty miles from Fairfield, and had been told that Mrs. Burden had gone to Los Angeles. Usually, brief out-of-state visits by divorce petitioners are not considered violations of the residency rules, hence it would have been possible for Mrs. Burden to have flown to Boston without jeopardizing her suit.

were far from exemplary. We are not concerned here with Ted Kennedy's morality or its effects upon his political career and the fortunes of the Kennedy supporters.

What *does* matter is the impact upon Joan. It was devastating.

3. Joan's Ordeal

WHATEVER WAS HAPPENING, this much was clear to Joan Kennedy's friends: She was plainly in distress, perhaps the deepest and most painful of her life.

She looked terrible: Her eyes had lost their luster; she was careless in her appearance and grooming. She bit her nails. Once her hands shook so much that her manicurist (Leonarda Medina, an Argentinian woman at the Dann J. Hopkins salon in Georgetown) had to give up. A hairdresser, now at another shop, recalls she came in several times looking like a bedraggled heroine of a Jacqueline Susann novel.

A news reporter who covered her during the 1964 campaign: "Her face seems hard now. She doesn't smile as much and she doesn't seem to give a shit any more. A couple of times I saw her she looked like she had crawled through a rathole. The old Joan wasn't like that, never in a million years. The old Joan was always so beautifully dressed, always took great care of herself. Jesus, the old Joan would have charmed a bird out of a tree, but there's something very wrong about her now. She just doesn't seem to give a damn."

She was humiliated by the gossip, whispered and published. To escape the pressures, she visited California several times, staying with a friend from college days at the beach in Santa Monica. Here she had an opportunity to rest and recoup her energies before returning once again to Washington and the problems of her life. To a close friend of the family she appeared "a classic case of the long-suffering wife—but how much longer she is willing to suffer in silence I don't know."

Kandy Stroud, the Washington newswoman, notes: "She became extremely hypertense and there were some who said she drank too much. She would never tell you she was feeling blue, but it was obvious in her behavior. She was also very, very nervous." Ms. Stroud, wife of a Georgetown pediatrician and the mother of two small children, is young, blonde, attractive and always stunningly turned out, which must be borne in mind as we listen to her account of an experience with Joan Kennedy. We should also remember that Joan once told Kandy: "You're just about the only newswoman in Washington I would trust." Nonetheless, this:

Kandy: "I was covering Teddy's campaign trip for George McGovern's candidacy that summer, from Minneapolis on to New York. Joan was to link up with Ted in Detroit. Kennedy and many of the media people, including me, were staying at the Sheraton-Cadillac on Washington Boulevard.

"One morning, I happened to be in the elevator with Kennedy when she entered the hotel. She saw me and almost fell over. She hadn't known I was going on the trip and, in that one quick look, it seemed to her as though I was there alone with her husband. I remember recording in my mind that what she was going through must have left her with a terrible suspicion of other women, even of someone she considered fairly friendly.

"I tried to talk to her: 'Hey, how are you?' She was recoiling. She looked nervous, very jittery, very who-the-hell-are-you-to-be-here-with-my-husband? Strange, because she has always been up front with me, never hostile.

I kept talking to her, asking her how she liked the convention in Florida that July, and if she were still doing twenty laps a day. But she was looking at me, like you know, *you bitch, what are you doing here in the elevator with my husband?*

"It struck me that Amanda Burden must have been on her mind, that she felt threatened by any other woman who is passably young and attractive.

"He hasn't proved himself to be the staunch, loyal husband. She never knows who is going to be around next."

To ease the strains, Joan took tranquilizers and, on occasion, a drink. A number of times she appeared in public looking as though she were drunk.

Stories of her reputed drinking episodes spread rapidly, finding their way into print and even onto a television talk show via a variety of journalistic devices ranging from coy to straight-out statement of fact.

Cosmopolitan magazine's reporter let the reader know what was being noised about but pleaded innocent: "I was breathlessly informed by 'in' reporters that any stewardess on the shuttle between New York and Washington could tell of Joan's drunken escapades with businessmen whom she dragged home because she is so lonely. Personally, I found nary a stewardess (after a total of eight flights at four girls per) who would begin to verify such a rumor, nor can I conceive of a face so fresh and a figure so well-kept as Joan's surviving the amount of alcohol she is reported to imbibe (when we finally *did* meet, we had a high old time—on iced tea).

Burton Hersh, one of Senator Kennedy's biographers, minced no words in *The Education of Edward Kennedy*: "Joan—fresh-faced and cheerily uninterested in liquor at all in Manhattanville—had proceeded from smilingly refusing any to enjoying a drink now and again to—as the sixties thickened—needing a drink badly at times, too badly."

Some twenty to thirty million television viewers watched and heard a lively discussion of Joan's drinking and Ted's behavior in mid-1972. The "David Susskind Show," which is syndicated to forty cities, brought together four news and magazine writers for a session devoted to gossip. This from James A. Brady, former publisher of *Women's Wear Daily* and currently a writer of "inside news" for *New York* magazine:

"Teddy is now a case for someone professionally qualified to analyze him. Teddy is on a self-destructive track that I just can't believe . . . [he] doesn't seem to care any more what he does and what people's reaction is to his actions. I would think that a man who is obviously odds-on for the Democratic nomination in 1976 would be behaving himself a little bit more than he is. What I hear is that Ted is wilder than ever in his private and personal behavior.

"The other night there was a party at Jean and Steve Smith's house here in New York, a birthday party for Teddy. Apparently an awful lot of alcoholic beverages was consumed. Mrs. Kennedy, Joan, apparently fell flat on the ground leaving the party. There were things said which could not be repeated either on the air or in private without a libel or slander suit having been brought between the Kennedys and others . . ." *

---

* Joan was reported to have talked about her sexual problems and frustrations in the presence of some of the guests. *Women's Wear Daily*, which devoted a full column to the party, a "barn dance," which celebrated Ted's forty-first birthday, reported that Joan, upon leaving near 3 A.M., "caught her heel on the doormat and fell on the sidewalk outside the apartment building." Ted helped her up and they left in a cab, the account said.

Joan's friends were furious at Ted for his treatment of her. One said: "He almost drives her crazy. He expects her to be there when he wants her to, and she obeys. The other Kennedys, John and Bobby, never made fools of their wives as Teddy has done.

"John Kennedy had been charmingly flirtatious, somewhat like a naughty boulevardier. He did it, as he did everything else, with grace and class. You knew that Jackie was a sophisticated woman who came from a background that understood such things. She was also a strong person, very self-sufficient, who could take what was probably happening without falling apart.

"Joan is very different. She was unused to this kind of behavior and was shattered by it."

Kandy Stroud: "Here was a man who after Chappaquiddick was supposedly a penitent, who had been through the ruination of his presidential hopes after being the king, the candidate-designate. He blew the whole thing and on top of that gets involved with Amanda Burden. As if Joan hadn't already forgiven enough!

"If I were her husband, I would protect her and help her and not ruin her life any more than it's already been ruined."

Not mentioned in the story was the accident that befell a baby donkey someone had brought up to the apartment in the service elevator to enliven the party. Jean Smith must have been everlastingly grateful that she had rolled back her carpet and spread sawdust on the floor for the hoedown, for the burro did what burros generally do on a barnyard floor and was summarily banished.

13

Joansie

1. *Herself*

IF SHE HAD her way she would be a full-time mother and let all the rest go. That was why her son Teddy's illness was the cruelest torment of all. She loves being a mother. "It was always what she wanted to be most," her sister, Candy, says. "She's terrific at it."

She has always tried to get it all in, all the birthday parties, the field days at school, the plays and concerts in which her children perform. She will rush from an obligatory interview in her little car to the school where Kara, in a long blue gown, is singing in the class choir. She will worry about their grades, their homework, and—believe this—whether Patrick would be able to get into a good school. When the child was barely three, she told a visitor: "I'm interested in sending him to a Montessori nursery school. I have an interview on Friday. I suppose it won't be a big ordeal like taking college boards, but I know from my girl friends how hard it is to get children into schools. They say if you don't get them into the right nursery school, you can't get them into the right kindergarten—and on up to college." Kara and Teddy, Jr., are in a "good" school, the National Cathedral School for Girls and its brother institution, St. Albans, probably Washington's best. Lucy Baines and Lynda Bird Johnson, daughters of the late President, are alumnae; so are the daughters of Wernher von Braun, House Speaker Carl Albert, and many dozens of the Capital's elite.

Her child-rearing formula is eclectic, a mix of things she has read and heard and what comes naturally. She believes in stern discipline enforced with light punishment for transgressors, low allowances, plenty of responsibility and all the time and attention she can possibly spare. She will break away early from a meeting to rush home and swim with them or play tennis or talk.

Servants or no, the children make their own beds, clear the table after meals, hang up their clothes and perform other chores. And when they do not, or misbehave, Mommy doesn't choke down her wrath but will let loose with a burst of temper. ("I don't agree with mothers who think they have to be on their best behavior at all times, who do not show their emotions. After all, we're human too and the children might just as well know it early. So every once in a while I get mad at them and I always tell them why.") Her biggest concern is that the children might be spoiled by the Kennedy wealth and the spotlight none could ever avoid. ("Ted and I are very much on guard about this and keep telling them how lucky they are. Maybe we tell them too many times, but we're always reminding them how fortunate they are that they have the best of everything.") Each time they go to a hotel, Joan will let them know how much the room costs; when they go skiing, she informs them that the lift alone is $9 a day. ("When they hear, they're bug-eyed.") If they lose their ski hats, Joan will make them buy new ones out of their allowances, so much down, so much a week.

Like all the Kennedy children, and unlike Joan herself, Kara and Teddy have been receiving instruction in current affairs ever since they were old enough to go to school.

Joan and the senator, when he is home, watch the news on television with them, explaining and discussing the events afterward, explaining and discussing too what each parent did that day in public life. As a result, both children are considerably more aware of what's going on in the world than most youngsters their age.

Religion, too, is a family affair. The Kennedys regularly attend ten o'clock mass at Holy Trinity in Georgetown; either Ted or Joan will go to catechism class prior to mass with the children, along with other parents. Joan is not a daily communicant like Rose and Ethel, though she has a strong commitment to her faith. At Lent, she will usually spend a weekend at a religious retreat. ("I want religion to be meaningful, not mechanical for my children. I'm all for Church reform. It's important to educate the parents as well as the children so that they can answer the tough questions kids ask. For instance, Kara and Teddy have asked me if they'll see Uncle Jack and Uncle Bob in heaven.")

Perhaps it is in the genes or, more likely, the example of a kind and gentle woman; the fact remains that Joan's children are not of the Kennedy mold. Around Joan's house there is none of the unleashed tornado effect one found up the road at Ethel's. For Ethel and Bobby's children were an untamed lot growing up. Some visitors, among them the most eminent persons in the land, never appreciated the charm of being pounced upon in exuberance, tugged into games, occasionally squirted by water guns and nipped by the animals at Hickory Hill.

Joan's children are different in temperament and behavior. Young Teddy, blond like his mother with her soft features, was always a good athlete: before his illness, he swam, played tennis and, best of all, loved to go camping and sailing. There is a sweetness about him, an endearing shyness, a look—yes—of vulnerability. One has the feeling that sharp words spoken to him will bring tears. He talks to strangers with eyes cast down; he blushes charmingly at a compliment. His younger brother Patrick, wraith-thin at six, has the same air of sensitivity; he does not catapult himself about the house and grounds but will play quietly for hours on end. Kara, too, a pretty teenager, seems more subdued than most of the other Kennedys.

Joan's motherliness extends to other people's youngsters too. She heaped gobs of advice on the teen-aged Tommy Joyce during their lengthy automobile trips on the campaigns, ranging from his career to love and marriage. ("She told me the kind of things you get from your mother," Tommy remembers.) When it comes to girls, she advised—"Don't just pick a sexy one. Look below the surface, look for intelligence and real consideration. Don't be swept away by flash, otherwise you'll have trouble. Remember, Tommy, you'll have to live with her the rest of your life, so choose very, very carefully."

A friend who knew her in 1969 during her trips to New York found her "very naïve—she would believe anything anyone said."

"I found out," he says, "that she was very limited in what she knew about life. She had never gone on a roller coaster in Palisades Park. She went on a yacht but had never been on a Staten Island ferry for a nickel." She surely was not at the level of sophistication of the New York women who would patronize a bistro, since defunct, called Cerebrum, where the female guests would be asked to remove their clothing and don a white angel's robe. ("It was sort of like a happening," the friend said, "all kinds of touching and shared experiences.") Joan apparently didn't care to share some of the experiences. She did not undress, though a man in the place, who did not recognize her, kept urging her so insistently that her companion got in a fight over her, an incident the fan magazines and Sunday tabloids would have smacked their lips over had they known.

"Somehow," the friend says, "I felt it virtually impossible to be at ease with her." He insisted she never wear her mink coat or jewelry—"Just her wedding ring but no diamonds, no nothing." Even so: "I could not remove her from the glamour and the glitter." She remained, for him, "a curiosity," never a friend.

"She's not a true Kennedy," he says. "That's why she doesn't get along with them. She's a nice chick. I'm talking basic. Joan doesn't know where she's at and never will. Zorba said you've got to be a little mad to cut the rope; that is, to get off the treadmill, to screw it all and take the bread and go somewhere. She would like to say that and she almost did before Chappaquiddick because she was under the most incredible pressure, but the accident made her a Kennedy forever.

"The woman was under incredible pressure," he recalls, "pressure that you and I cannot possibly conceive. She was cracking under the strain. She was seeing two psychiatrists, one on a Tuesday, one on a Wednesday. She wanted to confirm one's analysis with the other, one's dialogue with the other's. This went on for a year.

"Then she began pulling out. I don't think it was psychiatry that did it. I think what really pulled her out, what really turned her around, was Chappaquiddick.

"Before Chappaquiddick, she was only an adornment, but afterward she was the only ally Ted Kennedy had. He needed her desperately, and she knew it, and she rose to the occasion."

Even though she had been welcomed into the family by

the other Kennedy women, Joan has never established warm personal relations with any of them.

She has great admiration for the brisk, competent Eunice but has never become chummy with her. Nor has she developed a closeness with Ethel; they are too different. Ethel the extrovert, who, at forty-six, has the incredible energy of a teen-ager, who still plays her practical jokes and darts around an athletic field like one possessed, who leaps on tables at parties and does a song and dance, comes on too strong for her. Though less than a decade older, Ethel is a generation behind Joan in many of her attitudes. Square as an alphabet block, Ethel does not understand, and certainly disapproves of, the changing climate in which young people are growing up. The new attitudes toward everything from sex to religion confuse and often anger her. Her children, faced with the inevitable problems and pressures of adolescence and beyond, find it easier to talk to Aunt Joan, who is more in tune with the world of today.

Of them all, Joan likes Jackie best. One commentator, writer Liz Smith, observes in *Pageant* magazine: "Joan admires Jackie's bright culture, taste and most of all her witty bitchery." For her part, Jackie has a great fondness for the less sophisticated Joan and has delighted in teasing her on occasion for her naïveté.

Once she whispered a question to Jackie: That famous, charming author friend, the one with the high-pitched voice and slow delivery—was he really, well, *queer?* Jackie pretended she didn't understand. "Queer?" Joan, blushing: "You know—gay." Jackie roared. "Gay?" she said. "He's gay as paint. Oh Joan, you're hopeless. We'll never corrupt you."

They see each other seldom now and there is less opportunity for the little acts of friendliness they once shared. Once at Hyannis Port, when Joan was recovering from an illness, Jackie, then the First Lady, dropped in with an armful of books she thought Joan would enjoy reading. Telling the story, Joan's sister, Candy, remarks: "Joan thought it was such an unusual and thoughtful thing to do, taking the trouble to find out what books she would like, and going to get them, instead of just bringing flowers or candy." Jackie didn't purchase the books. She got them from the local library. When Joan was finished with them, she came by again, collected them and took them back.

The newest blow—Teddy's illness—came just as the gossip about Joan and her husband, which had been simmering hotly in private, finally boiled over into the newspapers.

In the fall of 1973, the air in Washington was heavy with rumors of a separation after Ted and Joan had spent much of the summer apart. Ted vacationed in Colorado with John Tunney, Representative William J. Green of Pennsylvania, Representative Wayne Owens of Utah and their sons. Ted Kennedy, Jr., was there, with Teddy Tunney, Billy Green and Douglas Owens. The four fathers and the four sons jumped the rapids of the boiling Colorado on a raft.

Meanwhile, Joan went to Europe with Kara and one of her little friends—"strictly a mother-daughter time." In a rented Peugeot, youthful-looking in blue jeans, she drove the youngsters through France, shopping and sightseeing. In July they lunched with actor Yves Montand at a small restaurant near St. Paul-de-Vence. Usually, mother and daughter were in bed by ten each night. ("It couldn't have been more innocent," she said.)

It was a long vacation, and a strange summer and fall. She returned to the United States, remained for only two weeks, staying at Squaw Island most of the time, and was back in Europe by late August. This time it was the picture-book city of Salzburg in Austria, birthplace of her beloved Mozart and the setting for the famed annual Festival of Music and Drama. Ted called Leonard Bernstein, the conductor and composer, who arranged for highly prized tickets. Asked later why Ted didn't accompany her, she replied: "You have to admit Teddy's not crazy about classical music."

In September Joan attended the fashionable Volpi ball, the year's biggest bash for the celebrated and uninhibited jet-setters. Here, among the six hundred revelers at the Venice palazzo of Giovanni Volpi, the wealthy bachelor son of an Italian financier, she danced until past 6 A.M. Wrote *Women's Wear Daily:* "It was a night-through of coquetry . . . and Joan Kennedy did not seem out of place. In a simple black dress she caught the eye of a number of Italians who kept her dancing." She was photographed dancing with Giorgio Pavone, a Roman publicist. Asked where Teddy was, she told an interviewer: "Back in Hyannis Port, baby-sitting."

The Pavone incident also snowballed. "I didn't even know the name of the man I was supposed to be dancing with or who he was," she said. "He was just a man who cut in, but I checked around and discovered he is a PR agent from Rome who used to work for Count Crespi. Why they used my picture with him I don't understand, because I danced and had my picture taken with so many other exciting people, including Prince Rainier. It must have been a set-up. Besides, he's fifty-five years old and not even attractive."

The remarks, published in *Women's Wear Daily,* enraged Pavone, who fired off a letter to the newspaper insisting: "I am not 'just a man who cut in' since we had been formally introduced (and the color pictures of Mrs. Kennedy and I [sic] show this very clearly . . .)." The published photos would indeed seem to corroborate this. They show Joan standing alone with Pavone and designer Yves St. Laurent, Joan smiling at Pavone as she dances with him.

In Rome, Giorgio Pavone insisted that he had been introduced to Joan and named the person who introduced them—the actress Elsa Martinelli. He expressed wonder at Joan's denial and brushed aside her reference to him as fifty-five years old and not especially attractive. "Yes, I am about that age," he admitted, "but I know my physical value." Gallantly: "She is a charming girl. We talked about the beauty of the evening, Venice, the gondolas, the lights."

Maxine Cheshire, a Washington-based newswoman specializing in "inside" stories on public figures, wrote that Joan and Ted had reached an informal agreement under which she would lead "a life of her own and pursue her own interests," these interests having little to do with politics. Henceforth, Ms. Cheshire said, Joan would make only major appearances at Ted's side if he ran for the Presidency or other office but would no longer go off campaigning by herself.

From his Washington office, Senator Kennedy denied that a separation or even a rift was in the offing. "It would come as a surprise to me," he said.

Joan remained silent, continuing to vacation in Europe. Then, in November, came a message from home. Teddy, Jr., was sick.

She has become an avid antiques collector, a hobby

started years before. She has made a deep study of the field, narrowing her interest to New England and English antiques. Earlier, she would go out with experts to guide her; now she feels capable of going alone, buying with extreme care, studying each object thoroughly. On her jaunts through the countryside around Boston and Washington, she will haggle with dealers over price. Sometimes she will get them to come down; often she will walk away from items she would like to have because she feels they are too expensive.

She has an excellent collection of handcrafted Sandwich glass, pewter and china. When she finds something special, she will buy it for Ted for a birthday present. A recent gift: an 1820 Staffordshire pitcher bearing the legend "Bad Luck to the Manchester Butchers." It cost $80. She has begun a collection of signed letters from all the United States senators from Massachusetts; fine furniture, metalwork, pottery and, her real pride, an excellent collection of hand-carved duck decoys she has been gathering for years and which have increased enormously in value. She tapes the bottoms so she can identify them. Beneath a huge Merganser is a note in neat script saying it was carved by "Joe" between 1890 and 1910.

She generally gives small dinners, rarely for more than one or two dozen guests. She and Ted will often dine alone, too, or invite a guest or two. Once, when Gerry Doherty was in town, Joan called him: "Come on over, we're having a big treat. It's cook's night out and Ted's going to make the dinner." Ted whipped up his specialty —scrambled eggs. Doherty, unfortunately, was allergic to them. He couldn't offend them, ate the eggs and itched all night.

While she will never be a must-win athlete like Ethel, or as good, she has come a long way from teen years. She is still less than ecstatic over sailing, won't ride a horse, climb a mountain, shoot the rapids in a raft or risk a battering in a touch football game, but she has come to love tennis (she still takes lessons now and then), skiing and swimming. A cardinal health rule she follows religiously: She will swim twenty laps daily, the equivalent of one mile, in her own pool or at the Watergate when the weather turns cool. Afterward, her hair stuffed under a babushka, she will drive home. Once Kandy Stroud was vainly hunting a taxicab on Wisconsin Avenue in the rain. ("This beat-up little car stopped and somebody waved at me. Here was this great beauty of the Kennedy family, her hair dripping, who was grinning and couldn't care less how she looked. She drove me home.")

She still marvels at Ethel's inexhaustible energy. One recent summer at Squaw Island, she gestured toward the water where a small flotilla of sailboats was circling around a larger power boat in the center. "Look," she told a visitor on the terrace, "that's Ethel. She's out there with all the kids. I'd go out of my mind. I have enough trouble with my own. Can you imagine that Ethel?"

She is still frugal. Ted has offered her an expensive sports car but she sticks to the low or medium priced ones. A nun who comes to the house asking for a donation receives a dollar and some mumbled words about her husband giving at the office. She has never dieted but makes it a point to eat meals that are nutritionally balanced. Usually, on campaign trips, she eats enormous breakfasts and equally large lunches. The activity helps burn off the calories. She will not insist that Ted, who needs it, stick to a low-calorie diet. ("He's a mature man and can make his own decisions.") He does, and sometimes they are pretty dreadful calorically. Once, after finishing the main course at dinner, he asked if there was anything for dessert. Joan told Andrée, the French cook, to serve *pamplemousse*. When, already jowly, Ted discovered it meant grapefruit (75 calories per half), he cast a negative vote and called for cake topped with chocolate chip ice cream.

She is no longer the college girl who hated current events. She has read widely, listened well and developed opinions, though admitting there are still gaps in her knowledge and understanding. Unlike many professional politicians, she is able to say: "I'm not well informed on that [the drug problem] and I'd rather not speak out than sound stupid with some half-baked thing." She does, however, endorse stronger laws to keep drugs out of the hands of young people and additional government subsidies for rehabilitation clinics. She also told me candidly that she knows little about the women's liberation movement.

Joan: "I am in a special position where I do have certain freedoms. I have help at home and when Ted says to me, as he did recently, 'Would you like to come with me on a trip to Utah, Montana, South Dakota, North Dakota and Colorado, all those places,' I am able to say 'Oh, yes.' I can throw things in a suitcase and next morning I'm on a plane with him. And I don't have to make a living, so it's awfully hard for me to really feel what the liberationists feel, though intellectually I can empathize with them."

The movement confuses her, she remarked to a visitor a year before I talked to her about it. "I have yet to meet a women's lib member or enthusiast. Some of their demands are legitimate, like equal employment opportunities, but I don't agree with a lot." She does agree with a basic concept of the feminists, that women must be considered, not as sexual objects, but as human beings. ("I think that's beautiful.") She opposes "abortion on demand" but adds: "That's a personal view." Birth control, too, is "an emotional issue" with her.

She urges more federally funded programs for the arts and humanities. She believes sexual permissiveness is the greatest challenge facing a wife and mother today. ("Though I haven't encountered that with my children yet. They are still pretty young.") She looks upon day-care centers for pre-schoolers as valuable educational institutions but worries that herding a child off without parental involvement in the program may be harmful. Parents, she says, should visit a center regularly. "In this way, the parent can evaluate the child's experience and be on guard for any impersonal techniques which might be damaging to the child."

She has become highly skilled in the political arts.

Gerry Doherty: "She's politically hep now. Teddy trusts her judgment. He tries out his speeches on her and she makes good comments. When he was scheduled to appear on an interview show, he tried out some answers to possible questions; she listened, made suggestions on how to elaborate a point—stress this, soft-pedal that. She's no dumb blonde.

"She'd never throw anybody out of the house, and there are plenty of political wives who do. She's never turned the heat off, as some women have done, in order to get the people to leave and let her husband get to sleep. She would never walk into a conference late at night and yell, 'Say, when the hell are you guys going to go home? It's late!' Other wives do! When we were deep in a political discussion, there was never a telephone call for Teddy from an upstairs phone. I've seen it happen. The phone would ring and it would be a candidate's wife. 'Get those bastards the hell out of here,' a woman would tell her husband, 'it's one o'clock for God's sake!' "

By 1968 she had acquired enough poise in campaigning to tease brother-in-law Bobby at a press conference during his campaign for the presidential nomination. After his victory in Indiana, Bobby met with reporters at the Sheraton-Lincoln Hotel in Indianapolis. Joan, watching, asked a question: "If you were elected President, would you appoint your brother as Attorney General?" Quickly Bobby answered: "No, we tried that once." Straight-faced, he inquired: "Whom do you represent?" Joan grinned.

Joan's hair and clothing styles may have won wolf whistles from men and admiring glances from middle-American women on the campaign trails, but they have never impressed the experts who pronounce high fashion verdicts in New York and Washington. From these arbiters of elegance she has won generally low marks and some flunks. Kandy Stroud, the *Women's Wear Daily* fashion expert, is sharply critical.

Kandy Stroud: "To me, it's not a question of taste. She has none. My God, she wore those silver sequined mini skirts when mini skirts were *out*. Not only that, but she would take these mini skirt things with these long sleeves and have them made over, lengthened.

"I've seen her a thousand times in the same dress. I'd say to her, 'I've seen that dress before,' and she'd say, 'I know, but I love it.' And she'd wear it over and over. She was trying for so long to wear sex-symbol, Marilyn Monroe-type clothes that would catch Teddy's eye.

"At the opening of the Kennedy Center for the Performing Arts she wore that purple thing with those Filipino sleeves, the skirt slit up to here with the panties showing. It was ghastly! She was trying to be sexy and went overboard. She was trying to be chic and was too home-sewn pattern. It missed all the way around.

"She used to go to Mme. Paul, the little French dressmaker on Wisconsin Avenue in Georgetown, and always came off as sort of lower Slobovia. She wasn't editing her clothes properly. And it looked as though she never took time getting dressed. I would see her at a ball at night when she'd still have on suntan lotion."

Candy Jones, her former modeling mentor, not unkindly yet realistically, warns that time is catching up with Joan. Candy believes Joan is "the" beauty of the Kennedy women, shading Jackie, but she could—and should—be paying attention.

Candy: "Possibly she's so very busy that she couldn't care less about how she looks. Usually I've found that women who have been natural beauties all their lives really never had to do anything to remain attractive. But there comes a time when they had better start thinking about doing *something*. Joan could look better than she does. I think her hair is too straggly, too careless for her facial bone structure. She's twenty years behind with that hair the way it is. If she arranged it better, shortened it a bit, she could look years younger . . ."

Since 1940, Eleanor Lambert, a New York fashion publicist, has conducted the International Best Dressed Poll, sending twenty-five hundred ballots to fashion editors, designers, socialites and others considered expert in the field. Joan has never made the list of twelve best-dressed women. In Ms. Lambert's view, she does not have a "sure instinct" for clothes, has suffered from the "freakout" syndrome and looked ridiculous at times, "tacky" at others.

Joan herself has admitted that clothes shopping bored her. "It's not that I'm cheap, I'm lazy," she has said. "I'd rather pull out a four- or five-year-old dress. It's just so much easier to hang on to clothes. And there are other things I'd like to be doing."

But she changed, suddenly and dramatically, in the summer of 1972. Even as a new Joan emerged psychologically, a more tastefully attired and groomed young woman began appearing on the scene, and perhaps the two are not coincidental.

Kandy Stroud: "She was getting to look so awful that finally Lorraine Cooper [Mrs. John Sherman Cooper, wife of the former Republican senator from Kentucky] and I sat down to figure out what we could do about Joan's appearance. Lorraine wanted me to call Joan and suggest that she, Lorraine, would take her to Dior in Paris. I didn't have the nerve to do that. It was at that point that Joan was introduced to Alice Dineen of the Saks Fifth Avenue couture department, a remarkable woman with superb taste, and from then on the change was amazing.

"Now that Alice is dressing her, Joan is much more with it. In summer, she would wear a little body sweater, collars, turned up cuffs; she had good shoes, a good handbag, and it all worked together, *edited.* She wore things that fit right and hung right. When she arrived at the convention in Miami, she wore a perfect outfit, clog shoes that looked wonderful with those great legs of hers, and her hair was fabulous."

Dann Hopkins had taken care of the hair. Hopkins, a blond man well over six feet tall, wears skintight jeans and T-shirts, and presides over a Georgetown salon reconverted from a town house. Decorated completely in black and white, with a zebra-striped floor, white walls and furniture and colorful abstracts on the walls, it caters to the elite of the area. Hopkins toned down the bright yellow, gradually adding layer upon layer of gold, doing it all slowly so nobody would notice a startling change. He cut it to shoulder length and allowed it to fall in soft waves.

Eleanor Lambert has taken notice too. "She has become more elegant. She doesn't look like a chorus girl any more."

2. *Fear*

How is she getting it all together as the seventies advance toward the election that could—that just could—
put her in the White House as another Kennedy First
Lady?

McLean, Virginia—*The picture-taking is over. She sits
in the family room on the blue and purple tweed couch,
one of a pair flanking the tall stone fireplace. Her arms are
crossed across her chest, right hand cupping the left elbow,
the way a woman will hold herself when she walks against
the cold. She is leaning forward, not looking at the visitor
who is alongside, and she is crying.*

"*We're naked here,*" *she says.* "*Naked. Look at us.
Listen.*" *She raises her head. There is no sound in the big
house.* "*Here we are with the children. There's a maid.
Nobody else.*

"*You saw when you came in how close we are to the
main road. My God! Someone can come up across that
bridge, make that turn, come here. There's no name on the
mailbox but that doesn't hide us. The cabdrivers know
where. Every newspaper has printed where we live.*"

*Her voice is low but the words are coming out in bursts,
almost strangled by the strong emotion.*

"*I'm scared something will happen to him. There may
be a person out there trying to make a clean sweep of the
Kennedy brothers. Whatever has been written about that
is true. My husband knows it and I know it.*"

*The visitor is caught off-balance. There had been a ses-
sion of picture-taking during which she sat patiently and
chatted quietly while the photographer, Otto Stupakoff,
fussed with lights and angles. She had kept them waiting
more than an hour, selecting her clothes carefully, putting
on the makeup, brushing her hair back from her face into*

a neck-level wave and allowing the ends to flow over her shoulders. Finally, in a long-sleeved purple shirt, top two buttons undone, and light blue slacks, she had come down, apologizing.

A compassionate man, the visitor, a magazine editor, gropes for something to say, to offer some kind of consolation though at the same time recognizing how ineffectual and even fatuous his words, any words, could be.

Outside, in the big living room, Stupakoff, the young Brazilian fashion photographer, has packed his camera equipment and is leafing through a travel guide to Mexico, waiting.

"Joan," the editor says finally, "perhaps you're exaggerating, perhaps it isn't really the way you think. I'm sure the country is more mature than that . . ." Joan turns suddenly to face him on the couch. The tears spurt from her eyes and course down her cheeks and into her mouth. She makes no move to stop them. She unclasps her arms and reaches out to grasp both his hands.

"Exaggerate? Exaggerate?" She exhaled the word in sharp whispery bursts. "How can you say that? Let's get in my car and I'll drive you down the road just over a mile to Hickory Hill where Ethel lives. Let's go in there and you can look at a house filled with eleven children without a father, and then tell me if I exaggerate the dangers of being a Senator Kennedy!"

The editor is silent. ("What do you say to that?" he was to say later. "How do you comfort a person who must live with a reality like that? She was right and I was wrong. She had every reason to be afraid and I knew it.")

The phone rings. Ted Kennedy is calling from Montana where Mike Mansfield, the dour Senate Majority Leader, had asked him to address a civic meeting. Joan cradles the telephone between her uplifted arm and shoulder and whispers into it.

*The editor walks out of earshot to the tall glass door
that looks out upon the bare woods and hard ground just
beginning to soften under a March sun. Down a slope beyond the trees, winter thaw has filled up the Potomac. In
summer the river here is a brook where the Kennedy children and their friends will plunk big stones into the am-
bling water; now it was all white-water rapids, rushing
and roaring.*

*After three or four minutes, Joan hangs up. The emo-
tional mood, the resignation and the despair, has vanished.
She does not resume the discussion. The tears have dried on
her face.*

The terror is part of the misery, for she is deeply in
love with her husband.

She has lived with fear, she told me, "for a very long
time," ever since she had to face the harsh fact that three
of the Kennedy men accepted great risks of life and had
gone down, heroically, gloriously. She knows that "the
future of the fourth is darkly shadowed by doubts," Pearl
Buck's phrase. He is being propelled to candidacy by
forces he is unable to control—his debt to his heritage, the
strongest; his sense of history; his deep wish to help build
a nation along the liberal lines set down by his brothers.
He believes, with Robert, that "the future . . . will belong
to those who can blend passion, reason, and courage in a
personal commitment to the ideals and great enterprises
of American society." Against these is the force that is making him dig his heels into the ground to resist the pull: the
clear awareness of the risk and the knowledge that his
family is deeply frightened that the last Kennedy male
could be murdered.

In Florida, Harry Bennett, now divorced from Ginny,
says he talks to Joan each week, sometimes oftener.

Harry Bennett: "Nobody wants him to run, nobody in
the family on either side. They're all scared to death. Over

and over, Joan keeps saying she hopes he does not run. Can you blame her? But they all know, and Joan knows it too and this is what terrifies her, that he's got to do what he feels he must. But they all pray he doesn't."

Lem Billings: "None of his family or any of his close friends wants him to be President. Nobody who cares a damn about Teddy wants it for him. It's a dangerous job, more so for Teddy than anybody else because there are damned crazy fools in this country. We don't know where they are and they're very hard to avoid."

Once so very long ago, when they were the golden couple from Boston at the court of Camelot, everyone believed similar glowing words that she spoke to interviewers because they were so obviously true.

Now more and more are beginning to wonder: Are they just brave efforts to paper over what has become a hollow marriage? Is the Ted and Joan union to become—has it already become?—as empty as those other political marriages in which man and wife are remaining together solely because of his career and her dignity?

Right now, the hunt for answers is one of the biggest guessing games on the Washington party and cocktail circuit. Ted-and-Joan watchers note that he acts curiously toward her. One day he will ignore her, and the next be as attentive as a honeymooner. In Little Rock one cold and rainy evening, they sat side by side on the dais at the testimonial dinner for Representative Wilbur Mills. Ted spent most of the evening looking into Joan's eyes and whispering to her. Another time, however, at a tea dance in the home of Townsend Hoopes in McLean, he sat with the actress Cloris Leachman while Joan played a piano duet with Ann Hoopes. When she finished, the music began and couples rose to dance. Joan sat alone at the piano bench while Kennedy still chatted with Ms. Leachman.

One of Joan's friends, standing a few feet away, noticed what was happening and whispered angrily to her escort: "Why the hell does he let her sit there alone—why doesn't he dance with his wife?" Kennedy overheard, rose, went to Joan and whirled out on the floor with her.

"I am more in love with him than ever," she will tell a newswoman. And he with her? An interview with the rugged, plain-speaking, loyal Lem Billings:

Lem Billings: "From what I know of Joan, I think she would like to have a private family life. But that isn't what she has, and it's too bad because that's what she married. She married a political figure and she's got to live with it. She'd rather have a life like most other women, with a husband entirely to herself, but with a public figure this cannot be, especially one like Ted Kennedy.

"I have the feeling that she will never adjust to the fact that she has to share him. A lot of political figures have the same problem with their wives. It was probably very hard on Mrs. Onassis when she was first married to John Kennedy."

Question: "Is Joan unhappy because of this?"

Billings: "She's terribly in love with her husband, and anyone as much in love as she is and who enjoys her children as she does—how can she really be unhappy? If she's not a happy woman, I don't know what's wrong with her."

Question: "Is her husband as much in love with her as she with him?"

Billings: "I think he's a terribly busy guy. He's got to give so much more of his life to other things. It happens many times—he's the busy husband, she's the woman at home."

Question: "You haven't answered. Is he as much in love with her as she with him?"

Billings: "I couldn't answer that."

Old friends from other times and places have become very special to her. As she became more deeply involved in political life, she realized quite suddenly how far she had drifted from them. "I had to make an extra effort to let my friends know that I really needed their friendship more than ever," she told me. Periodically, on her trips to New York and Boston, she makes it a point to schedule a close visit with at least one—"not just shopping, or going to a museum but a real heart-to-heart sitdown, and maybe go out to their homes and have dinner with them and their families." She has four or five of these friends in the Boston area, and several more in New York and Washington, none prominent nationally, "all brides about the same time who went this way and that way with our husbands." Acting as contact is Sister Katherine Hargrove, a former Manhattanville dean who teaches theology and avant-garde films. ("She's very in with the ecumenical movement. She's not a nun-bunny like we used to think they all were in those days. I have a special relationship with her and she helps us all stay in touch.")

She has said many times that she did not want to see Ted in the White House or herself as First Lady. In 1970 she told a reporter: "I've been very close to it, the Presidency. I don't see it as glamorous and all that. I think of it as a lot of work. It's tough. It's risk-taking. It's everything I find unattractive." She told me in 1972 before the campaign: "I'd be happier if I had some more time, time to grow up, time with my children as children. Four years from now, I'll be more able to cope."

The Presidency, she said then, means loss of the precious privacy she wants for Ted, herself and the children as a family, but most of all her three youngsters. "At this time they are so young, so impressionable," she stressed.

"They need time to mature," Joan went on. She ticked off the ages of the Nixon and Johnson children when they were in the White House, indicating she had given the matter much thought. "The Johnson and Nixon girls were much older, of marriageable age, when their fathers became President. I certainly would do anything that Ted would want to do and I certainly wouldn't make it difficult for him if that's what he wanted." She paused briefly, then added: "Someday." And once again she said: "I hope it's not this year."

I had been in London in April of last year, researching my biography of Edward Kennedy, when Joan flew in, en route to Bonn, Germany, where she was to narrate "Peter and the Wolf" at a concert with the Boston Symphony Orchestra. I recall the headlines that greeted the statement she made to reporters at Heathrow Airport: "MRS. K. DOESN'T WANT TO CALL THE WHITE HOUSE HOME." "IT'S TOO TOUGH AT THE TOP, SAYS MRS. KENNEDY." "I have been very close to it," she was quoted as saying, ". . . I do not want the job."

Did she still feel the same way? The question she was asked that afternoon and her reply were not fully reported, she said. "It was the kind of question where the reporter, a woman, was really making a little speech. It went like this and it happens quite often to me: 'Well gosh, isn't it exciting your being in politics and just think, you just might be the luckiest girl in the world. You might get to be First Lady someday!' "

"They kind of get so excited about it themselves, and expect you to blurt out, 'Yes, yes oh yes! That's exactly what I want to be!' And instead I deflate the balloon in a sense, not really on purpose, but because I don't see it as all that glamorous. Having been so close, I see another side.

"I said just that and the woman said, 'Oh.' Then she asked me: 'What do you mean?' And I just said it's a lot of hard work, dedication, a lot of the other side of just the razzle-dazzle and the glamour and so-called excitement of the White House. I told her I've seen it firsthand and knew there were drawbacks.

"I was trying to point out that it wasn't all sweetness and light, that there were *problems*. You really have to give up almost your whole life."

Whether she is ready to do this is moot. If Ted runs, she will help; if he wins, she will be his First Lady. For she is cemented to the family by a triple seal of religion, politics and family. Divorce probably would not destroy Ted politically but can hurt him. Unlike other politicians, he has a playboy image, which a marriage breakup will sharpen. While Rose lives, a marital split affecting the dynesty's heir-apparent is the unspeakable act. After she is gone, the pressure by the family would be enormous, probably irresistible for Joan.

Psychotherapy has been helpful, she told me. "I feel more independent and self-confident," she said. "I feel so much better about everything."

The Kennedy experience came close to destroying her, but she is struggling to survive. There are ups and downs. In May, 1974, she was in a private psychiatric hospital, The Silver Hill Foundation in New Canaan, Connecticut. The Senator's office announced she "has been under continuous strain" following young Teddy's illness. She is seeking to come to terms with what has to be, Teddy's behavior included, and is learning the great lesson of humankind, adaptation. Eleanor Roosevelt once wrote: "You cannot live at all if you do not learn to adapt yourself to your life as it happens to be." No longer intimidated by the Kennedy name and dazzle, Joan is learning to be her own woman now, seeking fulfillment, not in what the family holds dear and expects, but in her friends, her music, her children, her own life.

Index

Abel, Bess, 129
Albert, Carl, 235
Alecks, Joseph, 160
Alphand, Mrs. Hervé, 103
Anderson, Jack, 110

Bain, Barbara, 31
Barry, Bill, 187, 188
Bayh, Birch, 79, 83, 87, 93, 113–114, 135, 152, 154, 157
Bayh, Marvella, 80, 83–84, 92–93, 113–114, 122, 135, 152, 154, 157–158
Beale, Betty, 145
Beene, Geoffrey, 133
Bellotti, Francis X., 152
Bennett, Agnes Pattie Smith, 20
Bennett, Candace, see McMurrey, Candace Bennett
Bennett, Harry Wiggin, Jr., 16, 19–21, 24–25, 27–28, 32, 36, 39, 50, 57, 170, 252–253
Bennett, Harry, Sr., 17–19, 20
Bennett, Virginia Joan Stead, 16, 21, 25–26, 32, 34, 36, 47–48, 252
Berlin, Irving, 37
Bernstein, Carl, 191
Bernstein, Leonard, 241
Biardi, Alan and Ann, 151
Billings, LeMoyne K., 50, 181, 253, 254
Birmingham, Stephen, 22, 37 n.
Boland, Edward P., 71, 158
Both Your Houses, 212

Bouvier, Janet, 111
Bouvier, John Vernon III, 111
Bouvier sisters, 37 n.
Boyle, Judge James A., 188 n.
Brady, James A., 232
Brokaw, Danne, 50
Bronxville, N.Y., 21–23
Brooks, Marty, 133
Brown, Barbara, 149
Brown, Jacqueline, 156
Brown, Pat, 87
Brussel, Dr. James A., 125
Buchwald, Art, 96
Buck, Pearl, 216–217, 218, 252
Burden, Amanda, 224–225, 226–228, 231, 233
Burden, Carter, 224

Caffrey, Patrick T., 137
Capehart, Homer, 93
Caper, Dr. Philip, 1–2, 6 n.
Capote, Truman, 145
Caprio, Dr. Frank, 145
Carter, Dr. Stephen K., 5–6
Cassini, Oleg, 97–98, 101
Cavanaugh, Father John, 48
Chappaquiddick Island incident, 8, 50, 176–191, 193, 211, 223, 225, 238
Cheshire, Maxine, 242
children of politicians, 141–143
Christy, Marian, 133–134
Clasby, Richard, 49–50
Clinch, Nancy G., 218, 219, 223

Connally, John, 138
Connally, Nelly, 138
Conover, Harry, 39, 43
Cooper, Lorraine, 249
Covalt, Dr. Donald A., 6–7
Crimmins, Jack, 151, 153–154, 169,
    188
Curlin, William P., Jr., 137
Curran, Robert, 110
Cusack, Dr. William J., 116

Dallas, Rita, 120
Davis, Sammy, Jr., 106
Day, Dorothy, 30–31
Debutante Cotillion, 35, 37
debutantes, 34–37
de Gaulle, Mme. Charles, 171
De Valera, Eamon, 122
Dever, Paul, 67
Didato, Dr. Salvatore V., 130, 134
Diefenbaker, John, 98
Dineen, Alice, 249
divorces in politics, 136–139
Doherty, Gerard, 63, 64, 66, 89–90,
    91, 152–153, 158, 243, 246
Dole, Phyllis, 138
Dole, Robert, 137–138
Dominick, Mrs. Peter, 121
Donovan, George, 3, 53
Donovan, Luella Hennessey, 2–3, 4,
    53–54, 113, 114–115, 116, 117,
    183, 185, 186–187, 193
Donovan, Robert J., 109
Dorsey, Jean, 136
Dowd, Donald J., 63–72, 151, 153,
    154–155
Dowd, Phoebe, 71, 72, 85, 151–153,
    154, 155
Drayne, Dick, 11
Dubbs, Theresa, 95, 104

*Education of Edward Kennedy,
    The,* 231–232
Egan, Arthur C., Jr., 74–83, 225–
    227, 228 n.
Eisenhower, Dwight D., 60
Eisenhower, Mamie, 133

Fiedler, Arthur, 82, 117

Finch, Robert, 128
Fitzgerald, John F. ("Honey
    Fitz"), 60, 61
Fitzgerald, Polly, 61
Fitzgerald, Robert, 67
Fitzgerald, Sally, 67, 68, 160
Fitzgerald, Thomas, 17
Ford, Betty, 142, 197
Ford, Gerald, 141, 197
Fosburgh, James W., 119–120
Fox, Tom, 206
Freidin, Seymour K., 222–223
Freud, Sigmund, 194–195

Galanos, 101
Gargan, Joseph, 50, 178, 188
Glaser, Vera, 132
Goldwater, Barry, 189–190
Green, William J., 240
Greene, Marie, 118–119
Gwirtzman, Milton, 149–150

Hall, Gordon Langley, 111–112
Harlow, Bryce, 128
Hartke, Vance, 90
Hartke, Mrs. Vance, 121
Hauser, Rita E., 133
Hayden, Carl, 213–214
Heckler, Mrs. Margaret, 134
Helm, Rosalie, 2, 10, 199
Hennessey, Luella, *see* Donovan,
    Luella Hennessey
Hersh, Burton, 231
Hollings, Ernest F., 137
Hooten, Claude E., Jr., 50, 169
Hopkins, Dann, 249
Houston, Bryan, 19, 20
Howar, Barbara, 121, 197
Humphrey, Hubert, 87, 88
Hyannis Port, Mass., 1, 22, 52, 100,
    121, 148, 149
Hyatt, Dr. George W., 3, 4

Irvine, Keith, 11

Jacobs, Andrew, Jr., 138
Janssen, Webster E., Jr., 50
Johnson, Lucy Baines, 234
Johnson, Lynda Bird, 234

Johnson, Lyndon B., 88, 102, 149, 157, 172
Jones, Candy, 39–44, 76, 248
Jordan, Dr. Sara, 195
Joyce, Tommy, 158, 159, 237

Kabis, Dorothy Elston, 133
Keating, Kenneth, 169
Kennedy, Caroline, 5, 109–110, 119, 127 n. 148–149, 181
Kennedy, Edward Moore, 119, 129–130, 131, 194, 202, 203, 204, 205–206, 251–252
and Chappaquiddick incident, 8, 50, 176–191, 223, 225, 233, 238
courtship and marriage of, 43–50
death of brothers and, 8, 149–150, 171–176, 252–253
eating habits of, 243, 244–245
left-liberalism of, 73–74
in plane crash, 78, 151–170
presidential intentions of, 13, 131–132, 174, 189, 232, 233, 242, 252–253, 255–257
and relation to John F., 51–52, 54–55
rumored infidelities of, 8, 14, 179–183, 216, 220–229, 232–233, 253–254
as senatorial candidate, 59, 60–91, 151, 158–170, 198
son's illness and, 1–7
Kennedy, Ethel Skakel, 5, 13, 22, 45, 46, 49, 56, 58, 61, 94, 101, 103, 104, 148, 150, 162, 172, 174, 175, 185, 209, 220
Joan compared with, 28, 84, 94, 100–101, 110–111, 112, 115, 121, 171, 192, 236, 239, 243–244
Kennedy, Jacqueline Bouvier, *see* Onassis, Jacqueline Kennedy
Kennedy, Joan Bennett:
beauty of, 9, 38, 39–41, 51, 75, 96, 128–129
campaign role of, 54, 62–91, 158–170, 192, 198–199, 201, 244, 246–247

Kennedy, Joan Bennett (*cont.*)
and Chappaquiddick incident, 176–191, 193, 238
childhood of, 23–31
clothing styles of, 97–98, 99–101, 126–131, 132–135, 241, 247–249
college education of, 32–34
compensation syndrome of, 125–135
in competition with Kennedy women, 113–121, 243–244
family background of, 13, 16–23
family size as concern of, 98, 116
family tragedies and, 147–176
fears of, 250–257
hobby collections of, 242–243
as homemaker, 56–57, 92–95
homes of, 11–12, 55, 57–58, 94–95, 121
as hostess, 56–57, 58, 100, 101–104, 243
indiscretions ascribed to, 230, 231–232, 241–242
ingenuousness of, 96–104, 135, 237–238, 239
Kennedy in-laws and, 106–112, 238–240
marital difficulties ascribed to, 8, 179–183, 229–233, 240–242, 253–254
marriage of, 45–59
merchandising of, 63–72
as model, 39–44, 76
as mother, 234–237
musical involvement of, 24, 33, 62–63, 86, 94, 104, 117–118, 162, 164, 197–209, 241
personality changes of, 31, 155–156, 170, 229, 243–249
pregnancies and miscarriages of, 8, 52–54, 58–59, 84, 116–117, 158, 177, 183, 185–186
as prospective First Lady, 131–132, 255–257
psychiatric experience of, 192–197, 257
social blunders of, 127–131, 132–135

social conscience and views of, 73, 74–82, 245–246
as Society debutante, 34–38
son's illness and, 1–7, 234, 240
thrift of, 99–100, 244
travels of, 1, 104–105, 122–124, 240–242
Washington arrival of, 92–95
Kennedy, John F., 7, 49, 60–61, 71, 96–97, 122, 123, 141, 159, 181, 194, 198, 233
assassination of, 3, 8, 14, 123, 148–150, 156, 171
in Berlin, 123–124
family tragedies and, 147–148
health of, 98–99
as president, 54–55, 108–110
presidential campaign of, 51–52, 54, 72–73, 109
rumored infidelities of, 216–217, 219–220
Kennedy, John F., Jr., 5, 119, 148–149, 181
Kennedy, Joseph, 172
Kennedy, Joseph P., 2, 3, 14, 19, 22, 24, 33, 45, 48, 53, 58, 60–61, 100, 107–108, 115, 174, 175, 194, 195, 216–219, 220
Kennedy, Joseph P., Jr., 194, 216
Kennedy, Kara Anne, 2, 54, 92, 148–149, 161, 163, 173, 185, 186, 234–236, 237, 240
Kennedy, Kathleen, 148
Kennedy, Mary Courtney, 148
Kennedy, Patrick, 2, 11, 161, 234, 237
Kennedy, Patrick Bouvier, 8, 147–148
Kennedy, Robert F., 45, 49, 74, 94, 101, 103, 104, 106, 119, 148, 150, 170, 192, 194, 198, 233, 236
assassination of, 1, 8, 14, 73, 171–176
campaigns of, 84, 86, 131, 169, 171, 246–247
rumored infidelities of, 216, 220, 227

Kennedy, Robert F., Jr., 172
Kennedy, Rose, 2, 4, 13, 25–26, 32, 33–34, 51, 53, 58, 60–61, 115, 118, 119, 121, 148, 164, 169, 170, 175, 178, 193, 194, 195, 198, 217–218, 228, 236, 257
Kennedy, Rosemary, 53 n., 194 n.
Kennedy, Teddy, Jr., 11–12, 58–59, 92, 116, 148–149, 161, 163, 173, 185, 186, 234–237
illness of, 1–7, 165, 234, 240, 242
Kennedy family:
athletics in, 7, 113–115, 243–244
vs. Bennetts, 19, 24–26, 33–34
effect of tragedies on, 147–176, 186–187, 194
machismo in, 216–229
as political campaigners, 60–62, 63, 84, 89
problems of marriage into, 106–121
religion in, 32–33, 110, 111, 194–195, 236
wealth of, 48, 63, 235
winning as goal in, 33–34
women of, 13, 48–49, 51, 54, 61–62, 63, 89, 99–101, 110–112, 113, 115–116, 117, 121, 162, 192–193, 200, 205, 209, 238–240
Keyes, Daniel M., Sr., 71
Keyes, Helen, 61
King, Edward J., 64, 65, 66
King, James, 170
King, Joan, 196–197
Kissinger, Henry A., 215
Knauer, Virginia, 133
Koonitz, Elizabeth D., 133
Kopechne, Gwen Jennings, 184–185, 190
Kopechne, Joseph, 184–185, 190
Kopechne, Mary Jo, 81, 177–179, 184, 187–188, 225

Laird, Mrs. Melvin E., 129
Lambert, Eleanor, 248, 249
Lane, Dr. Howard, 155
Lash, Joseph, 28
Latimer, Cary, 37

Laughlin, Larry, 66
Lawford, Christopher, 53, 109–110
Lawford, Patricia Kennedy, 53, 61,
    106, 110, 120, 121, 131, 148,
    162, 209, 228
Lawford, Peter, 53, 106–110
Lawford, Sir Sydney, 107
Leachman, Cloris, 253
LeHand, Marguerite (Missy), 218,
    219 n.
Lerner, Max, 220
Lodge, George, 91
Lodge, Henry Cabot, Jr., 61

McCarthy, Abigail, 141
McCarthy, Eugene, 141
McCloskey, Caroline, 144
McCloskey, Pete, 144
McCormack, Edward J., 66, 86,
    151
McCormack, John W., 66
McGarry, John, 85–86
McGovern, Eleanor, 141, 143
McGovern, George, 13, 141, 142–
    143, 230
McGovern, Steve, 142
McGovern, Terry, 142–143
McLean, Virginia, 250
McMurrey, Candace Bennett, 16,
    21, 25, 27, 29, 34, 50, 78, 86–87,
    116, 122, 124, 149, 150
McMurrey, Robert M., 31, 149,
    150
Mailer, Norman, 209–210, 219, 220
Manchester, William, 150
Mancini, Henry, 209
Mandel, Barbara Overfield, 136
Mandel, Marvin, 136
Manhattanville College of the
    Sacred Heart, 32–33
Mansfield, Mike, 102, 251–252
Marcos, Mrs. Ferdinand, 133
Markham, Paul, 178, 188
Martin, Dean, 106
Martin, Edward, 158, 169
Martinelli, Elsa, 242
Mayer, Louis B., 108

Menninger, Karl A., 196
Mesta, Perle, 101, 102
Michaelson, Abe, 86
Mitchell, John, 136–137
Mitchell, Martha, 136–137
Mondale, Joan, 143
Mondale, Walter F., 143
Monroe, Marilyn, 220
Montand, Yves, 240
Moore, Deedee, 89
Morton, Rogers C. B., 128
Moss, Edward, 152, 156
Muguet, Marguerite, 149

Neville, Mike, 61
Newcomb, Pat, 202
New York, Society in, 34–37
Nixon, Pat, 128, 130, 133
Nixon, Richard M., 74, 87, 102,
    128, 144, 189
Noland, Cornelia, 217

O'Connell, Archbishop William,
    48
O'Mara, Margot Murray, 45, 46–
    47, 50
Onassis, Jacqueline Kennedy, 13,
    37 n., 49, 94, 119–120, 131, 148,
    156, 172, 175, 181, 254
    as First Lady, 131–132, 240
    Joan Kennedy and, 99–100, 111–
    112, 115–116, 121, 156, 239–240

Parker, John F., 26, 112
Parnis, Molly, 101
Pavone, Giorgio, 241–242
Peabody, Endicott, 88, 152
Peabody, Toni, 88, 91
Peerce, Jan, 203, 204, 206
Percy Charles, 140
Perry, Maude, 24
Pinchot, Ann, 111–112
Polatin, Dr. Phillip, 214
Powers, Dave, 147–148, 159
Powers, John E., 60
Powers, John Robert, 39
Proxmire, Ellen, 138, 143–144

Proxmire, William, 137, 139

Quinn, Sally, 215–216

Radziwill, Princess Lee, 37 n., 111
"rat pack," 106, 109
Reagan, Ronald, 87
Reid, Mrs. Ogden, 128
Riegle, Donald W., Jr., 137–138,
   141, 212–213, 214
Riegle, Nancy, 141–142
Robertson, Nan, 89
Rockefeller, Jay, 140–141
Rockefeller, Laurence, 37
Rockefeller, Nelson, 137
Rockefeller, Sharon Percy, 140–141
Rogers, Robert, 117–118
Roosevelt, Eleanor, 218 n.–219 n.,
   257
Roosevelt, Franklin D., 218, 219 n.
Rusk, Dr. Howard A., 7
Ryan, Mary Kennedy, 122, 123

Schlesinger, Arthur M., Jr., 132
Scott, Hugh, 128, 129
Shapp, Milton, 198, 203–204, 206
Shaw, Carolyn Hagner, 129
Shriver, Eunice Kennedy, 13, 32,
   60, 61, 103, 115, 120, 121, 148,
   150, 162, 170, 171, 172, 193,
   209
Shriver, Sargent, 13, 103, 150, 171,
   172
Simpson, Adele, 101
Sinatra, Frank, 106, 109
Skakel, George, 46
Smathers, George, 184
Smith, Agnes Pattie, 20
Smith, Deborah, 199, 203
Smith, Helen N., 130
Smith, Jean Kennedy, 33, 45–46,
   50, 51, 61, 121, 131, 162, 170,
   172, 185, 228, 232, 233 n.
Smith, Stephen, 46, 50, 172, 232
Smith, William, 199–201, 204–208
Spellman, Francis Cardinal, 36, 45,
   48, 77

Stead, William Albert, 21
Stephenson, Malvina, 132
Sternberg, William, 82
Stevenson, Adlai, 137
Stringfellow, Ethel, 112
Stoud, Kandy, 127, 179, 180, 230–
   231, 233, 244, 247, 249
Stupakoff, Otto, 250–251
Swanson, Gloria, 217, 218

Talmadge, Betty, 145–146
Talmadge, Herman, 145–146
Tate, James H. J., 203
Thayer, Mary Van Rensselaer, 119
Townsend, Kathleen and David
   Lee, 5
Town Topics, 35
Travell, Dr. Janet, 98
Tremblay, Mrs. E. Gerald, 56
Tunney, Gene, 138
Tunney, John Varrick, 50, 87, 122,
   137, 138, 169, 225–226, 227,
   240
Tunney, Mieke, 121–122, 129, 138,
   169, 225

Vanderpool, Ann, 122
Vanderpool, Wynant D., 122
Van Horne, Harriet, 134
Vietnam War, 88, 95, 144
Vitali, Andy, 169
Volpi, Giovanni, 241
von Braun, Wernher, 235
Voutselas, Angelique, 159

Wallace, George C., 88, 189
Washington, D.C.:
   Congressional swingers in, 211–
   216
   social life in, 93–94, 96, 100–103,
   127–131, 132–135, 145, 213
Watergate scandal, 136–137, 189,
   190, 191
Watt, Dr. Robert, 184
Weaver, Warren, Jr., 212, 213–214
Webster, Daniel, 207
Webster, Mrs. George, 128 n.

Whitmore, Howard, Jr., 169
Wiggin, Belle, 17
Wiggin, Thomas, 17
Williams, Harrison A., Jr., 137
wives, political, 92–93, 134, 135–146, 197
"Wives Manual," Republican, 139–140
Women's Lib, 91, 245

Women's Political Caucus, 140
Women's Wear Daily, 127, 179, 232 n.–233 n., 241–242, 247
Woodward, Bob, 191
Wright, Sylvia, 186
Wyeth, Andrew, 228

Young, Cindy, 38